WORKING WITH BRAIN INJURY

This book provides a hands-on resource for the development of essential skills and competencies in clinical neuropsychology. On a very practical level it addresses a question frequently asked by students, trainees, interns, and newly qualified psychologists: what do I need to know in order to perform the everyday tasks involved in clinical neuropsychology? The authors distil, from a vast knowledge base, the practical skills and knowledge needed to lay the foundations for working with brain-injured patients, especially within the developed and developing world where time and resources are limited.

The book is divided into three main sections: Basic Foundations, Clinical Practice, and Professional Issues. Together these sections cover 18 fundamental topics, each representing a key part of the life of a practitioner. Each chapter contains practical tips, points for reflective practice, and suggested further reading, with a particular emphasis on issues pertaining to working in under-resourced clinical environments. The book draws upon landmark academic papers and textbooks, and also the authors' experiences of working in state hospitals in both South Africa and the National Health Service in the United Kingdom.

Working with Brain Injury will be essential reading for clinical psychology trainees and their supervisors, for newly qualified psychologists in clinical settings, and for students and practitioners in other clinical professions seeking an introduction to clinical neuropsychology.

Rudi Coetzer is a Consultant Neuropsychologist and Head of Service with the North Wales Brain Injury Service, National Health Service (NHS) Wales, United Kingdom.

Ross Balchin is a Neuropsychologist and Postdoctoral Fellow in Neuropsychology at the University of Cape Town, South Africa.

WORKING WITH BRAIN INJURY

A primer for psychologists working in under-resourced settings

Rudi Coetzer and Ross Balchin

Psychology Press
Taylor & Francis Group

LONDON AND NEW YORK

First published 2014
by Psychology Press
27 Church Road, Hove, East Sussex BN3 2FA

and by Psychology Press
711 Third Avenue, New York, NY 10017

Psychology Press is an imprint of the Taylor & Francis Group, an informa business

British Library Cataloguing in Publication Data
A catalogue record for this book is available from the British Library

Library of Congress Cataloging in Publication Data
Coetzer, Rudi.
Working with brain injury : primer for psychologists working in
under-resourced settings / Rudi Coetzer and Ross Balchin. – 1 Edition.
 pages cm
 Includes bibliographical references and index.
 1. Brain damage. 2. Clinical neuropsychology. 3. Rehabilitation
 counselors. 4. Core competencies. I. Balchin, Ross. II. Title.
 RC387.5.C58 2014
 617.4'81044–dc23   2013044030

ISBN: 978-1-84872-332-0 (hbk)
ISBN: 978-1-84872-333-7 (pbk)
ISBN: 978-1-315-81643-2 (ebk)

Typeset in Bembo
by Wearset Ltd, Boldon, Tyne and Wear

Printed and bound in Great Britain by
TJ International Ltd, Padstow, Cornwall

'What wound did ever heal but by degrees?'

Othello, Act II, Scene iii
William Shakespeare

CONTENTS

FOREWORD

It is a special pleasure for me to be able to recommend this book. It addresses directly and precisely all the things I needed to know when I took my own first practical steps as a clinical neuropsychologist. If only this book had been available then!

It was in the mid-1980s. I had just completed the academic component of my neuropsychological training when my supervisor, Professor Michael Saling, took a sabbatical in Melbourne, Australia, in the department of Kevin Walsh. South Africa being what it was (and remains), namely a country with a woefully 'under-resourced' public health sector and with hopelessly sparse neuropsychological expertise, this left me high and dry, literally on my own, without anyone to turn to on my very first day at work.

I reported for duty that morning at Ward 7 – the neurosurgical ward – once I had found it in the sprawling grounds of Baragwanath Hospital in Soweto. Bara (as it was affectionately known) was the largest hospital in the Southern Hemisphere, a place like Charcot's Salpêtrière had been in the previous century, a vast sea of human misery.

In fact, I should say that I reported to Ward 7 only after I had found Baragwanath Hospital in the sprawling streets of Soweto. But that is another hair-raising story. Remember: this was the mid-1980s, during the height of apartheid; the people were angry, troops were in the townships and I was a little, lost white boy...

The ward must have had about 90 beds in it, spread across three sections, one each for men, women and children. I was met by a consultant neurosurgeon, Mr Percy Miller, a no-nonsense bird-like figure who talked faster than anyone could reasonably be expected to follow. He shook my hand, blurting out something like, 'it's good to have you, man, we've been really in need of you guys since Mike left', and then immediately took me on a ward round. My first ward round ever. I found myself standing next to him at the bedside of someone with an unrememberable name who was forty-something years old and was now suffering from a something or other (a kind of tumour?) that was going to be removed by an unpronounceable approach tomorrow and it would be good if I could take a look at him and get baseline measures before they did so. Then, reeling with this information overload, Percy led me to the next bed and started all over again: this is Mr So and So who is blah years old and suffering from such and such (what the hell is that?) which is being treated conservatively for now, but the team are considering doing a something or other once they have seen how well he responds to an unheard-of treatment (is that a drug?), so it was probably a good idea for me to get a measure of his current level of functioning in the relevant areas as soon as possible. Then within a few more seconds we were at the third bed. And so we went on, through the entire male section.

It was clear to me that this neurosurgeon assumed I knew things that I had never even heard of before. He talked a language that was entirely foreign to me, not only in its obscure technical terminology but also in the whole worldview upon which it rested; there was a hidden order to his thinking, completely obscure to me, with all sorts of assumptions about what is and is not relevant, about how one structures the report of a case history, about diseases and treatments and laboratory findings and clinical signs and the like, about all of which I knew next to nothing. Actually, about all of which I knew absolutely nothing.

Initially, I just did not want to embarrass myself; so I kept quiet, waiting for things to fall into place. They never did, and then we were onto the next case, and the next, by which time it was too late to say that I had not understood a word from the first moment onward, and so could we please go back to the beginning and start again, and could he please explain everything to me again, but in English this time, and could he also please not assume I know anything about anything, because the truth is, I don't.

What did neurosurgeons think we learned about in psychology departments? Did they think we studied medicine and surgery first and then added a bit of psychology afterwards? He seemed to think I knew all the things that he didn't know about the mind, but didn't realise that the same applied to me the other way around: I knew nothing about the body. Did he think we psychologists were taught about how hospitals and wards and doctors actually operate? Didn't he know that even the sight of these patients with those tubes sticking out of the Frankenstein-like gashes in their shaven heads makes me feel faint? And all the moans and groans, and the thrashing about, and the crazy behaviour of the patients … and the smells … all of this was something for which I was totally unprepared.

But now it was too late to tell him. So I had to start playing catch-up and really concentrate, and *remember*, because he seemed to assume I would remember all of the things he was saying when I returned to these patients and conducted all the assessments he was asking for. What was I going to do?

And then it hit me; it was even worse than I had realised. These were real patients with real diseases who were going to have real operations … tomorrow.

And I had mistakenly been placed in the middle of this team that was doing all these things. Except I didn't know what I was doing. It was clear: *I was going to kill someone*. Someone was going to die and it would be all my fault, just because I was too embarrassed to tell this nice surgeon that psychologists are not prepared for the real world of clinical neuropsychology.

(Remember: the book you are holding in your hands right now had not been published yet.)

I will spare you the details of what happened next. It was a very long day. I will mention only that the children's section was even worse than the men's. The sight of them was bad enough, but the sight of little children with tubes and holes in their heads, with heads far too big (or small) for their bodies, two of them joined together at the parietal bone, one of them with a bulbous mass hanging from the back of his neck, and so on, were simply too much for me. And they were crying and crying and crying. And worse: some of them were staring blankly through me, at the wall behind.

And then we entered the women's section, where further new shocks awaited. Didn't Percy Miller realise that I wasn't allowed to see women lying about in states of undress like that; I was just a psychologist!

So what did I do? After that nightmarish ward round, which seemed to last forever, I went back to the beds of the patients, one by one, found the notes in their bed-letters, and tried to make head or tail of them, in my own time. What was written there was just as incomprehensible as what Percy Miller had told me verbally, but at least I could go through it slowly now, and read everything twice, and gradually make some small amount of sense out of each case.

Then I started the assessment of my very first patient, the one who was having his operation tomorrow morning and therefore couldn't wait. I introduced myself, carefully explaining that I was the neuro*psychologist*, and asked him to describe his troubles to me. As he began to do so, naturally making no distinction between his physical and mental symptoms (how was he to know where the disciplinary boundaries are drawn?), all that I could make out was that he was not normal. The way he spoke and thought and behaved were grossly odd and unfamiliar. Oh my God; how I am supposed to differentiate the agnosia from the apraxia from the amnesia from the aphasia from the dysarthria from the … All I could say for sure was that he was abnormal. He was *brain damaged*. But I couldn't write that in the bed-letter! Did I have absolutely nothing to contribute?

Now I realised why Mike Saling had always told us in class that the psychometric approach to neuropsychology was so popular because it was so easy. All you had to do as a psychometrist (Mike Saling almost spat the word out) was sit the patient down in a quiet office, out of sight of the proper doctors, and force them to go through their paces, with your standardised battery of tests. You only had to ensure that all the instructions were complied with, stop the patient when they fail the requisite number of times, etc., and add up all the scores. Then you fill in the numbers in the blank report sheet and leave it in the folder. Mike Saling said this was the easy approach but that it didn't really contribute much because the scores did not reflect the performance, did not differentiate between the different reasons for failure. That is why psychometric score sheets normally remain in the folder, unread, he said. The task at hand was not merely to measure the neuropsychological problem but rather to understand it, to explain it. He explained that our approach to neuropsychology – the hypothetico-deductive, qualitative approach – was vastly superior, for the reason that it actually addresses clinical questions, actually answers them. Is this a case of this or that, asks the referral?... Let me see, let me examine the patient, says the neuropsychologist ... Ah, now I know; it's this, comes the answer!

Moreover, Mike Saling had explained that in a multilingual and multicultural society like ours, like most of the real world, a society in which many people are illiterate and have not even held a pen before, in such a society there is little place for psychometric testing. Everybody has to be measured against a different norm, in so many different respects simultaneously, that it makes no sense to even try to answer clinical questions that way. The only way to do neuropsychology in such contexts is to approach the mind in the same way as one would approach any other biological function (respiration, digestion, etc.) in internal medicine. One has to approach it in terms of *species-specific* expectations, on the basis of a sound *theoretical* knowledge of brain–behaviour relationships, and then *think* your way through the clinical problem till you have solved it.

On that first fateful day of my clinical life, I learned just how much easier this is to say than to do. After failing so dismally with my first case, managing only to write a list of the approximately 15 things that I could detect were wrong with him, I decided to defer the remaining referrals until the next morning.

I rushed back to the university, to the book store, where I bought *Stedman's Medical Dictionary*, a good textbook of clinical neurology (Adams & Victor) and, most useful of all, as it turned out, *Greenfield's Neuropathology*, as well as a companion volume – by Dorothy Russell, I think it was – on tumours of the nervous system.

(Remember: the book you are holding in your hands right now had not been published yet.)

I stayed up all night, trying to make retrospective sense of what I had seen that day and what I had been asked to do, and then I returned to work for Day Two ... this time with my four textbooks in tow.

And so I proceeded, day by day, case by case, stopping, reading, returning to the notes, and then to the books, and then to the patient and then back to the notes again, until slowly, slowly, ever so slowly, patient after patient, week after week, month after month, year after year, I gradually learned the things that a neuropsychologist really needs to know.

The book you are holding in your hands now will not spare you all the hard work that is required to become a good neuropsychological clinician. Only years and years of experience can do that, together with a gradual immersion in the knowledge of our sister disciplines, neurology, neurosurgery and psychiatry (not to mention paediatrics, geriatrics, radiology and so much more). But this book will spare you the panic. And it will spare you the chaos. And the embarrassment. It will set you off on your journey of life-long learning with a solid footing, a practical framework, a sound grasp of what is required of you and of how you should set about doing it, step by step, one patient at a time.

This book will, in short, provide you with the supervision that I so painfully lacked when I went through my trial by fire, all those years ago. The book you hold in your hands tells you what to do. For this, you, the reader of this wonderfully useful introduction to the practicalities of clinical neuropsychology, in the real world that most of us have to work in, have a lot to thank Rudi Coetzer and Ross Balchin for. I would like to congratulate them for their achievement and recommend this book to you as highly as I possibly can.

Mark Solms, Cape Town
November 2013

PREFACE

This book's primary aim is to provide a hands-on resource for the development of essential competencies and skills in clinical neuropsychology. The content is applicable to a wide range of contexts where clinical neuropsychology is practised, including publicly funded hospitals and clinics and community-based services. It is intended especially for students and healthcare professionals who work (or are training) in under-resourced settings in both the developed and the developing world. 'Under-resourced' settings in this context can be defined as: (1) settings where there are limited, or even non-existent, *physical resources* dedicated to neuropsychology and neurorehabilitation services including, among other things, neuropsychological rehabilitation; and (2) settings where there is either limited, or non-existent, *expertise* (specifically qualified and/or experienced neuropsychologists). A number of factors can result in a lack of or limited *physical resources*, for example limited funding, remoteness (rurality), poverty, the inherent design of national healthcare delivery systems, or a lack of infrastructure, thereby making it difficult for citizens to access healthcare. A lack of or limited *expertise* may also be the result of various factors, including limited/absent/inadequate provision of training programmes, regional recruitment difficulties, poor employment opportunities within specific healthcare systems, language and/or cultural barriers, and so forth.

Why is the focus on under-resourced settings in particular? It is here that practitioners are confronted by vast numbers of patients, but with only limited resources at their disposal. The infinite demands placed on finite state-provided health resources are a universal reality in most countries. While there are private healthcare providers that offer excellent services in some settings, the vast majority of patients simply cannot afford to pay. The result is a morally indefensible situation where one's health and social wellbeing depend on one's wealth. This situation is no different in brain-injury assessment and rehabilitation. Indeed, these are particularly salient issues in many developed and developing countries – often associated with contemporaneous or historical socio-political factors – where there are very high numbers of patients with various forms of acquired brain injury. Acquired brain injury is associated with very high levels of neuropsychological impairment and resulting chronic disability. For these patients, in many healthcare systems, there is very often almost no access to even the most basic neuropsychological assessment and rehabilitation. We hope this book will make a contribution towards redressing at least some of this situation.

Clinical neuropsychologists are low in numbers, and many do not work in publicly funded hospitals, for many reasons, including the fact that often there are simply no funded posts available. The everyday reality in the state/public sector, though, is that often many of the working clinicians are newly qualified psychologists, with little or no background in clinical neuropsychology. Some of these psychologists might eventually go on to train in clinical neuropsychology, but many have to make do without such training. In addition, irrespective of this, clinical realities dictate that practitioners who work in healthcare settings are often subjected at a very early stage to the 'one has to start somewhere' phenomenon. We hope that our book will at least help these practitioners to be able to provide the very basic input that patients with acquired brain injury need and deserve. We also hope that this book will stimulate more psychologists to decide to work towards more formal qualifications in clinical neuropsychology. While this book is aimed mainly at psychologists and students of psychology, most chapters should also have utility as an introduction to clinical neuropsychology for students and practitioners in other clinical professions, including, for example, house officers/medical interns, nurses, occupational therapists, psychiatrists and speech therapists.

What makes this book different? Practitioners who are new to clinical neuropsychology frequently find many of the voluminous textbooks on the topic overwhelming. Many may avoid the field for this reason. However, we feel that merely reducing material will not necessarily be helpful in itself. Instead, we feel that it is important to step back and attempt a fusion of the up-to-date science and practice in the field, and to synthesise this information in order to address some of the many practical realities and demands that are associated with working in publicly funded healthcare environments – including those in developing world settings. To achieve this, we have first attempted to extract and logically arrange the required information in order to lay an initial foundation for study and practice. We have drawn upon our prior experience of working in state hospitals in both South Africa and the United Kingdom (National Health Service) – we have both worked in underresourced settings in South Africa and have first-hand experience of the challenges associated with working in such contexts. We have then combined this knowledge with selected landmark academic papers and textbooks, upon which the foundations of each chapter are based. Each chapter has in turn been further developed for application to under-resourced clinical environments where there is little or no access to neuropsychology. Time is a relentless taskmaster in clinical practice – hence references have been deliberately kept to an absolute minimum. The main challenge was to define the broad areas that an aspiring clinical neuropsychologist needs to be familiar with. Based on an extensive trawl of the existing clinical literature, three areas have been identified. Accordingly, this book is divided into three parts: *Basic foundations*, *Clinical practice* and *Professional issues*.

On a very practical level, this book attempts to address a question frequently asked by students, trainees, interns and newly qualified psychologists: 'What do I need to know to be able to perform the everyday tasks involved in the job competently?' However, the intention was not at all to identify the minimum levels of knowledge and skill that a clinical neuropsychologist can get by with. Instead, it is an attempt to define the essential *praecognitum* information that exists in the vast field of clinical neuropsychology, which many psychologists will need to develop a knowledge of before they can embark on working in a first placement or job. Many of these jobs, internships or placements are in publicly funded hospital settings or similar environments, which receive unrelentingly high numbers of patient referrals. Clinical neuropsychology is a curious beast, representing equal measures of science and art. It encompasses the science of brain–behaviour relations and the art of understanding, as well as the application of these skills on many different levels. Neuropsychology can be very technical on the one hand, but can also demand extraordinary compassion and humanity on the other.

There are many ways to facilitate teaching and learning in clinical neuropsychology. Some of these include using algorithms and illustrative case vignettes (amalgams of actual cases to preserve confidentiality). Problem-based learning is also extremely useful, as is having a clear structure. The number of topics (chapters) used to cover the three broad areas of this book was deliberately limited to 18. In a similar vein, the chapters have been intentionally condensed in order to be, on average, the approximate length of a typical full-length journal paper. Furthermore, we set out to limit the number of references for suggested further reading that accompany each chapter. More generally, references have been carefully selected based on their utility in clinical settings. Hopefully, these strategies will help to hold the reader's attention, allowing him/her to remain focused on the core knowledge and thereby avoid the perennial problem of 'distraction by detail' – and the associated feelings of defeat and deflation. The references used contain the fundamental information reviewed in the chapter, and may also assist aspiring neuropsychologists and other professionals to further develop their clinical skills over time. In addition to these references, practical tips and discussion points are also provided at the end of each chapter.

While our primary aim was to create a self-study resource for the reflective practice of practical skills, we feel it can also function as a flexible teaching resource for an introductory-level teaching block. Such a teaching block can, for example, be delivered over 1 to 2 weeks. Alternatively, it can provide more in-depth teaching over a period of one to two semesters, by increasing the amount of self-directed learning through the use of the references for further reading. The suggested points for reflective practice can be used as topics for classroom discussion, or even for short essays.

In conclusion, we have attempted to distil, from a vast knowledge base, the practical skills and knowledge that have the potential to lay the early foundations for working with brain-injured patients – especially within contexts where both resources and time are limited. The focus is very much on clinical practice in these contexts, within both the developed and the developing worlds. There is, of course, also a very important ethical principle that has guided our thinking: a somewhat 'hidden' yet crucially important principle of evidence-based healthcare is that 'more' is not necessarily always 'better'. Put differently, practitioners need to be competent in the basics and capable of performing the fundamental tasks of their area of speciality well, and on a repeated basis, in order to positively influence the health and social status of many patients. For this reason, we feel that while this book focuses to some extent on neuropsychological skills for practitioners who work in under-resourced healthcare systems, some of the principles covered can hopefully be equally applied to many other brain-injury service providers too. We are grateful for the many patients, students, trainees, interns, researchers, supervisors and lecturers who, over more than three decades, implicitly and explicitly 'wrote' this book for us. We hope that this work can make a meaningful contribution, both directly and indirectly, to those patients who receive very little care and support following the devastating effects of acquired brain injury.

Dr Rudi Coetzer, DClinPsy CPsychol AFBPsS (BPS)
North Wales, United Kingdom, 2013
Ross Balchin, PhD
Cape Town, South Africa, 2013

PART I
Basic foundations

1

IDENTIFYING A KNOWLEDGE BASE

Think before you leap; it is very wise to stand back and clearly define what it is that one needs to learn before immersion (and drowning...) in studying it. It may sound like a false strategy to invest a whole chapter to the topic of deciding what to study, but bear with us and persevere. Clinical neuropsychology is an extremely fulfilling area in which to train and work. As part of the wider neuroscience disciplines, where many different professionals work, it offers much in the way of intellectual stimulation, while at the same time providing an opportunity to make a meaningful contribution to the lives of others. Not many jobs can equal the immense satisfaction that results from working in this unique area of healthcare. Unfortunately, neuropsychology is a scarce resource in most healthcare systems, in both acute diagnostic work and in post-acute rehabilitation.

Some of this lack of neuropsychological resources has to do with the length of time that training takes, along with the investment required. At a systemic level, in many countries there are simply not enough financial resources to provide extensive rehabilitation for patients with brain injury beyond the acute, life-saving stage of care (and even this critical service is not always available). This naturally affects the number of clinicians – including neuropsychologists – who work in publicly funded post-acute brain-injury rehabilitation. Consequently, in order to augment their existing clinical skills, many psychologists and other professionals find that developing core competencies in basic clinical neuropsychology can potentially make a big difference to their confidence and ability when providing care to this patient population.

While neuropsychologists rely heavily on a robust knowledge base, the prerequisite clinical skills are ultimately developed in practice, over time. In short, this entails *seeing patients on a daily basis*. Training in clinical neuropsychology varies widely across the world (see Chapter 15), leading to different emphases being placed on clinical skills and expertise. Nevertheless, there are probably two main strategic obstacles faced by aspiring clinical neuropsychologists, psychologists and other professionals who work in brain-injury services. The first obstacle is failure to prepare adequately for working in this specialist field. Starting clinical placements/first jobs without having received robust, direct teaching of academic knowledge is a bad strategy for any clinical profession. Inevitably, this scenario results in anxiety and, in many circumstances, avoidance of patient contact during what is a very formative period of professional development. The second obstacle is more problematic to control: after receiving foundation or specialist training, clinicians may sometimes not have the opportunity to see enough patients to develop the necessary clinical skills – if no clinical posts exist, for example. While these points may seem trivial, they are fundamental to understanding the potential stumbling blocks that one might initially face when embarking on a career or placement.

For clinicians in training who are new to hospital/clinic environments, such settings can be daunting and intimidating, especially when encountered for the first time – this can indeed be the experience of most healthcare professionals. Also, in many instances, psychologists in training are often only exposed to such environments and situations at masters or pre-doctoral level, which can make the adjustment more difficult. This is especially true when one considers the amount of new information that one has to adapt to quickly during such transitions. One is also required to learn the protocols and niceties that are involved in how hospitals/clinics function. The newfound sense of the responsibility that new practitioners experience when beginning to work in hospital/clinic settings can also be an initial source of anxiety. Something else that can be disconcerting, or make one feel insecure and/or out of place as a trainee psychologist or intern, is when one is a seeing patients for the first time and getting the sense that you are 'using' the patients for practice rather than offering them the clinical service they so badly need.

Another, perhaps more obvious stumbling block relates to the perceived complexity of clinical neuropsychology and the neurosciences in general. While neuropsychology is indeed a complex field, it is no more so than any other of the specialist fields within psychology. There are many areas of neuropsychology that most aspiring clinicians, and many other professionals who work in brain-injury rehabilitation settings, should ideally be familiar with. For this reason, it is not unusual to feel overwhelmed and anxious when embarking on a training programme, placement or career in neuropsychology, or any other clinical profession involved in service provision for patients with brain injuries. This problem is not only limited to the sheer depth of knowledge required in a given area, but also the fact that in order to be competent, several areas have to be mastered.

Topics that fall under the domain of neuropsychologists include, but are not limited to, *assessment, anatomy, report writing, rehabilitation techniques* and *neuropathology*. Adding to this, in multicultural/multilingual settings in countries, such as South Africa, the degree of diversity met in the patient population can be overwhelming at the best of times, especially for trainees and recently qualified professionals. As in most specialist areas, it is essential to organise and integrate the information that requires assimilation into a model that makes sense and facilitates learning. Perhaps then, the process of defining and organising is a good starting point for this book, not least to try to change the false perception that neuropsychology is overwhelmingly complex in terms of both its practice and the body of knowledge that it encompasses.

In everyday practice, practitioners tend to be immersed in the business of applying clinical techniques and skills. Over time, repetition starts to make these skills almost automatic and lessens some of the anxieties one may have. By default, clinicians are then set free from concentrating on technique and can instead focus on patients' clinical presentations – this can occur during assessment or rehabilitation endeavours once practitioners becomes less 'manual-bound'. Clinical tasks and the application of skills take place very much 'in the moment'. However, while performing these tasks, we draw on more fundamental academic knowledge. This body of core knowledge can, to some degree, be 'hidden' in the background – it informs and shapes the application of technique at an almost subconscious level.

There are also more delayed outputs of our application of techniques and skills. Some occur fairly soon after patient interventions, such as writing clinical notes and reports about patients' assessments. Other outputs are much more delayed or slow-moving. These are often in response to external, non-patient-related demands, such as the planning and maintenance of continuing professional development (CPD). Let us now return to the point about organising or structuring information in a progressive way, which facilitates learning and the development of practical skills. The first step is to identify key areas of clinical neuropsychology, before embarking on learning their essential content.

Three areas within clinical neuropsychology

How can the overwhelming amount of information that is potentially relevant to clinical neuropsychology be organised in order to reduce information overload? Can we facilitate a step-by-step approach to developing practical skills? There are almost certainly as many takes on the answers to these questions as there are teachers in the field! However, choosing to follow a stepped, problem-based learning approach, and then gradually increasing the information that is directly applicable to clinical practice, may help to simplify things somewhat. This way, it is possible to retain an overall perspective of what is being learned, while gauging one's progress. If ever there were a strategy protective of morale, this is it!

Learning applied skills in neuropsychology should not be a process creaking under the weight of labyrinthine complexities. First, there is a core body of knowledge needed as a foundation; this should cover the relevant basic sciences (foundations) required. These topics/subjects are in turn fundamental to the second general area – the clinical application of knowledge from the basic sciences. Finally, as the application of clinical skills becomes entrenched, everyday, ongoing professional practice issues then become increasingly important. Many training programmes do not have time to address these professional practice topics in great depth and, consequently, many newly qualified psychologists report that they find the transition from trainee or intern to their first job quite difficult – at least in part due to this potential gap in their training.

In this book, three broad parts – *Basic foundations*, *Clinical practice* and *Professional issues* – cover the topics outlined below. Here follow the knowledge areas that pertain to the basic sciences, which clinical neuropsychologists should have training in: *neuroanatomy* (note this is listed first); *neuropathology*; *pharmacology*; *neuropsychological theory*; *medical investigations*; and *psychopathology*. Building upon these basic foundations follow clinical practice skills, including: *clinical assessment*; *neuropsychological testing*; *neuropsychological rehabilitation*; *psychological therapy*; and *record keeping*. These skills are utilised daily, but clinical neuropsychologists also have more enduring tasks for which they need knowledge, skill and, importantly, experience. These tasks are covered in the third part of this book and include: *professional practice*; *ethics*; *supervision*; *research*; *team work*; *management*; and *service development*.

While these three parts build progressively from foundational knowledge through to everyday clinical skills and the more strategic skills and experience we ultimately learn to apply over time, this division is, at best, somewhat artificial. It is important to note that there is considerable overlap. Nevertheless, it is reasonable to posit that defining the outline in this way has potential benefits for organising specific neuropsychological topics. It is conducive to developing a curriculum for learning that can be applied to practice in under-resourced systems, across different cultures. Furthermore, this structured approach may help to identify and emphasise the 'absolute essentials' necessary to develop at least some neuropsychology in settings where no neuropsychologists are available – while limiting the 'nice to have' knowledge and skills.

A general observation about professional development

While we divide the areas of skill into sections, there is no expectation that, once completed, a specific section is 'done and dusted'. On the contrary, CPD is both an expectation and a prerequisite for practising clinicians, providing evidence that one is still competent. Furthermore, it is an ethical obligation to stay up to date with professional practice if you are providing a service to patients (see Chapters 14 and 16). However, is good CPD always necessarily about attending the latest research conference? Should we, in addition, not also aim to periodically revisit the basics, and should we not use supervision and other vehicles of CPD more proactively to achieve this goal?

We argue that this book's contents are not necessarily only for those in training or those working in under-resourced areas, or specifically for newly qualified clinical neuropsychologists embarking on their first hospital job. How important is it for various professionals, including psychologists, to regularly refresh their knowledge in these broad areas of neuropsychology? The answer is perhaps more than we realise. Colleagues often report that they derive enormous benefit from attending workshop-based training events and by rereading key textbooks on clinical neuropsychology. This is certainly a sensible and valuable approach to CPD in its own right. Perhaps this is CPD – continuous *practice* development – the perfect companion to lifelong continuing professional development.

Continuing professional development is a somewhat mercurial concept. Employers fund and support CPD and we assume that it is a natural part of professional life. Is CPD something that we engage in every year in order to learn about the latest research findings? Or is it equivalent to an 'MOT' (the vehicle-roadworthiness test in the United Kingdom), periodically ensuring that at least the basics are in place to guarantee safe functioning? Some might argue that it is much more representative of a process of reflection on current practice. CPD is probably all of these things combined and more. However, there is something to be said for *revision* being one of the more effective antidotes for staleness in clinical practice. The importance of remaining abreast of current best-practice policies, and the latest research findings, cannot be emphasised enough; this can only be achieved when a clinician has a sound, up-to-date knowledge base that can be used as a baseline against which to compare new ways of doing things. In essence, reflective practice involves considering what is essentially already historical, and how something was done in the past, with the purpose of learning from, and improving upon, current practice.

In countries where neuropsychology is either not an established or regulated profession, or where it is a new and emerging clinical discipline, colleagues from other fields may need to be educated as to what neuropsychology is, what the role of neuropsychologists is and what clinical skills and services neuropsychologists can provide. This may seem like a strange thing to say, but it is highly relevant to the field of neuropsychology. It comes from first-hand experience that often physicians, and even neurologists, for example, have very little knowledge or understanding as to what neuropsychologists do and what skills and services they offer. In more extreme environments, where even very basic resources (such as telephones, clean water and paper) are lacking, there is a more fundamental task required in informing people about what psychologists offer. At this level, community-based individuals, such as religious leaders and interpreters, will frequently need to be drawn upon to aid in the dissemination of information.

Neuropsychologists must be prepared to educate colleagues within the broader medical field and the general public, and to 'market' the profession. One of the best marketing strategies is to see as many patients as possible, thereby facilitating regular contact with other professionals. This often requires a gradual process of raising awareness by psychologists who work within multidisciplinary teams. Perhaps unsurprisingly, this task is often necessary in countries with relatively well-established neuropsychology services. Historically, the profession started to grow very gradually due to this process taking place in academic and clinical settings, often involving collaborative work with other professionals.

What can we learn from history?

Before proceeding to the next chapters, let us consider, very broadly, the practice of clinical neuropsychology and whether we can learn anything from the history of this field. It immediately becomes apparent that the dilemma is what to choose from an overwhelming selection of topics. Clinical neuropsychology, although a relatively young profession, already has a rich history. There are many pioneers in the field from whom one can learn. Interestingly, a fair proportion of these figures are not actually clinical neuropsychologists, or psychologists of whatever speciality for that matter. Nor are many of the other historically pertinent pockets of information in a sense exclusively 'owned' by the field of clinical neuropsychology. This is, of course, an entirely desirable situation. Clinical neuropsychology is almost always practised in multidisciplinary contexts. It is within these environments that important professional cross-pollination can take place. This is in fact one of the reasons why the 'toolbox' of the modern-day neuropsychologist is made up of such a diverse range of core knowledge and skills.

This book was written with the sole intention of briefly exploring the most salient and relevant practical information for aspiring clinical neuropsychologists and those psychologists or other professionals who work with brain injury and can therefore benefit from acquiring neuropsychological know-how. This is a difficult task to attempt and always an impossible one to achieve with any degree of perfection. There is always the risk of getting it wrong, for there are many experts who bring different perspectives. However, while over-inclusiveness would limit the number of 'enemies' made, it would also make considerably more difficult the lives of those starting out in the field, who need to gain practical knowledge fairly rapidly.

If there were space for only one historical topic, what would it be? Identifying a seminal figure in the field of neuropsychology is an extremely daunting task. However, we were fortunately relieved of this burden by remembering an important angle on the history of neuropsychology, which is: patients are inevitably central to everything. The *case report* remains, to this day, one of the most valuable tools for problem-based learning in the clinical professions. Case reports provide one of the best ways to get a real feel for a subject from very early on in one's training. We therefore felt that a seminal case report would be a better approach, and have chosen the case of Phineas Gage, which still serves as one of the very best for illustrating concepts that remain of great importance to the field of clinical neuropsychology.

The case of Phineas Gage

Phineas Gage was one of the earliest known survivors of a severe traumatic brain injury. Damasio (1994) provides one of the more detailed case reports concerning Gage. In short, Gage was severely injured in Vermont during the mid 19th century following a blasting accident involving a tamping iron. The accident was caused by explosives detonating unexpectedly, resulting in the tamping iron being blasted through the frontal region of his brain. Astonishingly, Phineas did not lose consciousness and was apparently taken by horse and cart to be seen by a Dr Harlow shortly after the accident. However, Gage apparently saw another doctor first, to whom he reportedly said: 'Doctor, here is business enough for you.'

Perhaps the most striking aspect regarding this case is Gage's subsequent (post-acute) clinical presentation. It is reported that, having made what was thought to be an amazing physical recovery, Gage started to present with personality changes and emotional problems. It was said by those who knew him well that 'Gage was no longer Gage'. Some authors have questioned if this was genuinely the case; was it not perhaps that, as time passed, people became more aware of his problems? Some of the doubts about Gage may simply be explained by either the lack of verifiable information (especially with regard to reliable pre-injury data) or perhaps by an over-interpretation of what little information is available today.

We may never know with certainty exactly what Gage was like before and after his injury, or exactly which brain regions were damaged (MacMillan, 2008). It is even possible that he might have made quite a good recovery – the primary sources of information about Gage are actually very limited (MacMillan, 2008). Furthermore, the first photograph of Gage taken after his injury was only very recently discovered (in 2009), and with it came speculation that his outcome might have been much better than thought. We can never be exactly sure of what aspects of this case represent sheer speculation. However, what we do now know is that the difficulties that Gage reportedly experienced are very common following severe traumatic brain injury. At the time, these insights/understandings into some of the effects of brain injury on behaviour did not exist. It is therefore understandable that many people found Gage's presentation rather puzzling.

There are many modern cases similar to Gage's. New technologies have now evolved to investigate the effect of dramatic injuries. Interestingly, a recent paper looked at the likely disruption of complex white matter pathways in Gage's case (Van Horn et al., 2012). To this day, even the most experienced clinicians can sometimes be taken by surprise by how difficult it can be to disentangle from the patient's presentation what the results of brain injury are likely to be, versus what is more representative of other factors, including pre-injury personality characteristics. While acquired brain injury is perhaps more of a fixed or constant factor, the individual's presentation is inevitably coloured by intrapersonal pre-injury factors.

There are also other factors to consider when looking at different presentations following similar injuries. Culture, language and access to healthcare, to mention but a few, are all potent modifiers of patients' clinical presentations. In this book, we have tried to juxtapose developed and developing world perspectives, while attempting to identify the universally applicable neuropsychological knowledge and skills that are important to practitioners who work with neurocognitively impaired patients. It is perhaps a truism that irrespective of the working environment – whether it is well resourced or under-resourced – there are certain fundamental skills that can potentially help to achieve the biggest impact for a substantial proportion of the patients one is likely to encounter.

Conclusion

As with all healthcare professions, developing skills in neuropsychology requires the rapid absorption of a phenomenal amount of information on a wide range of topics. Learning neuropsychology is to a large extent about balance: too slow and you have too little to forget, too fast and you forget too much. Learning has to be slow and, at the same time, fast. A possible way to achieve the precarious balance between pace of learning and retention of facts is to do some decluttering. The organisation of the information that needs to be covered can be done on two levels. First, define the broad areas of information, and then include the specific topics that make up these areas. Second, arrange the broad areas in such a way that there is an increasing flow towards more practice-based skills and knowledge. Then, once all of the necessary information has been covered, start with problem-based learning and supervised clinical practice as soon as possible.

Going over the essential information initially, and starting with practice, should be the fast part; repetition and more repetition will be the slow part. This will hopefully bring practice-derived clinical wisdom. Be comfortable with this slowness, as it is here that clinical memory and experience evolve over time into clinical intuition. Always consider history, not only in the sense of reflective practice, but also in terms of understanding what we can learn from the history of the profession. Never underestimate the power of learning from/hearing about patients' narratives through case reports. Finally, never hesitate to go back to the very beginning with regard to information and knowledge to ensure that the current way of doing things is as healthy as it can be. The following chapter starts with what many would think is the very foundation of clinical neuropsychology – *neuroanatomy*.

Practical tips

1. Read patients' accounts of brain injury – many excellent texts exist, such as *Injured Brains of Medical Minds*, by Narinder Kapur, and *The Man Who Mistook His Wife for a Hat*, by Oliver Sacks (see the 'Selected further reading' list at the end of this chapter).

2. Try to obtain a copy of Kevin Walsh's out-of-print classic *Understanding Brain Damage* (see the 'Selected further reading' list at the end of this chapter). Although somewhat dated (there are, however, more recent editions), it still contains great clinical wisdom.

3. Where possible, identify (early on) a fully qualified clinical neuropsychologist within your workplace who can: (i) oversee your professional development, (ii) serve as a mentor and (iii) supervise your clinical work.

Points for reflective practice

1. It was proposed that there are three broad areas that can provide the knowledge and skills base for the practice of clinical neuropsychology, namely *Basic foundations*, *Clinical practice* and *Professional issues*. How do these areas relate to each other, and are there other areas of knowledge that may be useful?
2. Discuss the following: the case of Phineas Gage is one of the most famous in neuropsychology and highlights many contentious points, including the potential discrepancy between lesion and clinical presentation, and the complexity surrounding the assessment of potential premorbid personality and post-injury personality change.
3. What is the purpose of continuing professional development (CPD), and how can we best achieve the aims of this process?

Selected further reading

Kapur, N. (1998). *Injured brains of medical minds*. Oxford: Oxford University Press.

MacMillan, M. (2008). Phineas Gage: Unravelling the myth. *The Psychologist*, *21*, 828–831.

Sacks, O. (1991). *The man who mistook his wife for a hat*. London: Picador.

Walsh, K. E. (1985). *Understanding brain damage: A primer of neuropsychological evaluation*. New York: Churchill Livingstone.

2

NEUROANATOMY

Introduction

Where does one begin to develop the basic knowledge base that is relevant to clinical neuropsychology? As highlighted in the previous chapter, there are several core topics that are fundamental to neuropsychology. But which of these represents a logical starting point for studying neuropsychology? What do we need to know first to make it easier to systematically and progressively develop our knowledge and clinical skills? It is probably best to grasp the inevitable nettle facing all aspiring neuropsychologists – and others embarking on a career in the neurosciences – which is the need to develop a reasonable understanding of *neuroanatomy* before anything else is attempted.

Neuroanatomy provides the foundations that are essential to understanding most concepts within neuroscience, particularly in neuropsychology. While studying neuroanatomy is generally a journey of fascinating discovery, it is also at times an enterprise that can make you think more clearly about what exactly it was that made you want to work within neuropsychology in the first place. Many of us have struggled with textbooks, often without very good results. Almost without fail, our hours of studying tend to disappear from memory, seemingly never to return – some experienced colleagues might even say that this is the nature of the beast when attempting to memorise neuroanatomy.

What works best then when it comes to studying neuroanatomy? To some extent, the answer depends on one's personal preference when it comes to memorising new material. A good textbook is for many an obvious starting point. Textbooks with photographs of actual brain structures can be far more useful than those that only include line sketches. For example, Crossman and Neary's excellent textbook is widely used across different disciplines – see 'Selected further reading' at the end of this chapter. What also helps is to use problem-based learning, linking structure, function and pathology right from the outset. What this implies is that it is probably unwise to separate learning about anatomical structures from knowing what the corresponding functions are (such as language and memory) that are associated with these brain regions. In clinical neuropsychology, these generally tend to be cognitive and behavioural functions, but not exclusively so. Some of the most important anatomical structures covered in this chapter, along with their main associated functions, are provided in Table 2.1. The common neuropathologies that affect these structures are also provided (see Chapter 3).

Ultimately, anatomy is something best learned in three dimensions. However, opportunities for learning through brain dissections are severely limited; nevertheless, there are fortunately alternatives. For example, the Internet and mobile phone apps offer some really impressive tools for studying neuroanatomy. The best combination to facilitate learning is perhaps the use of richly illustrated handbooks in conjunction with brain models that can be taken apart and attendance at brain dissections. Interestingly, in clinical practice, most of the time neuroanatomy is viewed and discussed by looking at scans, yet this aspect is often neglected when one is studying, or in under-resourced settings where scans may not be widely available. An excellent text addressing this issue is Atlas and Kaplan's (2001) pocket guide to brain MRI (see 'Selected further reading' at the end of this chapter) that can easily be used during ward rounds and case discussions. Finally, it is vital to persevere (and to revise!), as this is one of the most important topics for any aspiring clinical neuropsychologist to know. Studying neuroanatomy is always hard, but learning it in small chunks helps.

Basic neuroanatomy: the bony structures

The hard stuff is as good a starting point as any when it comes to studying neuroanatomy. Mercifully, there are few *bones* that need to be known by those aspiring to work in neuropsychology. Nevertheless, one does need to be aware of a bit more than just the fact that the brain, comprising soft tissue, is encased by the skull. The skull is made up of many separate bones, which fuse at a certain stage during a baby's early development. The brain has two hemispheres. In the vast majority of right-handers (dextrals), the left hemisphere is more involved in language and the right hemisphere in non-verbal functions, such as spatial cognition. There are four lobes to each brain hemisphere; working from the front (anterior) to the back (posterior), these are the *frontal lobes, temporal lobes, parietal lobes* and the *occipital lobes.*

Try this practical aid in order to both visualise and explain anatomical features. Make two fists with your thumbs pointing towards you. Imagine that the thumbs protruding towards you represent the two anterior poles of the frontal lobes. The first two knuckles represent the mid-temporal lobes, while immediately behind these (the next two knuckles) are the parietal lobes and, finally, pointing away from you, just above the wrist, the occipital lobes. By separating your fists, you can demonstrate the concept of the hemispheres and provide a midline view of internal structures, such as the ventricles and basal ganglia. If you do not have a brain model

TABLE 2.1 Brain anatomy, associated functions and commonly encountered neuropathology that affects neurocognitive functions

Anatomical area	Associated functions	Frequent concomitant neuropathology
Hypothalamus	Hormonal regulation; vegetative functions	Tumour
Cerebellum	Motor function, including coordination	Alcohol-related damage; stroke
Temporal lobes	Language and memory	Stroke; some dementias; traumatic brain injury; encephalitis; anoxia; epilepsy/seizures
Parietal lobes	Processing of perceptual information; spatial awareness; calculation; writing; bodily sensation (pain, touch, etc.)	Stroke; encephalitis; anoxia
Occipital lobes	Visual processing	Stroke; encephalitis; anoxia
Frontal lobes	Abstract thought; personality; planning; problem solving; inhibition/response suppression; working memory; movement; language (speech production)	Traumatic brain injury; encephalitis; anoxia; Pick's disease
Limbic system	Memory and emotion	Traumatic brain injury; encephalitis; stroke; alcohol-related damage
Cranial nerve I	Sense of smell	Traumatic brain injury; tumour
Cranial nerve II	Vision	Stroke; traumatic brain injury; tumour
Cranial nerve VIII	Hearing	Traumatic brain injury; tumour
Reticular formation	Processing of sensory and motor stimuli; sleep–wake cycle	Stroke; tumour
Ventricular system	Protective cushioning of brain provided by the cerebrospinal fluid (CSF)	Cysts; tumour; hydrocephalus; blocked shunts
Meninges	Protective mechanism	Meningitis; sub-arachnoid haemorrhage; sub-dural haemorrhage secondary to traumatic brain injury
Skull bones	Protective function	Depressed or linear fractures secondary to trauma; tumour
White matter	Connects regions of grey matter	Traumatic brain injury; degenerative conditions; stroke; tumour; alcohol or substance abuse; anoxia; HIV; Multiple sclerosis (MS)
Basal ganglia	Initiation and control of movement	Stroke; genetic conditions (e.g. Huntington's chorea), traumatic brain injury; Parkinson's disease (PD)
Corpus callosum	Connects the two cerebral hemispheres	Tumour; traumatic brain injury

and need to explain neuroanatomical concepts to patients, using your hand in this way as a visual aid may facilitate understanding and remembering. Alternatively, a simple drawing can be made. Visually based strategies are also invaluable when working in multicultural societies where at times, due to language barriers, one has to work through an interpreter who may not be completely familiar with scientific terminology.

Let us now return to the skull bones. The *skull base*, which is the part that the brain rests on, has an opening allowing the brainstem to link with the spinal cord. This hole is called the *foramen magnum*. During some types of acquired brain injury, most notably traumatic brain injury (TBI), the skull base may be damaged. Clinical signs associated with a skull base fracture include bleeding from the ear and hearing loss. Cranial nerve VIII (involved in hearing) is vulnerable to damage when the skull base is fractured. Such fractures do not always equate to a severe traumatic brain injury, but are of some importance as they can at least give some indication of the amount of mechanical force involved, or the amount of momentum transferred during the injury sustained. It is helpful when thinking about traumatic brain injury to consider the physics involved in momentum, where mass is multiplied with velocity.

The *temporal, occipital, parietal* and *frontal* bones are important too, and can also be fractured in a traumatic injury. The temporal bone is slightly thinner in places and can sometimes sustain a depressed fracture when, for example, someone is hit on the side of the head. This type of focal injury can sometimes result in post-traumatic epilepsy (especially when there are bone fragments in the brain tissue) and, if on the left, disturbances of language function – although one must also always be aware of *contrecoup* injuries involving the opposite side of the brain. Language disturbances following brain injury can be diagnostically confusing. Much of neuropsychological assessment is language-dependent. The patient's first/home language can further complicate matters: for example, in the case of an isiXhosa- or Welsh-speaking patient with a left temporal injury, admitted to a hospital where all the clinicians speak only English.

It is not only the physics of momentum that apply when considering brain injuries. Fractures frequently occur even where modest force has been transmitted to a very localised area of the skull, due to the concentration of the transfer of energy. For example, a penetrating injury can result from being hit on the head with a metal pipe or 'knobkerrie', or being stabbed. There are different types of skull fractures, including *hairline* fractures and *depressed* fractures. The latter are much more worrying, and can present a higher risk of post-traumatic seizures, for example.

The sharp bony protrusions (most notably the *sphenoid ridge*) upon which parts of the temporal and frontal lobes lie pose an obvious risk when the brain is moved violently during the deceleration/acceleration associated with high-velocity injuries. These bony protrusions can cause abrasions and contusions to the frontal and temporal lobes (most notably the anterior poles), which often show up on scans, with the neurocognitive consequences revealed upon neuropsychological testing.

Other skull bones are also occasionally referred to, most frequently the *facial bones*. The *orbital bones* (the bones around the eye) are often mentioned in medical notes and during case presentations – this is because they can be fractured during an assault or high-velocity injury. Again, this may provide valuable information to the clinician about the transfer of energy/force during the injury, which needs to be considered when determining severity. Knowledge of the bony structures, and how they react to the transfer of force through blunt objects or missiles involved in traumatic brain injuries, is important in neuropsychology. This is particularly salient when working in countries with high levels of violence, where an associated increase in the frequency of traumatic brain injuries occurs.

Brain topography and structures

The first-time dissector immediately observes that the brain has a unique outer appearance: the surface (*cortex*) consists of convolutions, or 'valleys' and 'hills'. These are known as *sulci* (the 'valleys') and *gyri* (the 'hills'), and their function is to maximise the surface area of the cortex. Once the inner brain structures are exposed, two features tend to stand out: the change in colour and the presence of rather large holes within the brain. While grey on the surface (constituting the cell bodies of the cortex), the adjacent tissue below is white. These white components are the nerve fibres (the *axons*, or 'tails' of the cell bodies) projecting throughout the brain. Axons get their white colour from the *myelin sheath* that covers them.

The above-mentioned projections serve as pathways between different brain regions, much like telecommunications cables. For example, vertical bundles of white matter fibres form the *internal capsule*, found almost in the middle (lateral to the midline) of each hemisphere. The *arcuate fasciculus* connects Broca's and Wernicke's areas, ensuring that areas which govern language comprehension (Wernicke's area) are connected to speech production areas (Broca's area). It is important to be aware of these fibres, as certain types of stroke, for example, involve the internal capsule. However, it is not only the cortex that contains grey matter – there are also islands of grey matter deeper within the brain. These are collectively referred to as the *basal ganglia*, the largest being the *corpus striatum*, which includes the *caudate nucleus*, *globus pallidus* and *putamen*. It is important for neuropsychologists to know about the basal ganglia because certain types of stroke in these areas can result in specific neurocognitive impairments, including memory problems.

One of the most important internal structures of the brain is the *limbic system*, which is generally considered to comprise the *cingulate gyrus*, *hippocampal formation*, *amygdala*, *septum*, *formix* and *hypothalamus*. The *Papez circuit* describes the pathways involved in the known functions of the limbic system, *memory*, *motivation* and *emotion*, among others. The hippocampus is involved with memory encoding. A lateralisation effect occurs where, in most right-handers, the left hippocampus is associated with verbal memory functions, whereas the right is responsible for visual memory. When both hippocampi are damaged, severe memory impairments can result, as in the classic case of 'HM'.

Some neuropathological conditions that involve the limbic system include *Korsakoff's psychosis*, *Klüver-Bucy syndrome*, *herpes simplex encephalitis* and *temporal lobe seizures*, among others. The hippocampus, due to its proximity to the *sphenoid ridge*, is also vulnerable to injury during high-velocity head trauma. Memory impairment severely limits patients' independence and increases the burden on families and communities. Fortunately, there are practical neuropsychological compensatory strategies that can be offered to try to limit patients' disability (see Chapter 11).

The second surprise encountered when dissecting a brain is that there are large 'holes' inside it. These holes comprise the ventricular system, made up of several fluid-filled spaces containing cerebrospinal fluid (CSF), which is produced in the ventricles by the *choroid plexus*. The lateral, third and fourth ventricles all produce CSF. The ventricular system communicates (meaning that it connects) the fluid between the brain and the skull, providing much-needed cushioning and protection for the brain. The largest of the ventricles are the two boomerang-shaped lateral ventricles in both hemispheres. The lateral ventricles connect downwards to the third ventricle in the midline by means of the *interventricular foramen*. The 'walls' on the sides of the third ventricle are provided by the *thalamus* and *hypothalamus*. The third ventricle connects downwards to the fourth ventricle via the *cerebral aqueduct*. The fourth ventricle lies between the brainstem and the cerebellum, and is connected to the subarachnoid space surrounding the brain by three apertures: in the midline the *foramen of Magendie* and laterally the two *foramina of Luschka*.

As previously mentioned, the skull base can be visualised as a 'bowl' containing the brain, with a hole (the *foramen magnum*) in the centre through which a 'pedestal' (the *brainstem*) protrudes, eventually becoming the spine. The brainstem is involved in maintaining vital, life-preserving functions, such as breathing. It consists (from the top down) of the *midbrain*, *pons* and *medulla oblongata*. The brainstem contains the *reticular formation*, which is directly involved in governing level of consciousness, among other critical functions. Ten of the 12 cranial nerves attach to the brainstem (numbers III to XII), connecting to some of the brainstem nuclei. The rear of the brainstem has four little 'bumps', the superior and inferior *colliculi*, which are associated with visual and auditory pathways.

The *cerebellum* lies posterior to the brainstem and has convolutions known as *folia*, similar to the sulci and gyri of the cortex, only smaller. The cerebellum contributes to the integration of movement, among other things, and may be associated with some memory functions. Motor integrity contributes to many functions and can affect performance on many neuropsychological tests. Motor impairment can, of course, also have a profound effect on patients' psychological wellbeing, especially in cultures where physical integrity of function is highly valued. Due to their anatomical location, the brainstem and cerebellum are well protected against direct force, but not against other dangers, such as stroke.

Besides the cushioning provided by CSF, how is direct contact between the soft cortex and the hard surface of the skull prevented? Three layers of membrane (*meninges*) cover the brain, providing protection. The *dura mater* lies directly under the skull, while below it is the *arachnoid mater*. The *pia mater* is attached to the brain's surface, closely following its convolutions. The dura mater is the tough outer layer (closest to the skull) and reaches down in the midline between the two hemispheres via the *falx cerebri* into the longitudinal fissure. From the rear of the brain, the dura mater reaches in horizontally via the *tentorium cerebelli*, protecting the cerebellum from movement. The *subarachnoid space*, containing CSF and blood vessels, lies between the arachnoid mater and pia mater.

These three layers are important for our understanding of certain pathologies, such as *subarachnoid haemorrhage*, *subdural haematoma*, *subdural haemorrhage* and *meningitis*. Meningitis is an infectious process and is particularly important to be aware of when working in countries where there are less robust public health systems – in particular, where there are no child inoculation programmes against some variants of this disease. Secondary (life-threatening) problems that may result from severe traumatic brain injury include subdural haemorrhage/haematomas, which can have very serious pressure effects on underlying brain tissue, which can increase as they enlarge (as bleeding occurs). We now turn our attention to some of the macro-anatomical structures of the brain.

The lobes and their functions

When viewed from the outside, the four lobes of each hemisphere form the most obvious macroscopic divisions of the brain. But how do we know where these lobes begin and end? Some of the major prominent sulci function almost like divisions between districts on a map, revealing where the different lobes begin and end. The frontal lobes start from immediately above the eye sockets, behind the frontal bone and extend backwards to the *central sulcus*. They do not extend below the *lateral fissure*, below which are the temporal lobes. The frontal lobes are of considerable interest to neuroscience, especially in light of cases such as Phineas Gage (Chapter 1). They are the seat of personality and are also associated with problem solving and abstract thought, planning, spontaneous initiative, set shifting, inhibition, curiosity, voluntary arousal and memory retrieval, among other functions – collectively referred to as *executive functions*. The frontal lobes are also involved in aspects of language (speech production involving Broca's area).

The temporal lobes are associated with several language and memory functions, including language comprehension involving Wernicke's area, axial memory (memory encoding) and learning, and emotion. The right *temporal lobe* is involved with visual memory, among many other functions, whereas the left is responsible for verbal memory. Anatomically, the lateral fissure delineates the temporal lobes; by extending this as an imaginary line towards roughly the middle of the area posterior to the central sulcus, we can upwardly define the boundary between the parietal and occipital lobes. *Heschl's gyrus* is found in the superior temporal lobe and is involved in auditory function. The *insula*, a hidden cortical area (unfortunately, without obvious landmarks), is located inside the lateral fissure. The occipital and parietal lobes are at the rear of the brain, separated by the *parieto-occipital sulcus*. The parietal lobes contain the primary *somatosensory cortex* and are associated with the processing of perceptual information, calculation, visuospatial functions, praxis, reading and bodily awareness, among other functions. The occipital lobes contribute to vision and visual processing – lesions can lead to a rare syndrome known as *Anton's syndrome*, where the patients are unaware of their blindness.

It should be remembered that the individual lobes serve many more functions than those briefly covered here. Moreover, the lobes do not function in isolation from each other – nor are they isolated from other brain structures, such as the brainstem and cerebellum. For example, patients with traumatic brain injury often present with cognitive impairment in several areas, due to a combination of focal lesions and the disruption of connections between different anatomical areas. Effective cognitive, behavioural and emotional functioning all very much depend on intact interconnected neural pathways. These pathways consist of more basic structures of the brain.

Brain cells

The brain is made up of *cells* called *neurons*, which are responsible for transmitting neuronal impulses via pathways. Neurons are generally comprised of a cell body, with a prominent tail called an *axon*. The cell body has several short arms (actually more like the branches of a tree) called *dendrites*. In contrast, the axon can be thought of as a single length of electrical cord. Bundles of axons make up white matter tracts or pathways. Impulses are transmitted via the neurons by means of *neurotransmitters*, such as *dopamine, serotonin, noradrenaline* and *acetylcholine*. Pathways can be interrupted by structural damage or altered biochemistry.

Neurons do not actually make direct contact: a gap called the *synapse* exists between them. The transmission of electrical impulses across this gap results from the release of neurotransmitters on the one side of the synapse, which affect receptors on the other side of the synapse; the synaptic gap is bridged, both chemically and electrically. The release of neurotransmitters changes the electrical properties or potential of the individual neurons. This is how impulses representing processed incoming perceptual stimuli via the senses – as well as cognition, behaviour, emotion and so forth – are transmitted, virtually instantaneously throughout the brain.

Why do individual neurons, and the brain itself, not simply 'fall apart' or 'fray'? Within the brain, there are cells, the *neuroglia*, that are not directly involved in the conduction of nerve impulses, but instead have a 'supporting role'. Metaphorically, neuroglia are the cement bonding the bricks together. *Oligodendroglia, microglia* and *astrocytes* are all examples of neuroglia. Many types of brain tumour result from the unexpected and undifferentiated growth (division) of neuroglia, resulting in an occupation of space within the brain, which in turn causes pressure on surrounding structures. In addition, neuroglia demand a 'fair share' of the nutrients carried by the blood, such as glucose and oxygen, thereby 'stealing' blood supply by default.

When brain injury has occurred (through trauma, for example), there can also be an increase in microglia in the area where the lesion occurred. Under other circumstances, for example, following a stroke, the blood associated with the stroke is eventually re-absorbed and the 'scar' that is left (which can be seen on neuroimaging) is composed mainly of water. It is important to realise that ultimately all cellular structures require a continuous supply of nutrients in order to continue to function and prevent cell death. This is achieved by means of a reliable and consistent blood supply.

Vascular structures

Many people struggle to understand what might be described as the 'plumbing' that supplies the brain with nutrients. However, it is crucially important to know the basics regarding the brain's blood supply – vascular pathology gives rise to fairly specific patterns of cognitive impairment and behavioural change, compared to traumatic brain injuries, for example. For some reason, the brain's vascular system tends to be a particularly difficult area of neuroanatomy to memorise. Perhaps this is similar to the lost motorist, who when receiving directions from someone almost inevitably promptly forgets everything after the third turn is described. It is likely that the motorist will be more successful if s/he is able to see the stepwise instructions and landmarks as a visual map in his/her mind's eye.

To help our three-dimensional visualisation of the brain's vasculature, we should turn it upside down. Imagine looking from underneath the brain, inwards. From the two pairs of vessels supplying blood to the brain, follow the vessels from there. There are two vascular 'dual carriageways' into the brain. First, the couple of *internal carotid arteries* make a few bends and go through the *cavernous sinus* before reaching the brain to the side of the optic chiasm (where cranial nerve II partially crosses). Here, branches create a circular flow ('traffic circle' or 'roundabout'), known as the *Circle of Willis*, which comprises both the *posterior* and *anterior communicating arteries*. From the Circle of Willis, the internal carotid divides into 'B-roads', the two *anterior cerebral arteries* and *middle cerebral arteries*. These 'roads' travel through some 'valleys'; the anterior cerebral arteries follow the longitudinal fissure and supply the medial (inside) part of the brain, whereas the middle cerebral arteries follow the lateral fissure, supplying the lateral parts of the hemispheres.

Two *vertebral arteries* are the second source of blood, entering the brain through a 'tunnel', the foramen magnum. Soon after the tunnel, this dual carriageway becomes a wide single road: the vertebral arteries join between the pons and medulla in the brainstem to form the *basilar artery*. Between the pons and midbrain, the basilar artery forms a 'junction' and divides into the *superior cerebellar arteries* and the *posterior cerebral arteries*. The posterior cerebral arteries are connected to the Circle of Willis (and thereby the internal carotid arteries) via the posterior communicating arteries. The posterior cerebral arteries irrigate the occipital lobes and a small portion of the lower temporal lobes.

Various other small arteries ('country lanes') leave the Circle of Willis and enter the brain's internal structures – known as *perforating arteries*. These perforating arteries provide blood to key structures (certainly from a neuropsychological perspective), such as the basal ganglia, the hypothalamus and the internal capsule.

Aneurysms in the Circle of Willis (for example, *anterior communicating artery aneurysms*) pose a great risk by potentially disrupting the blood supply to some of these crucial internal structures, which can in turn result in memory and executive impairment. Finally, the *superficial veins, deep veins* and the *dural venous sinuses* all perform the task of draining blood from the brain before it travels on its long journey back to the lungs to be resupplied with oxygen.

The cranial nerves

Some of the *cranial nerves* are of importance to neuropsychology; these will often be encountered in clinical notes. There are 12 cranial nerves. These are listed below, along with some of their corresponding functions.

I.   Olfactory nerve: smell
II.   Optic nerve: vision
III.   Oculomotor nerve: eye movement; pupil reaction
IV.   Trochlear nerve: eye movement
V.   Trigeminal nerve: sensation
VI.   Abducens nerve: eye movement
VII.   Facial nerve: facial movement; taste
VIII.   Vestibulocochlear nerve: hearing; sensation of head position
IX.   Glossopharyngeal nerve: sensation and taste; swallowing
X.   Vagus nerve: sensation; swallowing and speech; heart rate
XI.   Accessory nerve: head and shoulder movement
XII.   Hypoglossal nerve: tongue movement.

The following cranial nerves are of particular interest to neuropsychology. Cranial nerves I, II and VIII are important, especially in connection with traumatic brain injury – the loss of the sense of smell (*anosmia*) is a fairly reliable clinical marker of potential frontal lobe injury following head trauma and certain tumour types (olfactory groove meningiomas). The two *olfactory nerves* lie underneath (the base) and to the middle of the frontal lobes within the olfactory grooves, and are therefore vulnerable to shearing when subjected to rotational forces. The olfactory nerve comprises the *bulbus* and *tractus*. Visual problems can also occur following traumatic brain injury, but not typically due to cranial nerve (II) involvement: for example, blurred vision, unrelated to cranial nerve damage, is often reported.

 A skull base fracture that is associated with a traumatic brain injury can sometimes sever or bruise parts of cranial nerve VIII, resulting in hearing loss (sometimes unilaterally). This should not be confused with *tinnitus* (ringing in the ear), which can also occur following traumatic brain injury. Strokes can affect the functioning of cranial nerve VII, resulting in facial asymmetry (*Bell's palsy*). Acoustic neuromas (a tumour type) can affect cranial nerve VIII. Certain aneurysms or tumours can compress cranial nerve III, resulting in a disturbance of eye movement. The general neurological examination covers the assessment of the functioning of the cranial nerves and is performed by neurologists. One should be aware of any impairment associated with cranial nerve damage, as it may affect neuropsychological testing and rehabilitation, for example.

Conclusion

This chapter has provided a brief, introductory overview of the basic neuroanatomy relevant to clinical neuropsychology. What are the main practical messages? First, neuroanatomy is difficult to 'memorise'; but we feel this has a lot to do with not separating verbal memory from visualisation skills and strategies. With regard to verbal memory, perhaps one of the best ways to revise is to practise in an 'ecologically valid' environment. Can you comfortably explain relevant neuroanatomy to your patients? Can you explain it to students or trainees? The ultimate test would be if one could describe, for example, the anatomical damage that results from a severe traumatic brain injury ... through an interpreter. Can you visualise what is being discussed during a case presentation or on a ward round? The point is that at work in the hospital/clinic, neuroanatomy is, in the first instance, *talked* about (on ward rounds) and *written* about (in medical notes) all the time. An important skill to develop from very early on is the ability to visualise brain structures when no pictures/images are available.

When brain scans are viewed, use a pocket atlas as an aid, and learn to associate anatomical structures with neuropsychological functions, but not in a rigid way. In reality, brain lesions hardly ever match perfectly with the individual clinical presentations. Why is this the case? We of course do not fully understand the complex reasons for this, and there may be limitations to the technologies used to determine lesions (such as MRI) and to the tools used to determine and understand the patients' clinical presentations (such as neuropsychological tests). Nevertheless, there are three points that one should keep in mind. First, when it comes to lesions, disconnections are also important to consider. Second, the psychological aspects of brain injury can significantly colour the overall clinical presentation. And third, environmental factors, culture and language can all have a significant effect too. Some of these key issues are discussed later (see Chapter 7).

Practical tips

1. Purchase your own brain model (despite the better ones often being expensive) – preferably one that can be taken apart and that comes with a booklet or study aid.
2. Memorise neuroanatomy by practising drawing and identifying and, crucially, by explaining and describing brain structures.
3. Many find *The Human Coloring Book* by Diamond, Scheibel and Elson (1985) useful – or later developments of this approach to learning (such as Pinel & Edwards, 2007).
4. Do not become anxious if you forget the neuroanatomy you are trying to learn. This happens to most people. Therefore, revision is essential – even years after having qualified as a professional.

Points for reflective practice

1. Why do clinical neuropsychologists need a solid grounding in neuroanatomy if they do not actually become involved in the physical (biological) aspects of the diagnosis and treatment of patients?
2. Which is the most important lobe of the brain? Is there a lobe that is more important than the others?
3. Is there always a direct, causal link between neuroanatomical structure and human functioning, including cognition, behaviour and emotion?

Selected further reading

Atlas, S. W., & Kaplan, R. T. (2001). *Pocket atlas of cranial magnetic resonance imaging* (2nd ed.). Philadelphia: Lippincot, Williams & Wilkins.

Crossman, A. R., & Neary, D. (2010). *Neuroanatomy: An illustrated colour text* (4th ed.). Edinburgh: Churchill Livingstone.

Diamond, M. C., Scheibel, A. B., & Elson, L. M. (1985). *The human coloring book*. New York: HarperCollins.

Pinel, J. P. J., with Edwards, M. (2007). *A colorful introduction to the anatomy of the human brain: A brain and psychology coloring book* (2nd ed.). New York: Pearson.

3

NEUROPATHOLOGY

Introduction

Learning and understanding neuropathology requires a basic knowledge of neuro-anatomy. Neuropathology is the second area within the basic foundations that clinical neuropsychologists have to study and make sense of. As is the case with neuroanatomy, neuropathology also involves a substantial amount of information. A difficulty associated with studying neuropathology relates to the huge number of conditions that have been described. There is also great variation in how conditions are organised into an overall structure/diagnostic system. Hence, one of the first key steps is to define some clinically useful distinctions, which should ideally mirror the way clinical services are organised, as this may help practitioners to concentrate more on the conditions that they are most likely to encounter in clinical practice.

One of the most common (and certainly most practical) broad distinctions within the classification of neuropathology is to divide all neurological damage or illness into *acquired brain injury* versus *progressive conditions*. The former tends to include *traumatic brain injury*, *stroke* and *brain infections*. The latter often includes the *dementias*, *genetic conditions* (such as *Huntington's chorea*) and diagnoses such as *Multiple sclerosis*, *Parkinson's disease* and *Guillain-Barré syndrome*. Other distinctions within classification systems are based on, for example, conditions requiring neurosurgery, such as tumours, aneurysms and complications from traumatic brain injury. Epilepsies, or brain injuries that result from substance abuse (such as *Korsakoff's psychosis*), are other examples of such distinctions.

There is huge overlap and many grey areas when dealing with diagnostic divisions. For example, what is and what is not genetically determined is not always entirely clear. Some dementias may result from a previous head injury. Learning disabilities can and do result from acquired brain injury, and often have co-morbidity with acquired brain injury or other genetic conditions, as do almost all the other diagnostic entities. However, learning difficulties may often be associated with socio-political factors, such as educational and cultural deprivation, which of course cluster with poverty and other non-biological factors.

It is not always possible, despite exhaustive investigations, to actually identify a definite biological aetiology for a patient's impairment, whether it takes the form of cognitive decline, personality change or a behavioural disorder. In some cases, what seems to have been a relatively minor biological event then appears to result in major cognitive impairment – again this makes the classification of the presenting condition more complex. Here, one of the most common examples would be patients who sustain what appears to be a minor head injury or concussion with no loss of consciousness or post-traumatic amnesia, but who nevertheless present with severe and enduring cognitive impairment. With these diagnostic complexities in mind, what follows is a brief overview of the most common types of pathology that practitioners are likely to encounter.

Traumatic brain injury

Traumatic brain injury (TBI) is frequently encountered. It is generally prevalent in most countries, but particularly in developing countries (due to over-population, lawlessness, unroadworthy vehicles and other contributing factors), which places huge demands on already overburdened healthcare systems. In countries such as South Africa, road accidents and violent crime affect many citizens, resulting in extremely high incidence rates of head trauma. Long-term outcomes following TBI are often poor, placing significant burdens on families and communities. Neuropsychologists usually encounter TBI in the context of requests for neuropsychological testing and cognitive rehabilitation.

Traumatic brain injury is a leading cause of death and disability around the world. It frequently has a tri-modal distribution: young children, young adults (mostly males) and the elderly. Traumatic brain injuries result from the transfer of force or momentum to brain tissue, usually due to severe acceleration or deceleration. The most common causes of TBI are motor vehicle accidents (MVAs), assaults and sporting injuries. A general distinction within neuropathological classification is as follows. Head injuries that result from trauma can be either *closed* or *open*. Another category is blast-induced TBI, the so called 'signature injury' of recent wars.

Open head injuries usually result from missile wounds (such as bullet wounds) or from events where the skull has been fractured and the brain exposed. Generally speaking, severe closed TBI associated with the transfer of external force tends to result in contusions of the anterior poles of the frontal and temporal lobes, diffuse axonal injury (DAI) and *haemorrhages* inside the brain. Bleeding between the brain and the *meninges* can also occur. Blast-induced TBI may have three distinct mechanisms of injury: (1) transmission of the energy associated with the actual blast wave; (2) objects (shrapnel) penetrating the brain; and (3) acceleration/deceleration as the person is propelled through the air, along with their sudden stopping (hitting the ground or a stationary object).

The ability to determine the severity of a TBI is an important clinical skill; however, it is unfortunately not easy to master. Neuropsychologists (especially those who work in the post-acute setting) frequently have to make a retrospective determination as to what the severity of a patient's TBI was likely to have been. There is an association, although not as robust as many would say, between severity and impairment and associated disability, as well as with long-term outcome. This is why it is important to have a method for determining severity. Four clinical markers are generally used: (1) the duration of loss of consciousness; (2) depth of coma; (3) length of post-traumatic amnesia (PTA) and; (4) the presence of anatomical abnormalities on brain scans – for more information on scans and TBI, see Bigler and Maxwell (2011) (see 'Selected further reading' at the end of this chapter). Unfortunately, some of this information is sometimes missing/not recorded, making a retrospective judgement of severity more difficult. In clinical practice it is not uncommon to see patients with very severe injuries who present with subtle impairment of cognition and other functions, while conversely, patients with supposedly mild to moderate injuries may present with quite profound cognitive impairment and other difficulties. While there is a fairly general pattern of presentation that typically follows TBI, substantial individual variation also frequently occurs.

Clinical presentations following moderate to severe TBI tend to be a combination of *cognitive impairment, behavioural change* and *emotional difficulties*. A period of PTA is common. The length of time that a patient remains in PTA offers the best indicator of the prognosis. The typical picture of neurocognitive impairment following TBI involves *executive dysfunction*. Memory impairment (especially frontal amnesia – memory retrieval problems on an executive basis) is common, and in some cases, language difficulties occur, including word-finding difficulties.

Frequently, the most problematic symptoms following TBI involve behavioural and personality changes and various aspects of executive impairment, including: poor judgement; lack of awareness of impairments/deficits or the implications thereof; impaired problem-solving ability and concrete thought processes (inability to think abstractly); reduced social skills; lack of inhibition; poor initiation; and reduced emotional control (for example, an outburst of rage in response to a minor stimulus). Impulsivity is also common. Physical problems (such as sensory loss and loss of motor function) are slightly less common, but do occur in many severe TBI cases. Post-traumatic epilepsy also sometimes occurs. Mild TBI (including more severe post-concussion syndromes), on the other hand, tends to present with reduced capacity for information processing, headaches, anxiety, dizziness, irritability and vertigo, among other symptoms.

Cerebrovascular accidents (stroke)

Cerebrovascular accidents, commonly known as *strokes*, tend to present in older adults (especially those over 65) more frequently than in young adults and children. There are many classifications, but Lishman (1998) has divided stroke into two broad pathological processes: *haemorrhage* (including *intracerebral haemorrhage* and *subarachnoid haemorrhage*) and *infarction* (including *thrombosis* and *embolism*). Infarcts are more common than haemorrhages. An infarct is dead brain tissue that results from a lack of oxygen supply to cells. Infarction is caused by the disruption of blood supply to a brain region due to either a *thrombus* (a blood clot/thromboembolism) or an *embolus* (such as a detached piece of arterial plaque). Thrombosis generally results from *arteriosclerosis*, where blood vessels become progressively occluded as plaques thicken. Embolism occurs when a piece of debris, such as an arterial plaque, dislodges and is pumped through the bloodstream, becoming plugged in a blood vessel, causing a blockage.

Brain haemorrhages are often caused by burst *aneurysms*. An aneurysm is the bulging of a blood vessel, forming a balloon-like protrusion in its wall. When aneurysms burst or, alternatively, in the absence of an aneurysm, when a blood vessel bursts because of a weakness in its wall, bleeding into the surrounding brain tissue occurs. This is known as an intracerebral haemorrhage. In addition, *arteriovenous malformations*, which are 'bird's-nests' of abnormal blood vessels, may also result in haemorrhage should they rupture, or, alternatively, they may result in reduced blood flow to surrounding brain tissue when intact. Finally, subarachnoid haemorrhage is the occurrence of bleeding between the *pia mater* and *arachnoid mater*.

What patterns of impairment are usually associated with stroke? Generally speaking, strokes tend to result in disrupted blood flow to specific brain regions, depriving tissue of essential oxygen and glucose. While not always true, in stroke, lesions tend to be more circumscribed compared to the diffuse lesions that can follow brain infection or traumatic brain injury, for example. Accordingly, the impairments that result from a stroke tend to be more specific. Almost any domain of cognitive function, or combination of domains, can be affected by a stroke, along with physical, emotional and/or behavioural changes.

Some strokes have an almost asymptomatic presentation, with little discernable impairment of physical, cognitive or behavioural function. Strokes involving the left temporal area are likely to affect language (especially in right-handers). Similarly, strokes affecting the frontal regions either directly, or indirectly, may result in executive impairment and personality changes. With stroke, as with other focal lesions, it is not only the functions associated with the lesion site that can be affected, but also those distant to the lesion (a phenomenon known as *diaschisis*) due to disconnected pathways/interrupted blood flow. This is particularly important in Circle of Willis aneurysms, for example.

A brief case vignette illustrates the effect of diaschisis. John, a 55-year-old engineer, suffered a ruptured anterior communicating artery aneurysm. Following lifesaving emergency neurosurgery, he made a complete physical recovery. After three months, John returned to work, but was dismissed after only two months due to interpersonal conflict resulting from gross social misjudgements with clients. Such behaviour was completely uncharacteristic, as John was always a shy man. Neuropsychological testing, when performed, revealed profound executive impairment. Anterior communicating artery aneurysms impact directly on the *basal ganglia*, but also on the distant frontal cortex due to disruption of the complex basal–striatal–cortical pathways.

Other cerebrovascular conditions that are relatively frequently encountered include *transient ischaemic attacks* (TIAs) and *lacunar infarcts*. A TIA is a brief (by definition usually 24 hours or less) presentation of focal neurological deficits due to temporary occlusion or reduced blood flow within the vessels. TIAs are thought to resolve completely in most cases, although this is somewhat controversial – at least from a neuropsychological perspective. With careful neuropsychological testing, subtle cognitive deficits may sometimes be identified in patients who have suffered TIAs, and abnormalities on brain scans are also occasionally revealed. In some cases, TIAs may be an early sign of a more severe stroke to follow.

Lacunar infarcts usually result from occlusions and tend to occur in the basal ganglia and surrounding white matter. Lacunar infarcts can be asymptomatic, or result in sensory and motor problems. They sometimes occur gradually over time, and can be associated with an insidious onset that ultimately progresses to *dementia*. In *Binswanger's disease*, lacunar infarcts occur in the *periventricular white matter*, thus affecting some of the pathways to the frontal cortex. Binswanger's disease may therefore, in addition to problems with walking and incontinence, also present with impaired executive functioning. There are of course a multitude of other cerebrovascular pathologies, but these are probably less frequently encountered unless one works full-time in a specialist stroke unit.

Brain infections

Brain infections include *encephalitis, meningitis, acquired immunodeficiency syndrome (AIDS), neurosyphilis, cerebral abscesses* and *cerebral malaria* (Lishman, 1998). There are many varieties of encephalitis (acute inflammation of the brain), a primary disease caused by a virus. Interestingly, a viral aetiology is often assumed, rather than evidenced by virological testing. However, it is sometimes the presence of an infection elsewhere in the body that causes a reaction in the brain, rather than the direct presence of a virus within the brain. Some examples of encephalitis include *herpes simplex encephalitis, Japanese encephalitis* and *herpes zoster encephalitis*. Herpes simplex encephalitis is probably the most commonly encountered encephalitis.

Another important example of a viral disease likely to cause an inflammation of the brain is *acquired immunodeficiency syndrome (AIDS)*, which stems from the *human immunodeficiency virus (HIV)*. Acquired immunodeficiency syndrome involves compromised immunity and the presence of an active disease process. It remains a major health concern in both the developed and developing world, with most cases in the sub-Saharan region of Africa. Acquired immunodeficiency syndrome also frequently carries the risk of cognitive impairments due to encephalopathy, which can lead to *AIDS dementia complex (ADC)* or *HIV dementia*. Much research is currently being undertaken to try to understand the various cognitive presentations seen with HIV/AIDS and to learn how these profiles relate to CD4 counts, to the different clades of the virus and to highly active antiretroviral therapy (HAART) treatment (which many individuals in poorer countries do not have access to). Such endeavours are greatly complicated by the risk of *opportunistic infections* that occur with

HIV/AIDS and the associated difficulty of not being sure what symptoms and neurocognitive deficits are attributable to which pathological process.

Meningitis is an infection of the covering layers of membrane (the meninges) surrounding the brain – its cause can be either bacterial or viral. In countries such as South Africa, where *tuberculosis* is rife and not adequately treated and managed in a large number of the population, *tuberculosis meningitis* also occurs. With this disease, the tuberculosis bacteria invade the brain, affecting the membranes and the fluid surrounding the brain and spinal cord (*spinal tuberculosis*). Another reason for the high prevalence of this disease in developing countries (relative to first-world countries) is the presence of HIV/AIDS, which is rife in many areas and creates a huge risk for opportunistic infections.

Cerebral malaria is seen in parts of Africa and Asia and patients with associated neuropsychological deficits many be encountered. Neurosyphilis is also still seen in parts of the world and can result in a severe dementia many years after the primary infection.

The neurocognitive effects of brain infections vary enormously. To some degree, this depends on the areas affected by the disease. In some cases, the pattern of involvement and the corresponding impairments are more specific – most notably perhaps in herpes simplex encephalitis. In other infectious processes, such as AIDS, there is wide variation in the cognitive, physical and emotional impairments that can occur. Neurosyphilis has been called 'the great pretender' in view of its unpredictable pattern of presentations – variation can range from barely discernible cognitive change through to severe impairment resulting in dementia. Furthermore, any neuropsychiatric disorder may occur in the presence of neurosyphilis and AIDS, reflecting the variety of presentations associated with these diagnoses. In contrast, herpes simplex encephalitis, if untreated, tends to severely affect the medial temporal lobes (including the limbic system), along with the mesial parts of the frontal lobes, typically resulting in axial amnesia and executive dysfunction.

A short case vignette illustrates some of the above points. Precious was 29 years old when she was admitted to a psychiatric ward following increasingly out-of-character behaviour. She was reported to have become very suspicious of neighbours and terrified that witchcraft was being used to transmit derogatory voices through the walls of her shack. Precious responded well to antipsychotic medication and was soon discharged. However, she had to be readmitted 12 months later when she became increasingly disoriented for time and unable to remember even the names of people in her township who were previously very familiar to her. Brief bedside cognitive assessment revealed significant impairment of new learning and language. A CT brain scan showed widespread areas of signal change, while baseline blood tests were performed, revealing that she was HIV positive.

Brain tumours

Many *tumours* diagnosed in patients for the first time are cancerous (malignant). However, some are *benign* (not cancerous), such as *meningiomas* and *schwannomas*.

Cancer is, put simply, an undifferentiated and unchecked division (growth) of cells that then invade surrounding cells. Tumours can occur anywhere in the body, including the brain, and can produce various effects on the brain (Lishman, 1998). It can be difficult to separate the effects of the lesion (tumour site) from more distant pressure dynamics (possibly raised in intracranial pressure) and from disturbances in blood supply surrounding the tumour.

Victor and Ropper (2001) divide tumours into *primary* and *secondary brain tumours*. Primary brain tumours arise from the cells inside the brain. Secondary brain tumours originate from disease elsewhere in the body (the primary site), which then affects the brain (the secondary site). *Gliomas* are tumours that grow from the glial cells inside the brain, and are the most common type of primary brain tumour. The gliomas include *oligodendroglial tumours*, *astrocytomas* and *mixed gliomas*, of which astrocytomas are the most common. The most common sources of secondary brain tumours are the lungs and breasts, and skin cancer (*melanoma*). There are also tumours that are not inside the actual brain tissue, but nevertheless affect the brain – these are known as *meningiomas*, which grow (usually slowly) from the membranes covering the brain, and tend to have an effect by exerting pressure on underlying brain structures.

By considering the dynamic biomechanical effects of brain tumours, it should be clear that different patterns of cognitive impairment and behavioural change can occur, depending on tumour location. Tumours are in some ways similar to focal lesions: for example, tumours in the frontal lobes generally result in executive impairment and behavioural changes, as is the case with other frontal lobe pathologies. There are also important differences in the ways that tumours affect clinical presentation. Many dynamic factors can influence how patients present, including the rate of tumour growth, disturbances in blood supply surrounding the tumour and biochemical changes.

Furthermore, tumour treatment – including *brain surgery*, *chemotherapy* and *radiation* – can effect neurocognitive functioning. For this reason, psychologists may sometimes be asked to perform 'before treatment' and 'after treatment' neurocognitive testing. Sadly, though, especially in some developing countries, access to treatment may be severely limited. Under such circumstances, one may be asked to document a possible trajectory in neurocognitive function through bedside testing or to provide psychological support (as part of palliative care, for example). Receiving a cancer diagnosis can naturally be expected to result in significant anxiety and depression – which will contribute to patients' presentations and potentially influence performance on neuropsychological tests. It is often emotionally and ethically difficult for clinicians to determine what psychological input to offer under such circumstances, especially where resources are limited.

Hydrocephalus

The ventricular system can become blocked by a tumour, for example, or if reabsorption of CSF is too slow. Under such conditions there is an increase in pressure on the surrounding brain tissue – resulting in *hydrocephalus*. Broadly speaking, there are two main types of hydrocephalus: non-communicating (obstructive) hydrocephalus and communicating (non-obstructive) hydrocephalus. Normal pressure hydrocephalus, a type of communicating hydrocephalus, usually presents with a triad of symptoms: a magnetic gait (walking as if one's feet are stuck to the ground), urinary incontinence and cognitive impairment (most notably slowness and memory problems). Shunts are often employed to drain excess CSF, while surgery can be performed to remove tumours or cysts, for example.

Anoxia and hypoxia

Total or near total disruption of the brain's oxygen supply causes *anoxia*, resulting in severe damage within minutes – and even dementia in extreme cases. In *hypoxia*, blood oxygen levels are lowered (blood flow tends to continue) rather than oxygen supply being totally disrupted. The causes of anoxia or hypoxia include: *cardiac arrest*; cessation of breathing; near-drowning; accidents involving anaesthesia; *sleep apnoea*; carbon monoxide poisoning; *status epilepticus*; *hypoglycaemia*; and high altitude. Given the severity of the impairment associated with anoxia and the more serious cases of hypoxia, prevention or extremely early reversal or removal of the cause is vital.

Some of the more insidious onsets of chronic hypoxia (for example, gas leaks in homes) can potentially be detected through subtle symptoms before any permanent brain damage occurs, or may only result in relatively mild impairments. However, in acute onset situations, such as cardiac arrest, many patients do not regain consciousness. When patients do survive and brain damage occurs, neurocognitive deficits involving memory and other cognitive difficulties of varying degrees arise (including potential deficits of higher visual functioning), as well as behavioural changes. The long-term prognosis of what is likely to be chronic disability tends to be known much earlier following significant anoxic brain damage than it does in other forms of acquired brain injury, such as head trauma. The prognosis for the latter is generally that of continuing improvement, while the former can present with a more static pattern of impairment that reveals itself early on (within days or weeks). This makes the brain damage associated with anoxia particularly difficult for family members to come to terms with, and psychologists may be asked to provide support.

Dementia

Contrary to some classifications/definitions, *dementia* can occur at any age, not only in the elderly. Dementia's hallmark is severe cognitive impairment, such as memory loss and other cognitive difficulties that are significant enough to exert a clear and obvious effect on patients' activities of daily living (ADLs). The term *dementia* refers to the presence of *generalised cognitive impairment*, as opposed to localised/focal impairment. However, it is possible that the presentation may not be totally generalised, as it is always a case of relativity in judgement. For a diagnosis of dementia, neurocognitive symptoms should be *progressive* and loss of orientation should occur. Dementia should not to be confused with learning difficulties, although there may of course be some overlap. Dementia can stem from many pathologies, including: vascular disease; traumatic brain injury; toxins; substance abuse; genetic factors; and metabolic and other systemic disorders.

Public health issues can affect the incidence and prevalence of dementias. For example, AIDS-related dementia may become increasingly common if growing numbers of HIV-positive people in poorer countries have no access to treatment; or where alcohol abuse is endemic, long-term consequences may include an increased prevalence of Korsakoff's psychosis. However, it may sometimes (perhaps more than is realised) not be possible to identify the specific aetiology involved. Furthermore, it is perhaps somewhat artificial, in some diagnoses, to specifically separate out genetic disorders as the primary or only aetiology. Nowadays, many diseases are considered to have at lease some genetic contribution – if not a genetic disorder, then an important contributory role of genes in the evolution of a given disorder. Where then does one start in trying to understand this complex subgroup of disorders? From a practical perspective, *Alzheimer's disease* and *vascular dementia* are probably the most common dementias likely to be encountered by hospital-based practitioners.

Alzheimer's disease (AD) frequently occurs after the age of 65, but a fair proportion of patients are younger. The presence of *senile plaques* and *neurofibrillary tangles* in the brain is thought to underpin the aetiology of AD. Brain atrophy is observed most notably in the frontal and temporal lobes. The temporal lobes, including the *hippocampus* and surrounding areas, are usually affected more during the early stages of AD. However, while less common, there can also be other changes during AD, such as the presence of vascular pathology. Furthermore, there can be neuronal and synaptic loss. These changes can, of course, also be a function of normal ageing, and are seen in older adults. It is likely that genetics play a significant role in AD, but research findings have not been unequivocal in their support of a purely genetic basis for AD. Other risk factors are also relevant, including a history of traumatic brain injury, but the most significant risk factors appear to be age, a family history of AD and genetics (heredity).

A definite AD diagnosis with certainty and accuracy requires the direct examination of the brain at autopsy to confirm the characteristic histological changes. Therefore, psychologists should word their clinical impressions of such patients carefully, referring to the characteristic presentation, when identified, as being 'consistent with a dementia of the Alzheimer's type'. There is variation in the initial presentation and progression of the neurocognitive deficits associated with AD, but memory impairment is the most common complaint – impaired memory is often the first indication of the disease, particularly verbal memory. Of significance is the presence of a temporal gradient with respect to memory. Here, remote autobiographical memories are much more robust than new learning and the delayed recall of newly acquired material, which are particularly vulnerable.

Alzheimer's disease is often first noticed when patients (and/or loved ones) note 'everyday forgetfulness' beyond what is 'normal' for the individual. As AD progresses over time, other cognitive functions are also affected. Impairments seen include: language difficulties (typically starting with *anomia*); *inattention*; *topographical disorientation*; visuospatial problems; *apraxia*, *agnosia*; and *executive dysfunction* – often in this order. From the language perspective, word-finding difficulties (anomia) often appear early on, and can be apparent along with memory problems before other deficits appear. Personality changes (a 'vacuous personality') and behavioural difficulties occur in a large proportion of AD patients, but generally slightly later in the disease process than the initial memory difficulties. The universal theme of AD is one of progressive cognitive decline towards an end-stage where there is very severe impairment of most, if not all, domains of neurocognitive function. Institutionalisation is common, but in socio-economically deprived countries the burden of care often falls upon the family.

Vascular dementia is another dementia frequently encountered. The term vascular dementia encompasses different aetiologies, and the brain's large vessels can be affected. A distinction is sometimes made between conditions where cortical infarcts occur, as opposed to infarcts limited more to the subcortical regions of the brain (such as Binswanger's disease). *Multi-infarct dementia*, a type of vascular dementia, occurs when a patient suffers several infarcts, in different regions over time, resulting in impairment of a range of cognitive functions. Such patients typically have predisposing risk factors for vascular disease. Usually lots of little strokes occur in the small vessels (especially in the deep white matter). There is generally a *stepwise progression* to the presentation over time, associated with specific stroke episodes (infarcts) occurring, which result in different symptoms.

Delusions or paranoia may occur in patients with multi-infarct dementia, and, for reasons that are not altogether clear, *nocturnal confusion* is fairly common. The cognitive impairments that occur vary between patients with multi-infarct dementia, depending on the sites and distribution of the lesions, among other factors, such as age. Many patients retain insight for much longer than AD patients. Vascular dementia patients will typically present with intellectual inertia; a loss of creativity; adynamia; aspontaneity; a loss of curiosity; an inability to deal with new or complex problems or environments; and a flattened affect. Memory may be better preserved initially, as executive dysfunction (especially of deep white matter/subcortical functions) is the most common neurocognitive presentation seen with vascular dementia – but again this will depend on the distribution and localisation of lesions. Personality changes appear to occur later on in the course of multi-infarct dementia, and can include inappropriate mood, irritability and poor hygiene.

Other dementias and syndromes

Other neuropathological conditions that neuropsychologists see include: *Huntington's chorea*; *Wilson's disease*; *Parkinson's disease*; *Wernicke–Korsakoff syndrome* (*Wernicke's encephalopathy* and *Korsakoff's psychosis* together); and *Lewy body dementia*

(*Dementia with Lewy bodies*). Huntington's chorea is a genetic disorder that affects the head of the *caudate nucleus, putamen, hippocampus* and *cortex*. Huntington's chorea presents with characteristic changes in motor function (*choreiform movements*), cognitive impairment and behavioural changes. Given the brain regions involved, it is unsurprising that memory and executive impairment are common. It usually presents during midlife and progressive impairment continues until death. Wilson's disease is another genetic condition that affects *copper* metabolism, resulting in widespread brain damage, especially in the basal ganglia. A distinct clinical sign is *Kayser–Fleischer rings* near the edge of the corneas of the eyes. Wilson's disease tends to present in younger individuals, with memory impairment and executive dysfunction, along with behavioural and emotional difficulties.

Parkinson's disease (PD) involves reduced dopamine in the basal ganglia, specifically the *substantia nigra*. It is classified as a movement disorder, presenting with involuntary shaking (including a *tremor* at rest), loss of strength, slowing, difficulty initiating movements, *shuffling gait* and *cogwheel rigidity*. There may also be significant cognitive impairment in some patients, including impaired memory and executive function (especially difficulty with spontaneous initiative, problem solving and set shifting). Attention and language are likely to be relatively preserved; depression is common.

Lewy body dementia (Dementia with Lewy bodies) occurs when *Lewy bodies* (particularly associated with PD and AD) are found widespread in the cortex. Memory and other cognitive impairments are common, depending on the cortical distribution of the effects of the disease.

Wernicke–Korsakoff syndrome results from severe alcohol abuse coupled with lack of *thiamine (vitamin B1)*, normally due to dietary deficiency. It affects some of the brain's medial structures, most notable the *mamillary bodies* and *diencephalic structures*. Wernicke–Korsakoff syndrome involves both Wernicke's encephalopathy and Korsakoff's psychosis, which can also occur independently. Korsakoff's psychosis usually presents with severe memory impairment, characterised by *confabulation* and both *retrograde* and *anterograde amnesia*, along with confusion and loss of insight.

In developing countries, where more people may be suffering from malnourishment, the occurrence of Wernicke–Korsakoff presentations can be high. One reason for this is that such individuals are more likely to be thiamine (vitamin B1) deficient relative to more affluent populations who, broadly speaking, have better diets. Chronic alcohol abuse in more affluent populations tends to result in a different clinical presentation – atrophy of frontal cortex rather than the diencephalic involvement typically observed in the malnourished patient, who will typically have diencephalic and frontal atrophy. Many other toxins can produce profound brain damage, including through: the long-term abuse of illicit or prescription drugs; inhalation of solvents; exposure to pesticides (such as the *organophosphates*); and exposure to/ingesting a range of metals (such as lead).

A multitude of other conditions may result in cognitive impairment, such as *Multiple sclerosis (MS)*, which is thought to be an inflammatory disorder that primarily affects younger adults. It involves the destruction of the white matter *myelin sheath* of the axons. It may have either a progressive or relapsing–remitting course and tends to present with physical (motor) difficulties, but can lead to cognitive impairment in the domains of memory and attention. Fatigue is common. In the relapsing–remitting variant, impairments may fluctuate over time. There is great variability in presentation, but in some cases MS can progress to dementia – similar to other subcortical dementias in terms of presentation. Neuropsychological testing can help to document the disease course and help with the initial differential diagnosis. Some patients may benefit from psychological support in helping to adjust to the condition.

Only a small number of neuropathologies have been covered in this chapter, which has addressed some of the more frequently encountered. This should provide a good starting point for practitioners who are commencing with employment or placements in settings where patients with neuropathology are encountered. Identifying these particular conditions should allow one to work with the majority of patients with neuropathology who are routinely encountered in hospitals/clinics. Being familiar with some of the frequently encountered neuropathological diagnoses may assist attempts to develop knowledge and skills in other ways too. For example, this can help to improve the clinical reasoning skills that are so vital when working as a neuropsychologist. This skill incorporates information and knowledge from neuropathology, clinical findings, special investigations (such as brain scans), blood tests, neuropsychological testing and diagnostic classification systems. A good foundation in neuroanatomy will facilitate learning in neuropathology, helping practitioners to decide whether patients' symptoms 'fit' with clinical diagnoses. The following chapter provides an overview of one diagnostic classification system that is widely used within psychology and psychiatry.

Conclusion

There are many more neuropathological conditions than even the most experienced neuropsychologist will ever be able to develop an in-depth knowledge of. Therefore, it is probably more important to aim to develop a sound knowledge of the most frequently encountered conditions, upon which one can then build additional knowledge over time. Emphasis has to (to some degree) be placed on conditions that are most likely to place the greatest burden on healthcare systems in both developed and developing countries, especially where resources are limited. Learning about several conditions as a starting point, rather than becoming a super-specialist of one condition, has another very important benefit – it is one of the key pillars required for developing clinical reasoning (the ability to accurately think through, then answer, a clinical question in a logical manner, incorporating all aspects of the patient's history and presentation). Clinical reasoning follows the pattern of the clinical assessment. Here, performing neuropsychological testing where required, gathering other clinical data including findings from special investigations, considering the clinical features of a case and their relationship to known neuropathologies before making a differential diagnosis and doing the formulation that can inform treatment and rehabilitation are all linked intrinsically to clinical reasoning. Clinical reasoning is one of the most difficult skills to develop, but, over time, it can become an invaluable heuristic for everyday clinical practice.

Practical tips

1. If your hospital has a pathology museum, visit it.
2. Keep a notebook to make anonymous, short case descriptions every time you encounter neuropathological conditions for the first time.

Points for reflective practice

1. The categorisation of neuropathological conditions is artificial given that there is huge overlap in the clinical presentations of patients with different pathological diagnoses. What is the purpose of making diagnoses based on neuropathology?
2. How does knowledge of neuropathology relate to other areas within neuropsychology, and, in particular, how does this ultimately influence decisions regarding patients' care?

Selected further reading

Bigler, E. D., & Maxwell, W. L. (2011). Neuroimaging and neuropathology of TBI. *NeuroRehabilitation, 28*, 63–74.

Larner, A. J. (2008). *Neuropsychological neurology: The neurocognitive impairments of neurological disorders*. Cambridge: Cambridge University Press.

Lezak, M. D., Howieson, D. B., Bigler, E. D., & Tranel, D. (2012). *Neuropsychological assessment* (5th ed.). New York: Oxford University Press.

4

PSYCHOPATHOLOGY

Introduction

Clinical neuropsychology training varies widely across the world. Sometimes this is due to historical reasons, while in other cases it is to address the particular skills needs for healthcare systems in different countries. Private healthcare systems are likely to require skills that differ slightly from those in publicly funded hospitals/ clinics. For example, where there is a fee for service in private healthcare systems, there tends to be a far greater emphasis on more extensive neuropsychological testing and diagnostic codes. Diagnoses and their corresponding codes are used to secure payment. Neuropsychologists working in these systems would possibly be more extensively trained and experienced in diagnostic classification systems and neuropsychological assessment, including testing, than perhaps they would be in psychological therapies and their application to brain-injury rehabilitation, for example.

In some countries (such as Australia and the United States) neuropsychology is essentially a stand-alone doctoral training from beginning to end. In other countries (for example, the United Kingdom) it is a postdoctoral specialisation (usually following training in clinical psychology). In South Africa, neuropsychology has recently been recognised within the practice framework as a professional category, requiring a masters-level qualification to practise clinically. Moreover, many training programmes in clinical psychology offer clinical neuropsychology training blocks at introductory or more advanced levels, depending on the programme. A unifying area between many clinical psychology and clinical neuropsychology programmes is in the training of *psychopathology*. Most psychology courses, irrespective of specialism, provide some direct or indirect teaching of psychopathology.

Both clinical psychology and clinical neuropsychology programmes tend to offer psychopathology training as part of their respective curriculums, although perhaps with a differing focus. However, the amount and depth of psychopathology teaching offered by clinical psychology training programmes varies widely. Nevertheless, the majority of clinical neuropsychology training programmes incorporate basic training in aspects of psychopathology. There are several reasons for this, including the high incidence and prevalence of mental disorders following acquired brain injury and neurological illness. For example, it is important for psychologists working in settings where patients with neuropathology are seen to be able to identify anxiety or depression in such populations.

The existence of diagnostic criteria for disorders that include cognitive impairment as part of their symptomatology provides further justification for the need to have knowledge of psychopathology. These would include, for example, *dementia* and *delirium*, among others. In this chapter, the *Diagnostic and Statistical Manual of Mental Disorders*, 4th edition (*DSM-IV*) classification system is used (American Psychiatric Association, 1994). While the *DSM-V* was published in 2013, it has not yet been widely implemented in everyday clinical practice, and almost no research using *DSM-V* criteria in neuropsychology has been published to date. Clinicians working cross-culturally around the world should remember that there are many cultural factors to consider when attempting to use and interpret meaningfully those diagnostic systems of Western European or American origin, such as the *DSM-IV* (see the 'Cross-cultural factors in psychopathology' section below).

Even though the publication of the *DSM-V* was recent, current research and case reports on mental disorders following acquired brain injury and neurological illness are based on work using the *DSM-IV*, or earlier versions of the DSM. There is likely to be a considerable time lag before the *DSM-V* is fully implemented into clinical practice. Likewise, findings pertaining to neuropsychological research based on *DSM-V* diagnostic criteria will necessarily take time to be published. Neuropsychologists need to be familiar with psychopathology and diagnostic classification systems to ensure that they do not miss the presence of mental disorders in patients with neuropathology. The role of the neuropsychologist is, from a diagnostic perspective, not only to evaluate and document cognitive functioning, but also to provide an assessment of behaviour, emotion and other domains of function.

Assessment can potentially become a more subjective and scientifically less meaningful process without a diagnostic system to consult as a reference. In essence, one of the main reasons to perform a clinical assessment (see Chapter 8) is to be able to conclude with a diagnostic formulation. A diagnosis is simply the beginning of a process. Diagnoses made in isolation are potentially meaningless, as they do not explain why a mental illness is present: *formulation* explains why (see Chapter 10). Within a biopsychosocial formulation, diagnoses can be very useful to a multidisciplinary rehabilitation team. This formulation directly informs the treatment or rehabilitation plans for patients. Neuropsychology explains (or formulates) how, for example, impaired neurocognitive functioning might be associated with the evolution of anxiety or depression. Being familiar with diagnostic classification systems can also improve clinicians' ability to communicate with healthcare professionals working in other services dealing with neuropathology.

The *DSM-IV*

Published in 1994, the *DSM-IV* uses a *five-axial diagnostic system*. The central aim is to list the diagnostic criteria of mental disorders. *Axis I* is for the core mental disorders, excluding Mental Retardation (learning disability) and Personality Disorders. These are reported on *Axis II*. *Axis III* is used to document medical conditions. *Axis IV* is for psychosocial problems, while *Axis V* is for reporting patients' overall level of functioning. Reassuringly for neuropsychologists, while the term 'mental disorder' is used in the *DSM-IV*, a dualism between the physical and mental is actually not intended.

According to the *DSM-IV*, each of the mental disorders is viewed as representing a clinically significant level, or the presence of the behavioural or psychological patterns associated with distress, disability, increased risk of suffering or the loss of individual freedom. While the *DSM-IV* uses the proviso 'due to a General Medical Condition' as a term for mental disorders that are deemed to have resulted from a definite biological factor (including acquired brain injury and neurological illness), there is no intention to communicate that there is a basic difference between the same mental disorders with regard to clinical presentation when biological factors are present, as opposed to when they are not. In a way, the *DSM-IV* posits that from phenomenological and symptomatology viewpoints, mental disorders are similar irrespective of aetiology.

Nevertheless, while a patient may present clinically with sufficient diagnostic criteria to satisfy the requirements for a diagnosis of an Axis I mental disorder, the *DSM-IV* usually specifies that where a biological factor is deemed causative (based on laboratory findings, the patient's history or physical examination), it should be recorded. The recording of biological factors that are of aetiological relevance is performed as follows. The identified diagnosis (for example, *Generalized Anxiety Disorder*) is recorded on Axis I, but as an 'Anxiety Disorder due to a General Medical Condition'. The biological factor judged to have caused or triggered the mental disorder on Axis I is noted (for example, traumatic brain injury) and recorded on Axis III. A slight anomaly that one needs to be aware of is that *Personality Change* associated with either brain injury or neurological illness is not the same concept or diagnostic entity as a *Personality Disorder*. The latter is recorded on Axis II, the former on Axis I – again the relevant medical condition is noted on Axis III (in the case of 'Personality Change').

From a neuropsychological perspective, there are both benefits *and* limitations to the use of diagnostic systems such as the *DSM-IV*. A main benefit is that diagnostic systems can facilitate interprofessional communication between clinicians and researchers. These systems can facilitate the identification of treatable mental disorders following brain injury and neurological illness that may otherwise not have been a focus for clinical intervention, thereby having a potentially detrimental effect on outcome. The *DSM-IV* follows a biopsychosocial model. Mental disorders are viewed as constituting psychological, behavioural or biological dysfunction, or any combination of these. Mental illness is also affected by environmental and socio-political factors, such as poverty, oppressive political systems, war and the occurrence of natural disasters (for example, earthquakes and droughts).

A fundamental skill that neuropsychologists try to master and bring to the multi-disciplinary clinical team is that of integrating biological, social and psychological factors into a cohesive formulation and treatment plan. Many of the diagnostic categories actually specify the presence of cognitive impairment (and sometimes in which specific areas these impairments lie) as part of their criteria. Clearly, in the case of these diagnoses, the role of assessment is important for neuropsychologists. There are also significant limitations to diagnostic classification systems. A conceptual difficulty with the *DSM-IV* is the fact that there are not always clear distinctions between diagnostic categories, or even what does or does not constitute a mental disorder. It would be fair to posit that a diagnostic system cannot possibly accurately describe and include *all* of the complexities and richness of human behaviour, even if the focus is only on what is termed abnormal variants of behaviour.

Diagnoses, while viewed as part of good practice, do unfortunately sometimes become static, failing to stay dynamic as patients' clinical presentations emerge and evolve. This can result in an inaccurate diagnosis becoming part of a health system's narrative/record about a patient. Such patients can then potentially be seriously disadvantaged if all their symptoms are always seen as a function of mental illness. The influence of culture on the clinician's assessment methodology, or the algorithm that s/he uses before making a diagnosis, is another potentially limiting factor. A further, more pragmatic difficulty with diagnostic classification systems relates to training. In reality, even basic clinical skills in the use of such systems generally require a huge investment of resources in training, the formal assessment of knowledge and ongoing supervised practice in clinical settings. It is, in a way, perhaps counter-productive to overly criticise a complex diagnostic system such as the *DSM-IV*, when one of the main issues is in fact the availability of the necessary resources to achieve the required in-depth training beneficial to patient care. Such resources include time and experienced psychopathology teachers.

The *DSM-IV* and clinical neuropsychology

Not all diagnoses in the *DSM-IV* will be encountered on a regular basis when working with patients with neuropathology, and many might never be seen. Some of the diagnostic categories may also have very limited validity; this is an entirely valid criticism of the *DSM-IV* and similar diagnostic systems. Nevertheless, aspects of the *DSM-IV* do have important clinical utility in neuropsychology. Several authors have reviewed the incidence, prevalence and treatment options for mental disorders following acquired brain injury, such as Vaishnavi, Rao and Fann (2009) – see 'Selected further reading' at the end of this chapter – and Lishman (1998). In clinical neuropsychology practice, commonly encountered *DSM-IV* diagnoses will probably include: 'Delirium'; 'Dementia'; 'Mood Disorders'; some of the 'Anxiety Disorders'; 'Personality Change' due to a 'General Medical Condition'; and 'Cognitive Disorders'. Each of these is briefly described below.

In the *DSM-IV*, *dementia* is defined as the onset of cognitive impairment in several areas, including memory function, along with impairment of *executive function*, language function, *apraxia* and *agnosia*. These impairments have a significantly negative influence on daily functioning, in the private, social and occupational aspects of life. There should also be evidence of a decline from a previous level of functioning. The symptoms are the result of a biological factor or factors, for example, stroke, traumatic brain injury, substance abuse, genetics and other medical conditions. These symptoms are common to all dementias, but there is differentiation based on aetiology. Some of the diagnoses include: 'Dementia of the Alzheimer's Type'; 'Vascular Dementia'; 'Dementia Due to Head Trauma'; 'Dementia Due to Huntington's Disease'; 'Dementia Due to Pick's Disease'; and 'Dementia Due to Other General Medical Conditions'. There is also a category for circumstances where a definite aetiology cannot be determined.

Delirium is a condition that develops over a short period of time, and presents as a disturbance of consciousness characterised by impaired attention, distractibility and reduced awareness. A diagnostic hallmark of delirium is that it fluctuates; it is not uncommon to obtain very different results on examination for the same patient within a short space of time. The *DSM-IV* further specifies that the clinical picture of delirium is the direct result of a biological factor. Biological factors include, for example, medical conditions such as infection, head injury, stroke, diabetes, substance intoxication or withdrawal, or the use of medication – or a combination of these. There are also non-biological factors that may lead to a delirium, or at least contribute towards exaggerating its severity; the most common example being sensory deprivation. An example of when this can occur is where a patient's (typically the elderly) spectacles and hearing aids are removed during a hospital stay. It is important to note that delirium can co-exist with dementia. Delirium is frequently encountered in the context of head trauma and alcohol withdrawal.

The cognitive disorders listed in the *DSM-IV* include '*Amnestic Disorder Due to a General Medical Disorder*' and '*Cognitive Disorder Not Otherwise Specified*'. Memory impairment, specifically the inability to learn new information, or recall previously known information, is at the heart of an 'Amnestic Disorder Due to a General Medical Disorder'. This disorder does not only occur during delirium or dementia – an identified physical factor is responsible for the clinical picture. One of the most common conditions one is likely to encounter in this diagnostic category is *Korsakoff's psychosis*. The disorders under the category 'Cognitive Disorder Not Otherwise Specified' include impaired cognitive function identified on neuropsychological testing, associated with traumatic brain injury or stroke. Another important diagnostic entity is *Post-concussion syndrome*, for which the *DSM-IV* provides some diagnostic criteria, including: a history of head trauma resulting in concussion; attention and memory difficulties identified on neuropsychological testing; and various physical symptoms (including fatigue, headaches, dizziness, anxiety and depression, among several others).

'*Personality Change Due to a General Medical Condition*' is, according to *DSM-IV*, a change in a person's usual personality pattern, resulting from the direct physical effects of a medical condition. Some common symptoms include: aggression, poor impulse control, apathy, emotional reactions (such as rage, which is completely out of proportion to the precipitant's nature), lack of social sensitivity and poor judgement. It is often necessary to obtain collateral information from a reliable source (such as a patient's relative), who can provide a longitudinal perspective pertaining to any changes in the patient's behavioural patterns. 'Personality Change Due to a General Medical Condition' is often associated with frontal lobe involvement, which is seen, for example, following traumatic brain injury, frontal lobe tumours or anterior communicating artery aneurysms (which can disconnect crucial connections to the frontal cortex). Sometimes '*Manic or Hypomanic Episodes*' can mirror some of the clinical features of personality change in the context of brain injury, but these are not as constant over time as genuine changes in personality that are associated with brain injury. 'Personality Change Due to a General Medical Condition' is not coded on Axis II as a 'Personality Disorder', but on Axis I as a distinct diagnostic category.

Unsurprisingly, some anxiety disorders are fairly common following brain injury or neurological illness. These include '*Generalised Anxiety Disorder*' and '*Panic Disorder*'. Other diagnoses, such as '*Post-traumatic Stress Disorder*' and '*Obsessive-compulsive Disorder*', are not as common – although they are still seen in clinical practice. The *DSM-IV* diagnostic criteria for a 'Generalised Anxiety Disorder' include excessive anxiety about a number of activities that the patient finds difficult to control. Restlessness, fatigue, irritability, muscle tension and difficulty falling asleep are some of the associated symptoms. In addition, anxiety causes significant distress and may interfere with patients' occupational and/or social functioning. When this diagnosis is made in the presence of a confirmed brain injury or neurological illness, then, strictly speaking, an '*Anxiety Disorder due to a General Medical Condition*' should be diagnosed. In the *DSM-IV*, 'Panic Disorder' is defined as the occurrence of unexpected and recurrent panic attacks. A *panic attack* constitutes a distinct period of very significant anxiety, accompanied by symptoms such as palpitations, trembling, dizziness, fear of dying, nausea and sweating.

Disturbances of mood are also common following neurological illness and brain injury. In the *DSM-IV*, the core feature of a '*Major Depressive Disorder*' is the presence of one or more '*Major Depressive Episodes*'. A depressed mood, or loss of interest and pleasure in nearly all activities, is the essential feature of a 'Major Depressive Episode'. For a 'Major Depressive Episode' diagnosis, the duration of the depressed mood should be at least two weeks. Some other diagnostic criteria for a 'Major Depressive Episode' include: insomnia; significant weight loss (or gain); psychomotor agitation or retardation; fatigue; feelings of worthlessness or guilt; poor concentration; and in some instances, suicidal ideation. To meet the diagnostic criteria, these symptoms should result in significant distress or impairment of social and occupational functioning.

The *DSM-IV* specifies that the symptoms of a 'Major Depressive Disorder' should not be due to a medical condition, and that where this *is* the case within the context of acquired brain injury, a '*Mood Disorder due to a General Medical Condition*' should be diagnosed. Clearly, some of the symptoms listed in the diagnostic criteria for a 'Major Depressive Disorder' (and some of those listed for the 'Anxiety Disorders') could also form part of a normal or expected emotional and behavioural reaction to having a brain injury. This complicates these diagnoses in patients with neuropathology, and careful consideration should be given to each individual presentation. Here, the patient's level of insight, along with the degree and nature of the neurocognitive impairment, are of particular relevance. Having excellent insight into neurocognitive and physical impairment can be associated with an increase in anxiety and low mood. Coetzer (2010) provides discussion regarding the anxiety and mood disorders associated with traumatic brain injury; see 'Selected further reading' at the end of this chapter.

Cross-cultural factors in psychopathology

Most diagnostic systems are of Western origin, with their classification of diagnostic categories and symptomatology based largely on the Western medical model of diseases. The DSM system, for example, was designed in North America, primarily for psychiatrists working in that setting. After the *DSM-III* was widely criticised for being *universalist* and not giving enough weight to cultural factors, the *DSM-IV* was designed to be more accommodating of cultural considerations (Swartz, 1998). Clinicians should exercise due caution when attempting to use such tools in non-Western settings. There are many factors that can influence their use, especially when used cross-culturally. Even if many psychopathologies are indeed 'universal' in the way that they affect all human beings, the description, meaning and understanding of these conditions may vary widely across cultures. Language and socio-political factors are also important to bear in mind.

Even in psychopathologies that appear universal, there are cultural differences between the symptoms and patterns observed. For example, the rates of the symptom of *catatonia*, as seen in schizophrenic patients, differ between developed versus developing world settings, as does the symptom of guilt in depression (Louw & Edwards, 1998). Based on epidemiological evidence, there are some diseases that are far more prevalent in certain parts of the world relative to others. This can result in their being erroneously attributed to a pre-existing (often biological) framework for a disease that is prevalent in another country, or can even result in such diseases/symptoms being missed altogether. In countries with high levels of poverty or violence and limited access to healthcare, psychopathology may be more prevalent, or conversely, depending on cultural factors, it may be tempered by stoicism and community cohesion, for example. It is important not to have rigid, preconceived models when working in such environments.

It is interesting to note the way that language reflects some of the subtleties found in clinical presentations across different cultures. For example, the term 'depressed' does not translate exactly into Welsh, where the word is *digalon* (melancholic, disheartened, despondent), while in Afrikaans, the word is *bedruk* (heavy-hearted, dejected, crestfallen). In non-Western and developing world settings, patients may not have the vocabulary with which to be able to describe their symptoms to someone trained in the Western medical model. Such patients may describe symptoms differently and attach very different meanings to their symptoms due to their particular cultural beliefs, which may not be understood or recognised by a medical practitioner using a Western diagnostic system. Practitioners must therefore be mindful and knowledgeable of patients' cultural backgrounds and seek to understand symptoms and signs from this perspective by embracing and immersing themselves in these alternative belief systems.

Professionals working in cross-cultural settings need to be aware of alternatives to the Western-based approaches to psychopathology and how these vary from country to country. For example, traditional healers in Africa use their own distinct classification systems for psychological disorders, some of which are similar to Western categories, while others seem dissimilar or incomparable. In South Africa, *ukuphuthelwa* (with similar features to major depression), *phambana* (psychotic illness), *intloko engxolayo* (severe anxiety, with similar features to generalised anxiety disorders) and *isthuthwane* (referring to epileptic symptoms) are all similar to disorders known in Western diagnostic classification systems (Louw & Edwards, 1998). Alternatively, for example, two disorders known as *amafufunyana* (possession by evil spirits, with various symptoms, including disturbed dreams and angry outbursts) and *intwaso* (shamanic initiatory illness, with symptoms of visions when awake and strange dreams) do not appear to overlap with any Western classifications (Louw & Edwards, 1998). Such disorders are typically viewed in one of two ways: either as variations of similar disorders which are seen in the Western context, or as disorders that are unique to the cultures/settings from which they originate – referred to as culture-bound syndromes (Louw & Edwards, 1998).

Conclusion

Developing a working knowledge of psychopathology is an important task when providing neuropsychological input to patients with neuropathology. Psychologists must also be mindful of the setting in which psychopathology is diagnosed, and of whether the assessment tools being used are not in fact culturally inappropriate and diagnostically limited.

One of the most widely used diagnostic classification systems is the *DSM-IV*. While not as much part of everyday practice as it is in mental health settings, for example, psychopathology is nevertheless an area that neuropsychologists need to know a fair amount about – especially with regard to a few specific diagnostic entities. These include some of the anxiety and mood disorders, delirium, dementia, personality change and cognitive disorders. When these conditions are diagnosed and thought to be the direct consequence of acquired brain injury or neurological illness, they are recorded in the *DSM-IV* multi-axial diagnostic system.

While there are many potential benefits to using diagnostic classification systems for psychopathologies, including, for example, the prevention of the under-identification of the emotional and behavioural difficulties that are associated with brain injury, there are also very real problems associated with their use. These include, but are not limited to, the scant evidence for the occurrence of some of the diagnostic entities within the context of brain injury, and difficulties in distinguishing between what are normal behaviours and emotional reactions following brain injury and what constitutes organic pathology. Finally, there is limited utility in using diagnoses in isolation from more complex and richer individual case formulations, which is one of the specific and unique skills that neuropsychology can bring to the multidisciplinary team. Where there is limited access to neuropsychology, and to individual patient care, this is often one of the more valuable contributions that can be made.

Practical tips

1. Is obtaining a pocket DSM really worth it? The reality is that unless one works in a specialist neuropsychiatric unit, it is probably not something that will be used on a daily basis. Therefore, although it will perhaps be harder work, it is instead better to memorise the few diagnostic entities discussed in this chapter.
2. Be wary of questionnaires that purport to diagnose specific psychopathological conditions – patients should always be directly assessed, rather than one relying on data from questionnaires alone, particularly when working cross-culturally.

Points for reflective practice

1. What are the main benefits and limitations of using diagnostic classification systems such as the *DSM-IV*?
2. How would you distinguish between dementia and delirium? Describe how you would go about assessing a patient in order to make this diagnostic distinction.
3. Are patients with acquired brain injury or neurological illness depressed, or are there other possible explanations for this type of presentation under these circumstances?

Selected further reading

American Psychiatric Association. (1994). *Diagnostic and statistical manual of mental disorders* (4th ed.). Washington, DC: Author.

Coetzer, R. (2010). *Anxiety and mood disorders: Clinical assessment and psychotherapy*. London: Karnac Books.

Swartz, L. (1998). *Culture and mental health: A southern African view*. Cape Town: Oxford University Press.

Vaishnavi, S., Rao, V., & Fann, J. R. (2009). Neuropsychiatric problems after traumatic brain injury: Unravelling the silent epidemic. *Psychosomatics, 50*, 198–205.

5

PSYCHOPHARMACOLOGY

Introduction

Clinical neuropsychologists do not prescribe medication; their two main functions are, broadly speaking, the *assessment* and *rehabilitation* (where indicated) of individuals with brain injury and accompanying neurocognitive impairment. The possibility of psychologists prescribing drugs in a profession where psychological therapy is the (almost) exclusive treatment approach would clearly have the potential to create philosophical tensions and/or intellectual distraction. Expertise in psychological therapy is what defines the identity of many psychologists when it comes to patient treatment. The perseverance and long-term approach that is so fundamental to a non-pharmacological rehabilitation approach such as psychotherapy might be hindered if psychologists prescribed drugs.

There are many other reasons why psychologists do not prescribe drugs, including the breadth and depth of knowledge required in pharmacology, physiology, biochemistry and internal medicine, for example. Medication is not prescribed without considering biological factors in other areas, along with other health issues affecting patients. Having sound knowledge of drug side effects, and of drug interactions, is also crucial. Medication is therefore only prescribed by medical doctors who possess this expertise. There are both philosophical and technical reasons why psychologists do not prescribe drugs. This chapter does not provide any guidance about treatment with medication, nor is there any intention to do so. Inevitably, then, the question is: why do psychologists (and other non-medical professionals) who work with patients with neuropathology need to know anything at all about psychopharmacology?

The first reason why one needs to be aware of the medications that patients are taking has to do with one of neuropsychology's primary clinical functions: *assessment* – or, more specifically, neuropsychological testing. Medications can have an effect on neurocognitive functioning and can consequently influence neuropsychological test results. Medications can also have an influence on emotion and behaviour, again with the potential of colouring patients' presentations during assessments. Another reason why it is useful to have such knowledge is for patients who abuse substances. Illicit substance misuse and the abuse of prescription medication are fairly common co-morbidities of acquired brain injury. In these situations, knowledge of the psychopharmacological properties of drugs may be very useful in understanding patients' clinical presentations.

The second reason relates to *treatment*. Medications can positively affect some symptoms that patients may have, which can also have an effect on neuropsychological test results. It may sometimes be sensible to delay neuropsychological testing until patients have responded to pharmacotherapy. Pharmacological approaches play a very important and often central role in the treatment and rehabilitation of patients with acquired brain injuries and neurological illnesses. For example, post-stroke depression is common, and pharmacological interventions can make it more likely that patients will benefit from other non-pharmacological rehabilitation input. However, medication can also make it more difficult (often because of side effects) for patients to fully engage in rehabilitation activities. From a practical perspective, hospital-based neuropsychologists generally work in multidisciplinary teams/settings and therefore need a good understanding of the other, non-psychological components of patients' treatments.

Medication use sometimes varies quite significantly between countries. This can be related to financial factors, such as what can be afforded within publicly funded hospitals versus private healthcare systems. More generally, though, prescribers of drugs need to at least make some use of an evidence base in order to evaluate their clinical effectiveness. This can sometimes be summarised into a prescribing algorithm, or into guidelines to ensure some level of consistency of treatment approaches. Unfortunately, there is not always a robust evidence base in drug use for the mental and neurocognitive deficits that follow brain injury. There are other difficulties and differences when it comes to psychopharmacological practice around the world. Aside from the financial realities that plague many countries, there are also other major factors in the developing world.

In developing or under-resourced countries, problems are often encountered by patients from rural or impoverished areas, who are unable to reliably access the medical institutions capable of dispensing medication. Often such institutions only exist in specific (larger) urban centres, far from remote rural areas, which leaves patients stranded (frequently in situations where critical acute treatment is required). There are other potential problems too. In countries such as South Africa, where multiple languages are spoken, and many of the population are poorly educated, it can be extremely difficult to provide patients with the appropriate medication. In many instances, it is difficult for doctors to understand from patients exactly what their ailments are, in view of the potential language barriers. Such situations are sometimes made worse by the potential inaccuracy associated with being reliant on translators – things can get lost in translation. This problem also affects practitioners' ability to accurately explain to patients what their medication is for and, importantly, what the correct dosages and the correct administration procedures are. This is most important in order to reduce the potential for serious harm through either accidental overdose, or through non-compliance due to unexpected or poorly understood side effects.

Varying levels of education within the population mean that patients are often unable to understand the meaning and purpose for their prescribed drug. For example, a patient with very limited education who was seen in South Africa literally believed that her diabetes was caused by 'sugar being in her eye'. The education barrier that often exists between practitioner and patient, especially as is encountered in many disadvantaged settings, poses many obstacles to implementing effective psychopharmacological (and other) treatment. Significant differences in education levels and, by implication, wealth, create power imbalances between clinicians and patients. This imbalance can make it really difficult to engage with patients. Along with language and educational barriers, cultural factors also play a big role; many cultures have very different beliefs towards illness and health compared to Western medical models.

In many African countries, for example, traditional healers are the first port of call for many, and serve a vital function. In such settings, it may be difficult, or even inappropriate, to negotiate with or try to persuade patients with these cultural beliefs to use Western-derived psychopharmacological treatments. Rather, it is important for practitioners to embrace alternative traditions, and find ways to accommodate and work hand-in-hand with them. Where applicable, and in the best interest of patients, clinicians should consider incorporating traditional models and beliefs into existing clinical practice frameworks. Part of this process is to learn from each other, the pros and cons of each approach in terms of treating different symptoms 'medicinally'. Finally, history has also played a part – staying with the South African theme momentarily, in the country's relatively recent political (apartheid) past, where the government enforced racial segregation, African traditional healers were excluded from the formal healthcare system. This was of course totally counter-productive and served to alienate patients. For an overview of South African psychology within a historical and political context, the interested reader should consult Cooper and Nicholas (2012); see 'Selected further reading' at the end of this chapter.

Medication in patients with neuropathology

This chapter does not focus on the pharmacological agents used during the acute stage of acquired brain injury and neurological illnesses, such as *steroids* in the treatment of brain tumours, *thrombolysis* for stroke or *Mannitol* following head injury. Neuropsychologists do not become directly involved in these areas of clinical care, but it is important to know of their existence as they influence patients' outcomes. Mannitol is used to reduce the fluid build-up in the brain (osmotherapy), thereby reducing intracranial pressure. Steroids are used with brain tumours to reduce swelling. Thrombolysis is a clot-buster therapy used in the hours following an ischemic stroke to break up and dissolve blood clots.

The actual focus of this chapter is the post-acute use of pharmacology in patients with neuropathology, such as the use of *anticholinesterase inhibitors* in Alzheimer's disease and *antidepressants* in post-stroke mood disorders. Below follows a brief overview of some of these medications, including their use and possible effects on cognitive performance, that psychologists and other non-medical practitioners should be aware of, rather than have an in-depth knowledge of. Sadock and Sadock (2007) provide more detailed information regarding *psychotropic* medications; see 'Selected further reading' at the end of this chapter. Only some of the situations most likely to be encountered in brain-injury rehabilitation or in settings where patients with neuropathology are seen are covered here.

There are general issues to be aware of when it comes to the use of medication in patients with neurological illness or injury. Fleminger (2008) reviews the treatment of neuropsychiatric difficulties following traumatic brain injury and highlights some of the issues that pertain to the use of medication in patients with brain injury. These include: the limited evidence base that exists from randomised controlled trails regarding the medications used on this population; possible drug interactions; a slow upward titration; and the awareness that some medications may lower a patient's seizure threshold. It would be fair to say that the pharmacological treatment of the neurocognitive impairment, the behavioural changes and some of the more common emotional difficulties that follow acquired brain injury (such as head trauma, encephalitis or stroke) has had mixed results. In contrast, some of the physical difficulties, such as post-traumatic epilepsy, are now relatively well controlled by medication in many patients with a history of traumatic brain injury, which can often make a dramatic improvement to quality of life. There are also treatments for other physical problems: for example, for motor difficulties, such as *spasticity*, following a neurological illness.

In contrast to the relative uncertainty associated with some of the drug interventions for patients with traumatic brain injury, for example, there are many neurological conditions where pharmacological treatment in general has a much more important, and indeed established role. *Parkinson's disease*, for example, has been treated for several decades with *L-dopa*, which acts to address the problem of lowered *dopamine*, which has been directly implicated in some of the most troubling symptoms of the disease. Similarly, *Multiple sclerosis* has been treated symptomatically with established drugs, such as *beta interferons*, which reduce immune system response, thus lessening the intensity of symptoms. Additionally, *cholinesterase inhibitors* are now used to slow the rate of cognitive decline in some patients with *Alzheimer's disease*. With regard to substance-induced brain damage, *thiamine (vitamin B1)* can, in some cases, limit or improve some of the memory difficulties associated with *Korsakoff's psychosis/Wernicke's encephalopathy/Wernicke–Korsakoff syndrome*.

Classification of medication

Medications can be classified in various ways. They can be classified according to what condition/s they are intended to treat. For example, *antidepressants* such as *selective serotonin reuptake inhibitors (SSRIs)* and *tricyclic antidepressants* are used to treat mood disorders, while *anticonvulsants* such as *Carbamazepine* are used to treat seizures. Other examples include: *anxiolytic* medications, such as the *benzodiazepines*, for the very short-term management of acute-onset anxiety; *antipsychotics*, such as *Haloperidol* and *Risperidone*, for treating psychosis; and *mood stabilisers*, such as *Lithium*, to treat mood disorders where instability of mood is a core feature of the presentation. There is, however, a problem with this approach. Many drugs may have more than one indication, often across different diagnoses. For example, Lithium is used for mood disorders, but anticonvulsants are also sometimes used as mood stabilisers. As a further illustration, a drug such as *Carbamazepine* can be used as both an anticonvulsant for controlling seizures and as a mood stabiliser for treating lability of mood or aggression following traumatic brain injury.

Another approach is to group medications by their pharmacological structure and action. For example, the family of drugs known as the benzodiazepines can be used to treat some types of anxiety – patients may occasionally be prescribed these drugs for a very short period of time for acute-onset anxiety, panic attacks or insomnia. The many different variants of the benzodiazepines all have a similar molecular structure and mode of action. However, these subtle variations in molecular structure may result in slightly different side effects. With regard to the benzodiazepines, this includes different half-lives of metabolism, resulting in different clinical indications and therapeutic potentials. The same applies to antidepressants, for example, where an activating side-effect profile might be preferable to a sedating one for some patients, and vice versa. For psychologists who merely need to develop an awareness of medication-related issues, this type of classification is probably not as relevant as it is to medical practitioners, who need to understand mechanisms of action and so forth.

In practice, what psychologists are likely to encounter with regard to prescribed medications varies widely according to the clinical setting where they work. Nevertheless, many psychologists and other members of the clinical team are likely to see at least some patients who may have been prescribed medication from the following groups of drugs.

The *antidepressants* include: *selective serotonin reuptake inhibitors (SSRIs)*, *tricyclics*, *monoamine oxidase inhibitors*, *noradrenaline reuptake inhibitors* and *Mirtazapine*. With regard to side-effect profiles, some antidepressants are sedative, whereas others are more activating in nature. Any of these drugs may be prescribed to patients with depressed mood, but the newer generation antidepressant drugs are now more widely used, in part due to their more acceptable side-effect profiles.

Psychologists working with brain injury need to be aware of the possible effect that those antidepressants with a significant sedative profile may have on neuropsychological test performance. Under these circumstances, it can be a challenge to disentangle what aspects of a patient's presentation are due to impaired cognition resulting from brain injury versus his/her premorbid cognitive ability and the side effects of the medication that s/he is taking. Add to this language barriers, cultural differences and the need to work as economically as possible in an under-resourced health environment (no luxury of eight hours of testing spread over a fortnight here...), and the clinical reasoning task becomes truly formidable. Furthermore, some of the older antidepressants, which tend to have more pronounced side effects, are also used for other difficulties that are experienced following brain injury. For example, tricyclic antidepressants are used to treat *neuralgia* (nerve pain) and other forms of pain. Some *selective serotonin reuptake inhibitors* are also used in the management of anxiety disorders; these generally tend to have a less problematic cognitive side-effect profile.

There are older (first generation) and newer (second generation and others) *antipsychotics*. First-generation antipsychotics include *Haloperidol* and *Chlorpromazine*, for example. Second-generation antipsychotics include *Olanzapine*, *Risperidone* and *Quetiapine*, among others. While antipsychotics are, in general, primarily used in psychiatry for the treatment of psychotic disorders, such as *schizophrenia*, they have other indications too. Some patients with brain injury present as restless and/or agitated (usually during the acute hospital phase) and are therefore sometimes prescribed antipsychotics. It is important for psychologists to know that these drugs can affect cognition and thereby influence the results of neuropsychological testing.

The anti-anxiety medications known as the benzodiazepines (see above) are sometimes used to treat acute agitation, restlessness and aggression, and include *Lorazepam* and *Diazepam*. The benzodiazepines carry with them the potential risk of causing drug dependence, and psychologists should be aware when testing patients who are prescribed benzodiazepines that they can have noticeable negative effects on neurocognitive performance.

Patients with neuropathology may sometimes be prescribed mood stabilisers, including *Lithium* and *Sodium valproate*. Lithium is generally used in psychiatry to treat *bipolar disorder*. Sodium valproate is classed as a mood stabiliser, but is actually an anticonvulsant. Anticonvulsants are used to treat *epilepsy (seizures)* and, hence, the chances are good that psychologists might have to test or work therapeutically with patients who are taking such medication. Other anticonvulsants include *Carbamazepine*, *Gabapentin* and *Topiramate*. Successful anticonvulsant treatment following brain injury significantly improves quality of life, and can decrease patients' dependence on social support systems within communities.

The anticonvulsants, while primarily used to treat epilepsy, are also used as mood stabilisers or for treating aggression in patients with traumatic brain injury, for example. However, the anticonvulsants have had less success in managing aggression in neurological patients, and behaviour modification and environmental manipulation may be more productive for some patients. There are many other medications that patients with neurological conditions may be receiving, such as *L-dopa* for *Parkinson's disease*, *cholinesterase inhibitors* for *Alzheimer's disease* or even *beta-blockers* for aggression associated with traumatic brain injury. To further facilitate awareness, some hypothetical clinical situations are described below to illustrate, more practically, the neuropsychological issues related to prescription medication and patients with neuropathology. Finally, an amalgamated case vignette is provided to further illustrate some clinical dilemmas within neuropsychology.

Illustrative clinical situations

Many patients with traumatic brain injury (TBI) present with behavioural, emotional, cognitive and physical difficulties. Accordingly, patients may be prescribed medication for seizures, depression, anxiety, aggression and so forth. *Aggression* is one of the most disabling symptoms associated with TBI. Such behaviour has been a focus of pharmacological intervention, including the use of beta blockers, antipsychotics and anticonvulsants as mood stabilisers. Of particular importance is the fact that some of these medications can unfortunately have negative effects on cognitive functioning (especially *attention*). The clinical dilemma here is that *both* poor attention and excessive aggression can affect cognition functioning and influence whether patients can take part in rehabilitation programmes. If one of these symptoms is left untreated, the other will become problematic.

In clinical practice, TBI patients can present with depression, and some are treated with antidepressant drugs, such as one of the *SSRIs*. Certain SSRIs can produce side effects of anxiety and apathy, which can negatively influence neurocognitive functioning. Conversely, effective treatment of depression can make some patients more receptive to psychological therapy and help to improve their performance on neurocognitive testing. Depressed individuals perform poorly on neuropsychological tests if they are not given plenty of encouragement and many rest breaks – which are not always easy to provide in environments where there is little time for neuropsychological input.

Stroke patients present fairly frequently with anxiety and depression (in addition to other symptoms), and are often prescribed medication for these symptoms. One of the most troublesome difficulties related to both depression and anxiety is disturbed sleep. In some cases, patients may be taking one of the benzodiazepines to treat *insomnia*, and in other cases for *anxiety* (although this is probably less common in view of the potential risk of becoming addicted to benzodiazepines). This group of drugs can have significant negative effects on concentration, and it may be sensible to postpone neurocognitive assessment. However, problems with attention are not only to be reckoned with when testing patients – they should also be considered in patients who are receiving psychological therapy or other forms of rehabilitation. Poor attention inevitably results in reduced retention, thereby hampering the recall of significant points covered during rehabilitation sessions. This becomes more salient when one considers that many patients with stroke (and other forms of brain injury) may have already had significant problems with attention prior to starting a course of medication, as a result of the brain injury itself.

An amalgam of different aspects of various cases (to preserve confidentiality) may help to construct a topical clinical case to illustrate the central point of this chapter.

In neuropsychology, we need to be aware of the medications patients are taking so that we can incorporate the important factor of potential medication effects into our own investigations, especially when conducting neuropsychological testing. Thus, while neuropsychologists have absolutely no involvement in the prescribing of any medication, a working knowledge of what drugs are, what they do and what their side effects are is of considerable practical clinical utility. The following short case report attempts to illustrate this fundamental point.

A right-handed male, aged 36, who worked as a professional engineer, was referred for baseline neuropsychological testing prior to planned neurosurgery. He was diagnosed with a left frontal meningioma. He had no history of any other neurological or psychiatric difficulties, no substance abuse, no major surgical procedures and no other illnesses of note. He was married, with three children, and had been in the same employment with a state department of civil engineering for the past eight years, providing low-cost housing solutions for impoverished areas. The initial presentation involved out-of-character behaviour, first noticed at work. In addition, some of his language functions had become subtly impaired, which alarmed his family. However, these signs were either ignored or ascribed to stress. Consequently, he first came to the attention of his doctor when he had a seizure while working in the garden.

He was offered an extended outpatient appointment that consisted of two standard one-hour appointments to try to perform an assessment of key cognitive functions. The central hypothesis that required investigation during neuropsychological testing, based on his history, was that the cognitive functions served by the left frontal regions might be impaired. Accordingly, in addition to a selection of short tests and sub-tests that were used to briefly cover most of the neurocognitive domains, more time was spent on the testing of executive and language functions. To the surprise of the neuropsychologist, though, the results did not provide robust evidence of specific neurocognitive impairment in either the executive or language domains. While the scores for tests of these functions were lower relative to the patient's projected premorbid abilities, most other functions were *also* below the expected range.

On closer inspection of the scores and distributions, this patient showed a much-reduced performance on tests of attention. Clearly, there are many possible factors that may have contributed to his test performance, including anxiety, the role of the frontal lobes in attention, and so forth. However, another important factor that should be included in the formulation when discussing his neuropsychological test profile is the possible effects of his medication. With the onset of his seizures, he was prescribed an anticonvulsant, which had been increased to the maximum dose in response to poor seizure control just prior to his neurocognitive assessment. He was seizure-free thereafter. However, for the purpose of interpreting the neuropsychological test profile, some anticonvulsants are known to affect cognitive performance, including attention, in a global way (that is, they globally subdue the brain). Poor attention can of course also reduce performance on most other cognitive tests, and psychologists need to be aware of this.

Conclusion

Pharmacological interventions form an important part of the treatment plan for patients with neuropathology. Such interventions are in many cases the only treatment provided, especially in poorly resourced healthcare systems. Psychologists are not involved in the prescription of medication. The only knowledge related to pharmacological interventions that is of major relevance to neuropsychological practice involves understanding possible drug side effects – most importantly with respect to cognition. This is directly relevant when performing neuropsychological testing and interpreting the results, and when observing patients' behaviour. Drug side effects can significantly colour clinical presentations and test results.

The risk of misinterpreting a patient's neurocognitive presentation is high if one does not have a working knowledge of the effects of medications, and if one does not consider the potential impact of medication on test performance. It is equally important for clinicians to consider the fact that even moderately effective pharmacological treatment – for difficulties such as anxiety or depression – can potentially make patients just that bit more amenable to engaging in psychological therapy, thereby opening up other avenues of rehabilitation as part of an integrated approach to treatment. Finally, effective pharmacological treatment for some physical difficulties, such as post-traumatic epilepsy, may dramatically improve patients' quality of life, and again increase the likelihood of their being able to engage with psychological therapy – or with the more functional interventions used to increase patient independence, such as occupational therapy.

Practical tips

1. Find out where the *British National Formulary, MIMS* or equivalent medication reference text is kept at your workplace. This way you can easily look up any medication side effects prior to assessing patients.
2. The best practical way to develop a working knowledge of this complex area is to ask and learn about medications when patients are presented at ward rounds.

Points for reflective practice

1. Realistically, does a clinical neuropsychologist really need to know anything at all about psychopharmacology?
2. Can pharmacological and psychological approaches to rehabilitation following brain injury be used on the same patient simultaneously?

Selected further reading

Cooper, S., & Nicholas, L. (2012). An overview of South African psychology. *International Journal of Psychology, 47,* 89–101.

Fleminger, S. (2008). Long-term psychiatric disorders after traumatic brain injury. *European Journal of Anaesthesiology, 42,* 123–130.

Sadock, B. J., & Sadock, V. A. (2007). *Kaplan & Sadock's synopsis of psychiatry* (10th ed.). London: Wolters Cluver/Lippincott Williams & Wilkins.

6

NEUROPSYCHOLOGICAL THEORY

Introduction

How valid is a theoretical model when it is applied across cultures? Do we even have the luxury of indulgence in theory when resource limitations demand that our every minute is spent caring for patients? It is always important to clarify the purpose of studying particular theories – this is no different in neuropsychology. Among its many functions, theory can help increase our understanding of naturally occurring phenomena and manipulated events. To date, there remains no unifying theory within the natural sciences. The same holds true for neuropsychology. Generally speaking, theory drives the development of new hypotheses, which then require testing. However, for theory to have even more utility in clinical professions, it needs to inform practice at the level of service delivery.

Theoretical models need to improve clinical care with regard to outcomes for patients and with respect to efficiency, which is especially relevant in the context of under-resourced healthcare systems. This may include theories concerning: normal cognitive functioning; cognitive impairment following brain injury; recovery following brain injury; cross-cultural perspectives; and theories relating to the rehabilitation of patients with acquired brain injury, to name but a few. These areas are stimulated by theoretical developments that have ultimately transformed some aspects of patient assessment and rehabilitation. This chapter only covers some areas of theory – those that have had a bearing on understanding the organisation of cognitive processes in humans and on understandings pertaining to rehabilitation and recovery following brain injury, for example. So, which of the many theoretical developments in brain–behaviour relationships can help those who are new to neuropsychology to develop a better understanding of some of the important clinical questions in the field?

The work of A. R. Luria

Alexander Romanov Luria was one of the most famous Russian psychologists of the 20th century. His seminal work has profoundly influenced the field of neuropsychology and its related disciplines. Luria's theory of brain functioning continues to directly influence our understanding of brain–behaviour relations and the rehabilitation of patients with acquired brain injury. In essence, Luria (1973) described *three principal functional units* operating within the human brain. The first functional unit is for *regulating tone* or waking, the second for *obtaining, processing and storing* information arriving from the outside world and the third for *programming, regulating and verifying* mental activity.

Each functional unit is hierarchical in its structural organisation. The brain's primary (projection) areas receive or send impulses to the periphery, whereas the secondary (projection-association) areas process incoming information and prepare programmes. The tertiary (overlapping zones) brain regions are involved with the most complex forms of human behaviour and mental activity; processes requiring the participation of many different interconnected cortical areas in a fluid manner. Each functional system includes several functionally integrated anatomical structures. To this day, the concept of functional integration of neurocognitive functions remains central to our understanding of brain–behaviour relationships. One of the more recent applications of this idea, now increasingly substantiated by functional brain imaging, is the importance of considering brain functioning holistically rather than only focusing on specific anatomical areas.

It is important to view 'higher cortical processes as complex, dynamically localised, functional systems that are affected differently with lesions of different parts of the cerebral hemispheres' (Luria, 1966, p. 586). From this perspective, man's 'perception and action, his memory, speech and thinking, makes use of a highly complex system of concertedly working zones of cerebral cortex' (Luria, 1973, p. 341). Within this theory, the term 'functional system' refers to the interaction between various tissues, rather than just a single tissue (Luria, 1973; Solms & Turnbull, 2002). By way of analogy, just as the function of digestion in the human body involves multiple individual functions (such as the work of the bowel, stomach and intestine, all acting together), so too brain functioning operates in a similar manner, with the interaction of various neuroanatomical 'centres' throughout the brain contributing towards neurocognitive functioning (Hebben & Milberg, 2002; Luria, 1973; Solms & Turnbull, 2002; Walsh & Darby, 1999).

A clinical example may help to illustrate some of the central aspects of Luria's work. Let us consider the impairments of executive function, attention and memory that are characteristically seen with severe traumatic brain injury. To recap, the first functional unit is involved in attention and information processing, the second in memory (storage) and the third in goal-directed behaviour and problem solving. These cognitive functions are mutually dependent – they rely on interaction with each other and cannot be seen in isolation – mirroring how, in clinical practice, systems (and functions) are interdependent. For example, patients with severe traumatic brain injury, who present with impaired information processing, are very likely to have executive dysfunction too. Clinically, this may declare itself as erratic difficulty with problem solving. Hence, patients' clinical presentations can be better understood, and appropriate interventions thereby selected, by incorporating a theoretical perspective on where exactly the impairments stem from. In other words, it is essential to understand where individual cognitive functions break down and how this in turn affects other areas of functioning.

Many would say that Luria has made a truly remarkable contribution to our understanding of brain functioning. His theory continues to influence how we think about patient assessment and rehabilitation, especially when using the *hypothetico-deductive approach* to clinical assessment, as opposed to the *psychometric approach* (see Chapter 9). Some of the reasons for this extraordinary achievement include the fact that his theory moves beyond anatomical localisation by integrating areas of the human brain with functions. It is this focus on functions – and their hierarchical organisation – that provides the underpinnings of important aspects of assessment and rehabilitation endeavours. This approach may also eventually prove a better fit with regard to emerging findings about pathways, which have been achieved through functional brain imaging research.

The rapidly evolving field of human brain imaging has the potential to show, at a biological level, how neuronal networks and pathways between brain regions relate to cognitive, behavioural and emotional functioning. Findings from functional imaging studies have the potential to further stimulate the development of fundamental theoretical models of cognition, recovery following brain injury, and behaviour. Functional imaging can also shed further light not only on individual differences, but also on what constitutes spontaneous recovery versus restitution of function during intensive brain-injury rehabilitation – one of the core debates in this area. Light can also be shed on both the taking-over of function by adjacent brain areas, and on patients finding alternative strategies for performing mental tasks. The following section focuses more specifically on applied models of neuropsychological rehabilitation.

Neuropsychological models of rehabilitation

The first important point to make is that many applied models of rehabilitation tend to evolve in clinical practice. Accordingly, it is unlikely that there are many brain-injury services that can claim a 'pure' or 'static' application of one specific model to their practice. Practice changes over time. Reflective professional practice has to do, at its core, with continual questioning and, where possible, with improving what we do as rehabilitation professionals. There are many models of neuropsychological rehabilitation. It can be overwhelming to have to make sense of the plethora of models that have been described over recent years. Therefore, a practical starting point is to try to gain an overall perspective of the broad theoretical directions that neuropsychological rehabilitation has taken. In this spirit, one of the most useful papers – although some might say by now a bit dated – remains the landmark overview and critique provided by Barbara Wilson (1997).

The first of the four models described by Wilson (1997) is the *cognitive re-training approach*. This approach focuses on cognitive retraining through exercises, making the assumption that cognitive deficits may be remediated by *practice, exercise* and *stimulation*. Patients are usually given a cognitive exercise (often a computer-based task) regime that targets a specific neuropsychological impairment. Attention is one of the most commonly targeted cognitive functions when using this model. Often the task that is intended to improve attention will involve repeated practice with the aim of reducing reaction times. Some of the difficulties associated with this model include: a lack of robust evidence for its clinical effectiveness and for the generalisability of the gains made in rehabilitation; the failure to address problems of poor generalisation of gains beyond the laboratory or clinic; and its lack of theoretical underpinnings. In addition, this model does not address the emotional, behavioural or social consequences associated with brain injury, which is a serious shortcoming. It has only limited application in providing specific strategies to rehabilitate specific cognitive impairments, such as poor concentration.

According to Wilson (1997), the *cognitive neuropsychological approach* is a diagnostic system rather than a model per se. It describes a *remedial strategy* to overcome impairment. Accordingly, within a detailed model of cognitive functioning, specific deficits are identified through extensive neuropsychological testing. The essence of the model defines exactly where a cognitive function breaks down. With regard to its application to rehabilitation, treatment typically involves practise of the impaired component that is defined within the cognitive model. A significant difficulty with this approach is that it appears to identify what to treat without really providing adequate strategies for how to rehabilitate the impairments. Furthermore, in clinical practice, the majority of patients have multiple deficits, which is something that is not addressed in this model. The problem is that deficits tend to overlap, making it very difficult to identify where exactly a cognitive function breaks down. Additionally, this model does not address the emotional difficulties associated with brain injury. Finally, the ecological validity of the outcome measures (neuropsychological tests) used is doubtful. Frequently, improvements that have been demonstrated with psychometric scores have limited predictive power regarding functional outcome and, in addition, improved psychometric scores may sometimes represent spontaneous recovery or simply test practice effects.

Learning theory, cognitive psychology and neuropsychology form the core elements of rehabilitation strategies in the *combined approach* (Wilson, 1997). A *behavioural approach* provides treatment structure with regard to: (1) analysis of the presenting problems; (2) assessing everyday manifestations of difficulties; and (3) evaluating the efficiency of the treatments/outcomes. Many techniques from mainstream behaviour theory are adapted for use within this approach. Some of these may include principles derived from learning theory, such as *reinforcement* and *extinction*, among several other useful techniques. Cognitive psychology and neuropsychology are also integrated into the programmes to enhance clinicians' understandings of cognitive systems and the brain's functional organisation. While this model has been effective in certain rehabilitation settings, some questions still remain. There are two primary concerns, namely its perceived failure to address emotional needs and its failure to address a wider range of cognitive impairments. Nevertheless, certain components of this approach, most notably 'Cognitive behavioural therapy', may be useful in addressing some of the specific problems patients commonly experience, including anxiety, poor planning and chaotic daily routines.

In concluding her review, Wilson (1997) asserts that the *holistic approach* to neuropsychological rehabilitation integrates interventions. It is unhelpful to separate cognitive, functional and psychiatric consequences from the emotional problems that are associated with brain injury. In this approach, individual therapy, group therapy and meetings between staff and patients all focus on themes such as vocational counselling, issues related to awareness, cognitive remediation and the development of compensatory skills. Psychotherapy plays an important part in these programmes. Other therapies, such as speech therapy, language therapy and occupational therapy, are provided individually, as required, and a group for patients' relatives is regularly held. Work trials are often included during the later stages of these programmes. In an ideal world, from a clinician's perspective, there appear to be few concerns with this approach. While very expensive, research findings regarding outcomes indicate that these programmes are cost-effective. Nevertheless, there are other factors to consider, such as the role of natural recovery processes, and the role that community support (and individual support) might play in facilitating recovery (see the 'Cross-cultural considerations' section below).

Recovery and rehabilitation

What do we know about spontaneous recovery following acquired brain injury? Conversely, what do we know about cognitive decline in progressive conditions? How do these processes interact with rehabilitation interventions? Robertson (2005) provides a model of cognitive rehabilitation that incorporates the important role of neuronal function. In essence, Robertson links behaviour and biology in order to clarify how neuropsychological rehabilitation works – incorporating *restitution, compensation, Hebbian learning* ('neurons that fire together, wire together') and *brain plasticity*. Some of the arguments made are that there is some evidence that neurons can regenerate after injury. Therefore, compensatory strategies that are used to achieve improvement in behaviour or function by reorganisation (as propagated by Luria) are not always helpful. The point is that compensatory strategies can possibly be harmful under certain circumstances. In clinical practice, however, practical questions regularly arise regarding patient care: for example, are compensatory strategies best, or will a restitution approach be more successful in, say, a patient with aphasia following a stroke?

In developing the argument for restitution further, Robertson (2005) suggests that, based on Hebbian learning, there are some principles that are of great importance to rehabilitation practice and spontaneous recovery following brain injury. The first is that the brain can repair itself through *synaptic turnover*, which may in part actually depend on experience, and may thereby underpin learning and recovery following acquired brain injury. The second principle is that recovery may have similarities to learning processes. The third principle is that input (through the provision of experiences) to neural pathways may shape interconnections and thereby aid recovery. The final principle pertains to the study of normal plasticity in individuals with no neurological damage to inform our understanding of how rehabilitation interventions might facilitate recovery. Restitution may be particularly useful to attempt in rehabilitation in instances where some remaining intact function has been identified. Rehabilitation interventions should also work on trying to prevent the development of unhelpful behavioural patterns. Finally, rehabilitation interventions should be paced to match the patient's ability to sustain attention. In practice, this may translate to the provision of brief but more regular input.

Robertson (2005) provides some interesting theoretical perspectives regarding recovery and rehabilitation that may prove to have significant implications for models of service delivery. One of the most frequent dilemmas facing those working in neuropsychology concerns outcome following brain injury. Patients and their families often ask us how much recovery (or decline) will take place and over what time period, and whether rehabilitation will be effective. These are always incredibly difficult questions to answer. Even if we have some pointers provided to us by research (for example, the typical trajectory following a stroke), predicting the course in an individual case depends on many factors. Some of these factors are biological (for example, age), while others are psychological (for example, premorbid personality or motivation) or social/environmental (for example, family support or a sympathetic employer). The reality is that we frequently get our predictions wrong. A potentially far more useful strategy is to: (1) outline the general research findings; (2) go over the good and the poor prognostic factors; (3) admit that predictions are inevitably likely to be off the mark; and (4) suggest the mutual identification of rehabilitation goals that are relevant to patients, their families and the clinical team.

Cross-cultural considerations

The particular cultural and educational background of patients also has a bearing on rehabilitation outcomes. Patients and their families, especially those from under-resourced regions who have also been educationally deprived, may have great difficulty understanding the purpose of rehabilitation procedures and their role in them. It can be very difficult to provide any rehabilitation at all for patients in many developing world or under-resourced rural settings, where very often such programmes are simply unavailable. Under such circumstances, the relatively lucky patients who get some medical treatment are usually only seen in acute-care settings, from where they are quickly discharged. This harsh reality means that very often patients are left, post-brain injury, to rely on community and/or family support under very trying circumstances. In these circumstances, psychologists should attempt, wherever possible, to establish community-based rehabilitation support, including the training of colleagues such as social workers and lay counsellors, in the basics facts about the brain and brain injury.

The African concept of *ubuntu* (see Chapter 18) is an example of a factor that may augment spontaneous recovery, especially in instances where patients have little else to rely on. Support from members of patients' communities, such as assistance with activities of daily living, for example, is likely to improve the chances of better reintegration into society, thereby reducing dependence on limited or even non-existent state support. Clinicians working in such environments, especially in the developing world, need to be aware of these realities, along with an awareness of the effects that a lack of infrastructure, a poorly educated population and different cultural belief systems will have on patient rehabilitation. When practitioners do get the opportunity to do neuropsychological assessments and rehabilitative work in developing world or rural settings, an integrative approach, incorporating Luria's *hypothetico-deductive* thinking, is usually better suited to working with patients cross-culturally, where many other factors that may colour neurocognitive performance need to be considered.

Conclusion

One of the most influential theories in neuropsychology is that of the Russian Alexander Romanov Luria, whose work emphasised the importance of considering how the brain's functional systems interact in determining behaviour, cognition and emotion. Rehabilitation models have been influenced by this work and by more recent developments in the understanding of spontaneous recovery and learning processes. Nevertheless, when designing an individualised rehabilitation plan in clinical practice, the patient's presentation should always be as thoroughly assessed as is pragmatically possible before being considered in light of these and other theoretical models.

When working in under-resourced settings/systems, the following practical clinical strategies may prove to be some of the more productive and cost-effective. When performing neuropsychological testing, view cognitive functions as parts of an integrated circuit, rather than in isolation. Use compensatory strategies for obvious and specific impairments, such as memory problems. Never neglect patients' emotional difficulties – compassion and empathy are potent agents in engaging patients who are undergoing rehabilitation. Consider providing shorter sessions – many patients have information-processing difficulties. Always try to go with the ebb and flow of a different culture, rather than simply imposing a specific model or approach at all costs. When resources are limited, try, where possible, to translate all rehabilitation plans into ecologically valid outcomes so as to achieve decreased dependency on state or social security.

Practical tips

1. Never make specific predictions regarding recovery or decline in patients with neuropathology; never say, for example, 'After two years there will be no more improvement', or 'It will be five years before any significant memory problems appear'. Such predictions inevitably turn out to be inaccurate.
2. Try to think about which theories inform your clinical practice the most – doing this will benefit your case formulations.

Points for reflective practice

1. Describe the theoretical principles that would guide your rehabilitation plan for a young adult who presents with moderate cognitive impairment and a lack of motivation six months after suffering a severe traumatic brain injury.
2. If the same adult described in point (1) can only be seen for rehabilitation for five (one-hour) appointments due to limited resources, describe what you would do and how you would achieve this in the most effective way possible.
3. Discuss what possible factors may account for recovery/improvement following acquired brain injury.

Selected further reading

Luria, A. R. (1966). *Higher cortical functions in man*. London: Tavistock Publications.

Luria, A. R. (1973). *The working brain: An introduction to neuropsychology*. Aylesbury, UK: Penguin Books.

Wilson, B. A. (1997). Cognitive rehabilitation: How it is and how it might be. *Journal of the International Neuropsychological Society*, 3, 487–496.

7

SPECIAL INVESTIGATIONS

Introduction

Special clinical investigations often provide additional information crucial to the diagnostic process. These are investigations other than neuropsychological tests and assessments, and usually include medical investigations (most notably neuroimaging), studies of brain electrical activity, blood tests and X-rays, among many others. Special investigations are not limited to medical tests. Other clinicians working within the multidisciplinary team contribute to the assessment and diagnosis of patients with brain injury. For example, *speech therapists, occupational therapists, physiotherapists, dieticians, rehabilitation engineers* and other professions all conduct specialist assessments of their own – all of which provide very important clinical data. For example, in right-handers with left hemisphere strokes, the most valuable information to have access to will probably be brain scans and speech therapists' assessments. With traumatic brain injury, brain imaging data and markers of severity, such as the length of the period of post-traumatic amnesia (PTA), are essential.

Unfortunately, in numerous under-resourced settings – including in many rural areas, especially in the developing world – many special investigations are simply unavailable. This may be due to lack of financial resources, or skills shortages in certain disciplines, or both. In such settings, all clinicians, including psychologists, need to adapt to whatever resources *are* available. For example, where there is no brain imaging equipment, neuropsychological assessment (along with other clinical medical tests) will be required to ascertain lesion location, based entirely on clinical presentation. There may also not be a multidisciplinary team available, and practitioners may have to improvise in making clinical decisions that are best for patients. For example, a patient may present with mildly impaired hand strength, and have no access to a physiotherapist. Here, consider whether there are other hospital-based clinicians who might be able to at least provide advice to the patient, or think later-ally: is there a community sports centre or coach who may be able to help?

In neuropsychology, it is considered good practice to always obtain the medical files of newly referred patients. This is the first step in the assessment process fol-lowing the receipt of a referral. Generally it is here, in medical notes, that the results from special investigations are reported. These data provide an important context against which neuropsychological assessment and testing is subsequently performed, and ultimately interpreted. While there is certainly an art and skill to making sense of medical notes in the first instance, psychologists need a basic understanding of the relevant special investigations likely to be encountered in patients' folders/ files.

Very few textbooks are specifically written for psychologists to provide guidance on how to trawl copious amounts of medical information, or how to extract essen-tial information for subsequent neuropsychological assessments and interventions. It is probably true that most neuropsychologists develop these skills in a hands-on fashion during internships or during the early years of their clinical practice. In this chapter, the main sources of information are from McConnell (2006) and De Zubicaray (2006) – see 'Selected further reading' at the end of this chapter – coupled with the authors' own experience drawn from working as hospital-based clinical neuropsychologists. Information is also drawn from learning some of the skills involved in finding and understanding relevant clinical data from other profession-als. Most of the emphasis is placed on brain imaging, as this is the type of special investigation that clinical neuropsychologists most frequently access, and which they find useful for helping to understand patients' presentations and cognitive profiles.

Neuroimaging

For neuropsychologists, the two most frequently encountered neuroimaging inves-tigation techniques are *magnetic resonance imaging (MRI scan)* and *computed tomography (CT scan)*, although in many under-resourced clinical settings these techniques are unavailable due to financial realities. Put simplistically, CT scans are images pro-duced by a computer, using the data from a series of repeated X-rays. For a very good, short review of CT scans in neurology, see the Cross (2008) reference in 'Selected further reading' at the end of this chapter. MRI scans use nuclear mag-netic resonance to collect data about the alignment of brain nuclei. These data are then used by computer software to generate an image of the brain. The develop-ment and wider availability of these high-quality anatomical imaging technologies has contributed immensely to both the acute and post-acute management of various pathologies and procedures, including traumatic brain injury, stroke, brain tumour surgery and the diagnostic process (for example, in *Multiple sclerosis* and certain dementias).

In effect, modern neuroimaging has (where available) made the quest of ana-tomical localisation purely by means of neuropsychological testing alone somewhat redundant in everyday clinical practice in parts of the world. MRI and CT scans have provided significant opportunities for research and increased our understanding of some of the anatomical changes associated with neurological conditions. MRI and CT scans have different advantages relative to each other, and are often used for different clinical purposes. MRI scans are more expensive than CT scans, but generally provide more detailed images, in different planes – crucial for diagnosing certain conditions. Computed tomography is less expensive and more readily available in many larger hospitals around the world, and also has clinical advantages: for example, they are considered effective at detecting acute intracerebral bleeding and calcified lesions.

How can we make basic sense of brain images displayed during clinical case presentations? A practical approach is to understand, orientate correctly and then visualise the three-dimensional anatomical structure represented in black and white (and in two dimensions). The first step is to look for important 'landmarks', such as the *eyeballs*, the *cerebellum*, the *ventricles* or the vertex (top) of the brain, and so forth. Doing this helps to visualise and orientate in three dimensions what it is that is being viewed – the shapes of the eyeballs, the ventricles and so forth are easy to visualise. Next, it is important to understand what the colours black and white (or grey) represent: for example, white represents either bone or blood on a CT scan.

What about lesions – how do we recognise these? Obviously, brain scans are primarily there for interpretation by medical practitioners, such as radiologists, neurosurgeons and neurologists, not psychologists. However, it is extremely helpful for psychologists to be able to follow what is being discussed and to see the anatomical structures that are pointed out. The following are some practical tips for the detection of abnormalities on scans. First, look for any *asymmetries*: does the left hemisphere look essentially the same as the right – or does it appear that the midline may have shifted? This is especially important in cases of traumatic brain injury, brain tumours and other space-occupying lesions. Sometimes it can be helpful to stand back, further away from a scan, and look at it again from this different perspective to try to detect subtle asymmetries, suspicious shapes and/or unexpected changes in tone or darkness. Be aware that many non-medical factors have an influence on the types of brain injury seen: for example, when working in countries with high levels of firearm violence, look for foreign objects (usually bright white, indicating metal).

While brain imaging is probably the most important medically related special investigation for neuropsychologists, there are some important limitations to the data and information it produces. Bigler (2001) points out some of the caveats that clinicians should be aware of when presented with neuroimaging following traumatic brain injury. While these points pertain specifically to traumatic brain injury, some of the general principles also apply to other neuropathologies. One of the most important points is that '*the lesion is always bigger than the lesion*' (Bigler, 2001). What this effectively means is that there can often be significant disruption of brain function immediately surrounding the delineated area (on scan) of the anatomical lesion, as well as further away from the demonstrable lesion due to disconnection of crucial functional neuronal pathways (a phenomenon known as *diaschisis*).

Given some of the important limitations to the data produced by these brain scans (which, after all, provide static anatomical images), neuropsychologists tend also to have interest in other, newer techniques that probably have more application in research settings, in many instances, than in clinical environments. Some examples of these newer MRI techniques include: *functional MRI, magnetic resonance spectroscopy* and *MRI diffusion weighted imaging*. MRI diffusion weighted imaging has been used to provide imaging of *cerebrovascular accidents*, for example. Functional MRI is used more as a research tool to map activity in specific brain regions while the individual is engaged in specific cognitive (or other) tasks.

Functional MRI uses an association between increased oxygen and blood flow to generate images that correspond with presumed increases in brain activity. The interested reader can consult Lagopoulos (2007) for a helpful two-page overview of functional MRI (see 'Selected further reading' at the end of this chapter). Other examples of functional brain imaging are *single-photon emission positron computed tomography scans (SPECT scans)* and *positron emission tomography scans (PET scans)*, which use a radioactive substance that can safely cross the blood–brain barrier in order to map out regions of increased blood flow. While many of these techniques have more of a research application, they may also have direct relevance to the practice of neuropsychology in healthcare settings, although in developing or economically disadvantaged countries they are often unavailable.

As Bigler (2001) points out, the limitation with static anatomical images produced by CT and MRI scans, for example, is that these images only reveal structural and anatomical damage. The functional (metabolic) problems resulting from focal anatomical lesions are not revealed by CT or MRI scans, and can only be seen with some of the newer functional imaging techniques. For neuropsychology, the essential point is that these metabolic impairments are often distant from the focal, anatomical lesion/s. This may to some extent explain the limited convergence between neuropsychological test findings and data from anatomical scans. Nevertheless, CT and MRI scans, where available, remain hugely important to the everyday practice of neuropsychology. Where there is no functional brain imaging available, neuropsychologists normally consider other information to help make sense of complex neuropsychological test results. This information includes an understanding of the nature of the neuropathology, the skill of identifying the most relevant clinical symptoms and an awareness of the often considerable limitations of neuropsychological tests in assessing and localising specific cognitive functions.

Other special investigations

Electroencephalography (EEG) is reasonably widely used clinically, and has important research applications. EEG measures the electrical activity of underlying brain regions by means of electrodes superficially attached to the scalp. Perhaps the most common use of EEG is to help with the diagnosis of suspected *epilepsy*. However, it should be remembered that an epilepsy diagnosis is not entirely dependent on EEG findings – a normal EEG does not always exclude epilepsy or seizures, and an abnormal EEG does not necessarily confirm their presence either. Clinical signs and symptoms are always crucial in making the diagnosis and a reliable observer report of a seizure event is very helpful.

There are special types of EEG investigations, such as *EEG video telemetry*, where an extended EEG recording is simultaneously coupled with a video of the patient to try to correlate observed behavioural changes or motor symptoms with changes in the EEG pattern. However, these are often only available in well-funded, typically larger specialist hospitals/units. The association between EEG patterns and cognitive functions is sometimes of more direct interest to neuropsychologists. It is also relevant to consider impaired attentional processes and, in certain conditions, the association of EEG findings with other cognitive functions, such as memory or language. An example of the latter would be subtle word-finding difficulties in a right-hander with a left hemisphere EEG abnormality.

The following are other special clinical investigations performed in the hospital/clinic. In stroke medicine, the *angiogram* specifically depicts the brain's arteries, and is used in attempting to identify potential abnormalities, such as *aneurysms*. However, not all investigations rely on technology or specialist equipment. The *neurological examination* is a very important special investigation. For neuropsychologists, clinical notes concerning the neurological examination of patients are one of the most frequently encountered investigations found in medical folders. These notes sometimes include a brief examination of cognitive function, often in the form of a brief *screening*, using tools such as the Mini-Mental State Examination (MMSE) and the Montreal Cognitive Assessment (MoCA).

Some of the many other areas examined by neurologists include: *muscle power, gait, reflexes, sensory functions*, the *cranial nerves* and *motor movements*. Examples of possible positive findings on neurological examination include: the presence of brisk reflexes; loss of sensation in a specific bodily distribution; the presence of a *Babinski reflex*; reduced muscle *tone*; *ataxia*; loss of muscle bulk in a specific area; and the presence of a *tremor*. Such findings are interpreted by neurologists and are sometimes used to make a provisional diagnosis, which then serves as a guide to which additional special investigations will be required to confirm the diagnosis. For this reason, it is essential not to read neurology notes in isolation, but in conjunction with findings from other special investigations. Neurology is a scarce resource and often unavailable in peripheral hospitals and healthcare centres; however, other doctors also perform more basic neurological examinations.

Results from a huge number of *blood tests* can, in many cases, make it difficult for clinicians to trawl through medical records. It is not the role of neuropsychologists to decide which tests are relevant to the diagnosis or treatment of patients. Nevertheless, an awareness of which blood tests may be relevant can be helpful in forming a more complete picture of a patient and his/her presenting condition. This can be of particular importance when new patients are seen and little is known regarding their histories. Basic blood tests are usually widely available, even in more poorly resourced systems. Demographics, socio-political systems, financial resources and many environmental factors can all influence which of the most common blood tests are performed in different countries. For example, in some countries testing for *HIV/AIDS* or *malaria* may be extremely common, while much less so in other countries.

The following blood tests are relevant to neuropsychology. Raised *white blood cell* counts can be indicative of an infection, while lowered *red blood cells* and *haemoglobin* can indicate *anaemia*. Severe infections may result in *delirium* and associated changes in awareness and concentration. An infection can also involve the brain directly. *Platelet* counts can be reduced as a result of medication (for example, *anticonvulsants*) or due to alcohol abuse, which potentially makes patients more vulnerable to bleeding – including *intracerebral bleeds* (full blood count values can point towards intracerebral bleeds). *Thyroid* function tests are also important, as thyroid function abnormalities are associated with *anxiety*, *depression* and changes in cognitive function. Raised *prolactin* levels shortly after a reported *seizure* may help in confirming a diagnosis of *epilepsy*. Blood *glucose* levels are important in *diabetes mellitus* and can be associated with changes in attention and other cognitive functions.

Blood test results for metals, such as lead, mercury and copper (levels of the latter being raised in the case of *Wilson's disease*), are important because of the potential for neurotoxicity and its association with cognitive impairment and *dementia*. Raised *liver* functions may provide a clue as to a previously unidentified chronic alcohol abuse. Blood tests for HIV are important too, as this can result in a very wide variety of psychiatric presentations and cognitive impairments and, in some cases, *AIDS-related dementia*. Thiamine (*vitamin B1*), *folate* and *vitamin B12* levels are all important because of their potential relevance to memory and other cognitive functions.

Another important function that some blood tests serve is in the monitoring of the physiological effects of certain medications: for example, with liver function tests, where *electrolytes* and white blood cell and platelet counts can all be altered by some drugs prescribed to neurological patients. Platelet counts can decrease as a result of some anticonvulsant medications, for example.

Numerous other tests are important for patients with neuropathology, only some of which are mentioned here. *Urine* tests are used to detect illicit substance use, for *urinary tract infections* (which may make patients delirious, especially the elderly) and as a marker of potential *kidney disease*. Kidney disease may be a contraindication for the use of certain medications, including in patients with neurological illness. *Cerebrospinal fluid (CSF)* is sometimes drained from the spine and analysed to look for evidence of brain infection.

Chest X-rays may be important in some cases: for example, in patients with suspected (or confirmed) lung cancer, which (similar to certain other forms of cancer, such as breast cancer) has the potential for causing secondary brain *metastases*. *Cardiological tests* are of relevance in cases where reduced cardiac function may be implicated in secondary problems with cerebral blood flow and oxygenation. *Ophthalmological* examinations can be of crucial importance in detecting neurological illness, particularly where the presence of previously unidentified *papilloedema* is confirmed. Papilloedema is associated with *raised intracranial pressure*, and is seen in conditions such as *subarachnoid haemorrhage*, *brain abscesses* and *tumours*. Finally, patients with acquired brain injury or degenerative brain conditions may have been assessed and/or treated by physiotherapists, occupational therapists and speech therapists. Reports and clinical notes from such colleagues contain valuable information regarding patients' everyday difficulties and functional limitations.

Conclusion

Special investigations are hugely important to the diagnostic process. In neuropsychology, it is important to have a good working knowledge and understanding of the data generated by certain of these investigations. Unfortunately, many special investigations are unavailable in certain settings, especially in under-resourced areas in the developing world. The most frequently encountered investigation that is of direct relevance to neuropsychology is the brain scan. However, we need to consider whether, on occasion, clinicians perhaps lend too much weight to individual investigations when trying to explain the potential aetiologies that underpin certain conditions. For example, MRI and CT scans are often normal following severe traumatic brain injury (Bigler, 2001), which does not in any way mean that the patient did not suffer brain injury. From a rehabilitation perspective, there is the potential problem that an individual with a normal brain scan might not, under certain circumstances, be believed about his/her reported ongoing psychological difficulties. After all, the cutting-edge (and expensive) technology 'proved' that the patient was 'normal'. Patients report that, under these circumstances, it can sometimes feels as if they are being dismissed, and/or that they are pretending to experience more severe symptoms than they actually are in reality. This can clearly have a significant impact on early consultations with such patients and their families, especially when one is speculating about predicted outcome.

It may be more important to invest time in clinical interactions in order to address healthcare needs, rather than always using vast financial resources to purchase technology. Ideally, the findings from different investigations (such as brain scans, blood tests, EEG, neuropsychological test results and toxicology screens) should all be considered by the multidisciplinary team, and then integrated through a process of clinical reasoning, before any diagnostic conclusions are reached.

Practical tips

1. Obtain a computer disc of a normal brain scan and practise seeing whether you can identify the corresponding anatomical structures on a model of the human brain.
2. It can be very useful to have a pocket book containing information about special investigations, neuropathology, diagnostic entities and neuropsychology. One of the best currently available is the portable text by Snyder, Nussbaum and Robins (see the McConnell reference in 'Selected further reading', below).

Points for reflective practice

1. What are the limitations of anatomical brain imaging techniques such as MRI and CT scans?
2. What are the limitations of functional brain imaging techniques such as SPECT and functional MRI?
3. Can all neurocognitive impairment, motor or sensory dysfunction, personality change and emotional difficulties always be explained by the biological factors that are measured through special investigations?

Selected further reading

Bigler, E. D. (2001). The lesion(s) in traumatic brain injury: Implications for clinical neuropsychology. *Archives of Clinical Neuropsychology, 16*, 95–131.

Cross, J. (2008). Computed tomography in neurology. *ACNR, 8*, 22–27.

De Zubicaray, G. (2006). Neuroimaging and clinical neuropsychological practice. In P. J. Snyder, P. D. Nussbaum, & D. L. Robins (Eds.), *Clinical neuropsychology: A pocket handbook for assessment* (pp. 56–74). Washington, DC: American Psychological Association.

Lagopoulos, J. (2007). Functional MRI: An overview. *Acta Neuropsychiatrica, 19*, 64–65.

McConnell, H. W. (2006). Laboratory testing in neuropsychology. In P. J. Snyder, P. D. Nussbaum, & D. L. Robins (Eds.), *Clinical neuropsychology: A pocket handbook for assessment* (pp. 34–55). Washington, DC: American Psychological Association.

PART II

Clinical practice

8

CLINICAL ASSESSMENT IN NEUROPSYCHOLOGY

Introduction

By far the most frequently encountered aspect of neuropsychologists' daily work is to accept a referral to assess a patient, and then provide a professional opinion concerning the *diagnosis, formulation* and *management* of that patient. In large, busy hospitals, these requests usually occur on a daily basis. While this is especially true for hospital-based psychologists, it is generally the state of affairs in most other hospitals and private-practice settings too – it is a reality of everyday clinical practice that we simply cannot escape. This reality is also one that those who work in the field should never attempt to avoid, for the sake of remaining a clinically relevant, credible and sought-after professional resource. Besides professional credibility, there are also other reasons to remain as active as possible regarding patient assessment.

It is a far riskier strategy to decline referrals purely on the basis of the information contained in a single source of indirect information, such as a referral letter. Only a very limited amount can be learned about a patient's difficulties and clinical presentation from inspecting paperwork. It is often the subtleties of the patient's presentation that are important for providing clues regarding the possible presence or confirmation of brain injury. Colleagues who refer to us and then do not receive an opinion based on an assessment are usually unimpressed, understandably. In contrast, most referrers would normally fully understand and accept the reasons for declining (or accepting) a referral, based on a practitioner's clinical opinion *following* the assessment of a patient. The clinical examination of patients is possibly the most valuable, portable and transferable skill of the neuropsychologist; it is also a deceptively difficult skill to develop to a reasonable degree of competence.

Broadly speaking, clinical assessment can be divided into three main components: (1) determining and exploring patients' presenting complaints; (2) taking a thorough history; and (3) performing a bedside neuropsychological assessment of the patient, including a *mental status examination* and a *neurocognitive assessment*. These aspects of clinical assessment should ideally provide the clinical data that culminate in a diagnosis, differential diagnosis, case formulation or, in most situations, a combination of these components. Clinical assessment in neuropsychology often includes a bedside cognitive assessment and a mental status examination. The latter looks in particular at behavioural and emotional phenomena, but also at other areas, such as vegetative functions. The intended result of a treatment plan that is based on a diagnosis and/or case formulation is especially important, as without it, the whole process will most likely have little clinical utility for either the patient or practitioner. Below follows an overview of how some clinicians might perform the bedside clinical examination of patients with suspected or confirmed brain injury.

Overview of the assessment process

The bedside clinical assessment generally comprises the following steps, often performed in this sequence:

1. Carefully read over the referral letter and try to find the clinical markers of brain injury. A brief *screening* for cognitive deficits may already have been performed, using tools such as the Mini-Mental State Exam (MMSE), Montreal Cognitive Assessment (MoCA) or the Addenbrooke's Cognitive Examination (ACE-R). It is often useful to first familiarise yourself with these findings to gain an initial impression of what possible deficits to expect.

2. Always go over patients' medical records, making notes on all relevant clinical data pertaining to neuropathology, but also to other diseases: for example, kidney disease (as such diseases can indirectly affect the brain). Pay attention to reports outlining the findings of CT and MRI brain scans.

3. If using a printed database, or any other method of recording patient information, make sure you capture everything that you have gathered at this point before going to see the patient. This saves time by avoiding having to do the same task twice.

4. After introducing yourself to your patient, and having made sure that you have the correct clinical data for the correct patient, start to explore the reasons why s/he has come to hospital. While technique varies, and may be influenced by culture, it is often unhelpful to engage in small talk at this point, as it has the potential to make the patient anxious by overly delaying what is expected to happen.

5. Allow ample time to find out what the patient's most relevant presenting complaints are. Always ascertain when symptoms began and for how long they have lasted. Check if any environmental factors contribute to making the symptoms worse.

6. Take a thorough history, including a developmental history, an educational history, an employment history, a medical history and a family history. Do not take shortcuts – professionally speaking, we 'live and die' by how meticulous

our history-taking is. Adapt the history where necessary: for example, it may be essential to include a short forensic history in some situations.

7. Perform the neuropsychological assessment, including the mental status examination and cognitive testing, covering cognition, behaviour and emotion. Never assume that the 'obvious' can be skipped: for example, that the patient will know what the date is. What was not examined is not objective and will only have opinion value.

8. Where possible, and indicated, always interview a relative or friend who knows the patient well in order to obtain a collateral history. This is especially relevant where patients cannot give a reliable account themselves, which is not unusual in the context of brain injury. It is ideal (and advisable) that the person/s providing collateral perspective attend/s the patient's assessment.

9. Administer questionnaires where necessary, including baseline outcome measures. It is sometimes a more economical use of the clinician's time to leave questionnaires with patients for completion in the ward or at home – this can also manage patient fatigue.

10. Give patients and their families enough time to ask questions before you volunteer provisional feedback regarding your initial findings, and before you outline the likely course of further action.

11. Gather all the information together and write down a short case formulation that includes a provisional diagnostic formulation and a likely early treatment plan.

12. Write, or dictate, your report back to the referring party as soon as possible – the longer the delay, the more laborious this task will become due largely to your memory fading – which will necessitate continual checking of the information in the patient's file. The expression 'fresh in the head, clear on the tape' says it all.

Below follows a more detailed overview of some key aspects of the clinical assessment.

History-taking in clinical neuropsychology

Taking a patient's history is crucial to the practice of neuropsychology – this applies to most, if not all, clinical disciplines. The history provides the context for the patient's actual clinical presentation. If it is not possible to obtain a history directly from the patient, then interview relatives. Where possible, involving family members in the assessment process is doubly important given that they frequently have very different views of patients compared to how patients see themselves; and they are around the patient far more than the clinician is!

Patients' clinical symptoms, especially memory impairment, poor self-awareness and lack of insight, can seriously affect the history and mislead clinicians. For example, important events may be forgotten, such as a much more severe traumatic brain injury pre-dating the current brain injury, or having had *meningitis* as a child.

Such episodes are of course all potentially highly relevant when evaluating the significance of the pathology that leads to the referral. With this in mind, it is worth remembering that family members are usually the only people who have known the patient before the onset of the current clinical picture and, most importantly, they have also usually known the patient well enough to reliably confirm the presence or absence of any suspected changes in character or personality – as well as any 'hidden' aspects of the patient's more remote history.

Let us now return to the areas that ought to be covered during history-taking. Strub and Black (2000) identify four, including both the pre-injury/pre-pathology history, and the history as it specifically relates to the patient's presentation. These areas are: *behaviour changes, functional psychiatric disorders, premorbid functioning* and the patient's *general medical status*. Below follows an overview of the history-taking process, combining the model described by Strub and Black (2000) with the one generally used by the authors of this book in clinical practice.

Always review all information contained in referral letters and medical notes. If your team includes a physician, make sure that you attend his/her review of patients' brain scans. Collate all data and then arrange to see the patient. Once with the patient, invest as much time as possible in obtaining a detailed first-person report (narrative) of his/her current presentation. Ask as many *open-ended questions* as possible, before focusing on the onset and course of the current difficulties that s/he is experiencing – done using more specific questions. If the patient is able to provide reliable information (for example, if s/he did not suffer *amnesia* for the event/s), s/he may be asked how an injury was sustained or what the symptoms were during the acute onset of an illness. Alternatively, the patient may describe a more insidious onset of symptoms.

Where applicable, try to determine the severity of a brain insult by enquiring about the period of *loss of consciousness* (LOC), including its duration. Also ask about possible *post-traumatic amnesia* (PTA) and its duration, as this is a key prognostic indicator in such cases. Ask what the consequences, if any, of the injury or illness have been. Always specifically enquire about: (1) the date of onset; (2) all the symptoms experienced; and (3) any changes in behaviour and/or personality since the onset. Also record your initial observations: for example, if there is any impaired self-awareness, if memory problems are present, if the patient is impulsive or is displaying over-familiarity, or if any other behavioural manifestations are present.

Unfortunately, in an increasing number of clinical settings around the world, multicultural/multilingual patient populations mean that interviews and assessments have to be conducted either in the patient's and/or practitioner's second or even third language, or through interpreters. These scenarios pose many difficulties for the validity of both the information gained and patients' performances. The use of an interpreter also affects what is supposed to be an intimate and private relationship between clinician and patient.

After having evaluated the patient's clinical presentation and having judged its severity, it may be useful to indicate to the patient that you will now proceed to find out a bit more about his/her history. However, point out that if anything has been missed, you can of course return to exploring any other aspects again towards the end of the consultation. Generally speaking, it is often more productive to work through the history before proceeding to the mental status examination. This allows patients time to warm to what is going to be a potentially anxiety-provoking situation. Performing the mental status examination too early can sometimes result in underperformance on the bedside cognitive assessment due to factors such as anxiety. It would probably be fair to say that most people find it less anxiety provoking to talk about 'who they are', rather than being formally assessed or tested.

Start off the history-taking by obtaining a *developmental, educational* and *employment history*. Where possible, the following areas should be explored: *where the patient was born*; the *type of birth*; the *mother's health during pregnancy*; *achievement of developmental milestones*; *academic and social functioning at school* (and college/university if applicable); *qualifications obtained*; *employment history*; and *significant social relationships*. Listen carefully for clues – sometimes something as mundane as having worked in a certain type of job may provide clues to exposure to toxins, for example. The patient's socio-economic status can often provide important pointers towards relevant information that needs to be further explored. Review the patient's *family history*, searching for any *neurological or psychiatric illness, any major surgery*, and evidence of *any early cognitive decline* or *premature death*. Bear in mind that many patients who have been educationally deprived may struggle with detailed questioning; as practitioners we may have to greatly simplify our questions (this, of course, applies anyway when dealing with patients with severe neurocognitive impairments).

History-taking is typically concluded with the in-depth exploration of the patient's past medical history: for example, any head injuries that resulted in loss of consciousness or hospitalisation; any neurological illness; any investigations for unexplained symptoms; any psychiatric illness; any use of substances (both prescription medicines and illicit drugs); any major surgery; and any medical problems that may have had a bearing on the current clinical presentation. This may appear to be an over-inclusive approach to history-taking. Is it not in most cases quite obvious what the neurological diagnosis is? We should always remember that many patients that we are asked to assess have unexplained symptoms, or symptoms that are supposedly incompatible with the assumed underlying neurological illness, injury or progressive genetic condition. Additionally, in many situations, a neurological factor has not yet been identified or confirmed: for example, in patients referred via a mental-health service where they have been treated for psychiatric problems considered unrelated to neurological injury or illness.

It is important to bear in mind that often the way patients (and their relatives/carers) describe symptoms may actually mean something quite different when viewed in clinical terms – for example, patients with *anomia* (difficulty naming) often refer to this particular impairment as a 'memory problem', because to them it seems as if they cannot *remember* the word, when in actual fact in clinical terms it is a *language* problem. Culture and language also influence how symptoms are described. Clinically speaking, things are frequently never as straightforward or simple as one may first think, or as outlined in a short referral letter. Finally, having one neurological diagnosis (for

example, stroke) offers no protection against other events or illnesses (such as traumatic brain injury). Moreover, the clinical presentation of any brain injury or illness
should, ideally, always be considered within the context of the patient's unique biological, psychological and social history. The clinical assessment in neuropsychology
is covered in greater depth in the following section.

The clinical assessment in neuropsychology

When working in busy hospital/clinic environments, what practical information do
we need regarding patients' cognitive functions? Conversely, what functions are
required to be intact for patients to effectively think through and perform the multitude of everyday activities? Perhaps the following is somewhat of an oversimplifica-
tion, but the basic starting point of most bedside neuropsychological clinical
examinations is possibly provided by answering the following questions: *can this patient
attend for long enough for my examination to take place, can s/he comprehend the instructions
and then remember these instructions for long enough to weigh up the different factors, and/or
implement the steps required, before communicating his/her response?* It is interesting to note
the similarity between the 'steps' embedded in this question and the test of the capacity of a person to make decisions for him/herself contained in the United Kingdom's
Mental Capacity Act (2007). Indeed, in many other countries, very similar mechanisms or laws exist to help assess and protect, where necessary, vulnerable individuals
who are less able to make decisions and/or fend for themselves. For example, in
South Africa, the Mental Health Care Act (No. 17 of 2002) sets out guidelines, procedures and requirements for working with and assisting vulnerable patients (Section
26 refers to patients who are unable to make their own decisions).

The *mental status examination* is broadly divided into three areas: (1) objective behavioural observations made by clinicians; (2) assessment of emotional functions through
questioning in order to elicit subjective patient reports and make objective observations from which conclusions about certain levels of functioning are drawn; and (3)
assessment of cognitive functioning by performing brief tests. To help make these
areas clearer, the following examples are provided. Objective behavioural observations include, but are not limited to, the patient's handedness, level of arousal, motor
functioning that influences gait and speech, level of self-care, willingness to cooper-
ate, distractibility, eye contact, spontaneity, expression of affect, and volition.

With regard to emotional functioning, the patient may be asked to describe how
s/he has generally been feeling over the past week or month. Observations are
made about this narrative, including the patient's expression of affect, any possible
suicidal ideation, his/her future plans, and so forth, in order to make an objective
(relatively speaking) judgement about his/her inner emotional experience that
mirrors his/her mood. Likewise, one may ask about anxiety and listen for evidence
or descriptions of symptoms compatible with *panic attacks* or *phobias*. However,
emotion is not the only area that is considered; other areas are too, including: the
patient's thought processes (including *paranoia* or circumstantial ways of communicating) and his/her perceptual functions, such as *visual* or *auditory hallucinations*.

Somatic functions are also covered, such as sleep patterns, appetite and any weight changes. The mental status examination is key to practical risk assessment, and in particular to making informed clinical decisions about patients' potential to self-harm, their potential for violence and their vulnerability to exploitation, among other considerations.

With regard to the *bedside cognitive assessment*, a clear strategy can help to avoid many common pitfalls associated with the eventual interpretation of findings. One of the major strengths of Strub and Black's (2000) model relates to the hierarchical manner in which they recommend that it be performed – there is a bottom-up influence to consider when assessing cognitive functions. Clinicians should commence by covering the most fundamental/basic cognitive functions before proceeding to more complex functions. This is essential, as these more complex cognitive functions, such as executive function, rely heavily on the more fundamental functions, such as attention. An impairment of a basic cognitive function will almost inevitably have a direct bearing on the patient's performance on higher-level functions.

Never be tempted to 'neurologise': do not assume that a specific pattern of cognitive impairment will be present just because the aetiology is known (for example, thinking that all left hemisphere strokes will always involve language impairment). There are other potentially hidden, practical obstacles to assessment that one needs to be aware of. We should always be alert to the possible presence of impairment of the even more basic sensory and motor functions, such as hearing loss, loss of or changes in motor function (such as a *hemiplegia*), and visual problems (such as *hemianopia* or *blind spots*). Such impairments can profoundly influence assessment results.

There are two other important factors to be aware of concerning *attention*. First, attention tends to fluctuate significantly. This is especially true of patients with *delirium*, of those in pain and of older adults. One can start testing attention simply by asking patients to spell a word backwards. One can use cancellation tasks, with either visual or auditory input, and either motor or speech output. For example, give the instruction to the patient to tap a finger every time s/he hears the letter 'o' being said. Second, attention is notoriously influenced by anxiety and depression. For example, patients who have recently suffered strokes may actually have depressed mood, declaring itself as slowness of information processing or poor attention, whereas in reality this may be much more a function of poor drive, fatigue and loss of interest in activities. Hence, problems of attention and processing speed may also relate to other, perhaps less obvious or 'hidden' symptoms.

Before proceeding to assess language and other higher-level cognitive functions, be aware of the patient's level of attention (while considering any fluctuations in attention). It is also important to establish the patient's handedness. It is key to establish the patient's highest level of formal education, even though this can sometimes be a touchy subject to approach. And, many people, especially those from disadvantaged areas, may have little, if any, formal education and may therefore not be test-wise when it comes to completing psychological tests.

Establish the patient's first/home language. This is especially important in multicultural, multilingual societies. It may be necessary to use an interpreter for the assessment. This can be a very difficult and problematic exercise, as there are many pitfalls to being reliant on an interpreter. Interpreters may condense or summarise what has been said into what they thought was meant, thereby failing to accurately reflect the clinician's or patient's actual outputs. Interpreters might leave out important information during the assessment, or they may add in additional information, resulting in an invalidation of the outcome of tests being administered (Nell, 2000; Swartz, 1998). Interpreters might also make errors of substitution, replacing what was actually said with something that was not mentioned at all. Using an interpreter also breaks what is supposed to be an intimate, confidential and private relationship between clinician and patient.

When assessing *language*, generally speaking *comprehension*, *production*, *naming*, *reading*, *writing* and *repetition* are all covered. Listen closely to the patient's *spontaneous speech*, including *volume* and *speed*. First decide whether the speech is *fluent* or *non-fluent*, and then whether any *paraphasias* are present. Assess the patient's ability to comprehend in increasing complexity, up to three-step commands. Ask the patient to name objects, or parts of objects, as almost all aphasics have difficulty naming (*anomia*). To assess repetition, ask the patient to repeat after you various sentences of increasing length. Let the patient read a passage in order to assess reading (and make sure that s/he has comprehended what was read). Ask him/her to write his/her name, then a sentence to dictation, and a sentence/paragraph of his/her choice to assess writing ability.

Language assessment is extremely important, as impairments can have profoundly negative effects on everyday functioning. Aphasics will, for example, generally find it very difficult to perform tasks such as phoning for information or asking for items while shopping. Patients with comprehension problems may find it very difficult to deal with formal or official written or spoken communications to which they have to respond (from welfare or social services departments, for example). Unfortunately, society demands a high level of language communication skill, and if impaired, the resulting disability can be very severe, with a great dependency on others. Language impairment also invariably affects the assessment of other domains of function, given that most neurocognitive tests require intact language ability in order to comprehend their instructions and to respond to/complete their tasks.

Learning to be able to get around such obstacles when assessing language is an important clinical skill to acquire – rather than simply giving up and saying that the patient cannot be assessed. A practical approach is to consider adapting some bedside tests by altering the input (clinician) or output (patient response) requirements in attempting to overcome language difficulties to allow for a basic assessment of other cognitive functions. An example would be to consider using visual and motor functions, rather than speech, to enable a patient who cannot speak following a stroke to 'communicate' (assuming that s/he can comprehend instructions), instead of assuming s/he did not understand the question.

After language, *memory* (delayed recall) should be examined, including the assessment of short-term (immediate) memory (note: working memory is an executive function). A comprehensive (within the natural limits of the bedside examination)

examination should always be conducted wherever possible. Be mindful of the potentially significant effect that anxiety can have on memory performance. Many patients suspect that they have trouble remembering things and therefore find testing an anxiety-provoking experience.

It is important to test both immediate and delayed recall for both visually and verbally presented material. For assessing short-term/immediate memory, give patients increasing series of random digits to recall. For verbal (auditory) delayed recall, use a story, such as the Babcock Story, and ask patients to recall it over three trials (immediate recall, a second recall and a delayed recall). For immediate visual recall, use a culturally appropriate drawing and ask patients to copy it. Next, ask the patient to redraw it immediately from memory (incidental learning). The patient is not told initially (at the copy trial) that this is a memory test, so for the delayed trial, ask the patient to redraw the picture from his/her memory about 30 minutes after s/he did the copy.

If the above-mentioned memory tests prove too complex, simpler alternatives are available. For example, ask the patient to name four disparate objects, then hide the objects behind your back and ask him/her to recall what they were. Next, distract the patient with a question and repeat the task. Assuming that the patient could recall all four objects, hide the objects in various parts of the room and then, after a few minutes, ask what the objects were and where they were hidden. Another test is to give four words or names (of cities, for example) that the patient must then try to recall after a three-minute delay. It is useful to test autobiographical events, as well as recall of other more ecologically valid everyday events, such as asking patients what they had for lunch or about what they read in the newspaper.

Testing of *executive function* concludes the cognitive part of the mental status examination. When testing executive functions – and in fact during all of the examination – one needs to be alert to qualitative observations regarding, for example, *impulsivity, rule-breaking behaviour, poor error detection* and *impaired self-monitoring*. Executive functioning can be examined by assessing the *copying of motor programmes by hand, design fluency, copying designs* that may elicit *perseveration*, and tasks requiring *set shifting*, such as listing different types of fruit, alternating this with listing different animals. Assess *planning* and *problem-solving* ability by, for example, giving patients a complex design to copy and a multi-step mathematical problem to solve.

Always assess executive functioning thoroughly, as problems can have wide-ranging effects on cognitive, behavioural and emotional presentations. Executive impairment can be one of the biggest obstacles to community reintegration, including returning to work. Moreover, some neurological illnesses, such as *Huntington's chorea* and *Pick's disease*, can present initially with executive dysfunction. In traumatic brain injury, executive dysfunction is typically the telltale feature of the neurocognitive presentation. An important concluding remark about executive function is that it can, and of course does, influence other lower-order cognitive functions (a top-down influence). In summary, Table 8.1 provides the main cognitive domains assessed and their associated everyday manifestations.

The use of structured bedside cognitive screening is an area that sits between formal neuropsychological testing and clinical assessment (see Chapter 9 for a

TABLE 8.1 Bedside cognitive assessment, neuropsychological functions and associated manifestations

Cognitive function	Bedside assessment	Examples of everyday manifestations
Orientation	To time, place, situation/person	Confusion; missing appointments
Attention	Cancellation tasks; reverse spelling; digit span	Memory lapses when multi-tasking; irritability; unable to cope with busy environments; easily distracted; difficulty completing tasks
Language	Read a paragraph; write a sentence; verbal fluency tasks, such as describing a visual scene in story form; naming objects; comprehension of commands; sentence repetition	Problems communicating with others; difficulty completing forms; may be seen by others as a 'second language' speaker; stopping reading
Memory	Recall an address; recall four words or objects after distraction, and after 5 minutes	Missing appointments; misplacing items; forgetting to do tasks; forgetting people's names
Spatial cognition	Copy a complex figure; construct a square or pentagon using matches or paperclips; draw a given time on a clock; calculations involving spatial-loading	Struggling to assemble basic objects; cannot read maps; getting lost; cannot read or write properly
Mathematical ability	Basic calculations (addition and subtraction)	Inability to calculate the amount of money to pay, or the correct change when shopping
Executive functions	Alternate between naming foods and animals, or producing as many unique designs as possible using four lines; hand-sequencing tasks; squeezing and releasing the examiner's hand corresponding to the words 'red' and 'green', before switching the task; memory tasks that include multiple-choice options; digit span (backwards); problem-solving tasks	Impulsive behaviour; poor planning; difficulty with abstract thought; personality change; difficulty solving problems; loss of drive and motivation; cannot multi-task; inappropriate behaviour; memory problems

breakdown of the different approaches to assessment). For example, one of the most widely used (and abused and misunderstood) cognitive screening tools is the Mini Mental State Examination developed in 1975 by Folstein, Folstein and McHugh. This tool is popular among many clinicians and has application in clinical practice, provided clinicians understand how to interpret the results beyond the total score and within the individual patient's context. However, it should never be used in isolation, but rather as the starting point for an assessment (for initial tentative *screening* for cognitive deficits).

In 2009, Brown, Pengas, Dawson, Brown and Clatworthy reported the development of a self-administered, paper-and-pencil cognitive screening test – the Test Your Memory (TYM) for the detection of *Alzheimer's disease*. The TYM may significantly increase the number of individuals who are screened for cognitive impairment, especially where resources are limited. However, there are some limitations to this tool. Its administration still requires some supervision, albeit minimal, and there is the problem of language barriers – whereas the Montreal Cognitive Assessment (MoCA), for example, is available in many languages. The TYM is also potentially culturally biased, as it is somewhat Eurocentric (for example, one of its items asks who the prime minister is). It may also be misinterpreted, if used in isolation, potentially resulting in unnecessary anxiety and/or further (expensive and unnecessary) medical investigations. Finally, as a general point, clinicians must pay careful attention to which norms (and cut-off scores) are used when scoring such instruments, as patients' performances are likely to vary around the world depending on factors such as language, culture, differing levels and quality of education and variations in socio-economic status.

Conclusion

The clinical assessment in neuropsychology, including the mental status examination and bedside cognitive assessment, represents one of three major pillars of assessment. 'Bedside' is, of course, a bit of a misnomer in many contexts. In many situations, the assessment is performed in an office (far from a bed!), while at other times, especially in the developing world where resources are scare, it *will* have to take place at the bedside, or even in a remote clinic or township. Nevertheless, it is a practical and useful clinical investigation, especially in under-resourced systems where there is little or no access to formal neuropsychological testing or where no neuropsychologists are employed. Cultural background, language and education levels of patients are key factors that can all have a great bearing on the assessment process and its outcomes, and these factors should always be kept in mind.

Cognitive functions are organised in a hierarchical fashion, where basic functions, such as attention, form the foundation upon which higher-order functions depend. Together with the patient's history and presenting complaints, this information is used to inform the clinician's initial case formulation, including his/her differential diagnoses. There are limitations to the bedside cognitive assessment. In many situations, it reveals either nothing or very little of note. For example, patients with superior general intellectual ability may have enough cognitive reserve to 'mask' (compensate for) subtle difficulties. A bedside assessment may not be that useful where a baseline performance needs to be obtained for comparison purposes. This may be required in order to compare possible future decline against it – as may be necessary in patients suspected of presenting with early dementia, for example. Under these and other conditions, standardised, comprehensive neuropsychological testing is sometimes more useful (see Chapter 9).

Practical tips

1. Never rely exclusively on questionnaires in order to make a diagnosis.
2. Have a template for making notes that can be used to document the clinical examination.
3. Print and laminate a pyramid shape with the hierarchical organisation of cognitive functions displayed on it, which can then be used as a memory aid.
4. Always spend a bit more time exploring and probing the difficulties that patients report during the assessment – this strategy will pay off later.

Points for reflective practice

1. Discuss the pros and cons of using self-administered tests, such as the Test Your Memory, for identifying cognitive impairment in under-resourced health systems.
2. It can be said that the bedside assessment of cognitive functions serves no purpose because it is not norm-based. Think about the main arguments for and against this assertion.

Selected further reading

Nell, V. (2000). *Cross-cultural neuropsychological assessment: Theory and practice.* Mahwah, NJ: Lawrence Erlbaum Associates.

Strub, R. L., & Black, F. W. (2000). *The mental status examination in neurology* (4th ed.). Philadelphia: F. A. Davis Company.

Walsh, K. (1992). Some gnomes worth knowing. *The Clinical Neuropsychologist, 6,* 119–133.

9

NEUROPSYCHOLOGICAL TESTING

Introduction

Testing neurocognitive functions is one of the unique skills that psychologists possess, and one that clearly differentiates psychologists from other clinical professionals. Topics covered here, as they specifically relate to clinical neuropsychology, include: the different approaches to clinical assessment; test selection; test administration strategies; and the interpretation of test results. This book does not intend to provide any in-depth discussion of individual neuropsychological tests. All psychologists administer and interpret some of the core tests that are widely used in neuropsychology, such as scales of general intellectual ability and memory. Accordingly, the emphasis is instead on the application (and sometimes modification) of these heuristic test administration and interpretation skills, for use in populations with neurocognitive impairment. Particular emphasis is placed on making *qualitative observations* during testing, and on the importance of bearing in mind the effects of education, culture and language on test performance and clinical interpretation.

Learning to administer and interpret specific tests is better achieved through: (1) supervision and coaching in practice; (2) consulting the relevant test manuals; and (3) familiarising oneself with research findings by using textbooks on neuropsychological testing, such as Lezak, Howieson, Bigler and Tranel (2012). When it comes to neuropsychological tests, Muriel Lezak's texts on neuropsychological tests have long represented the 'gold standard' in the field. Furthermore, our book is about practical skills in clinical neuropsychology – the focus is on practice-related issues, rather than on being a resource for individual test characteristics and administration procedures (this information can be obtained in the specific tests' manuals). While tests become dated, the practical skills required remain largely unchanged.

Different approaches to clinical assessment

Before proceeding with some of the rudiments of assessment, it is important to be aware of the different clinical approaches to neuropsychological assessment that govern the way neuropsychological testing is practised around the world. Broadly speaking, there are two distinct paradigms that influence how assessments are conducted, along with combinations of these approaches (to varying degrees). These approaches are the *psychometric approach* and the *hypothetico-deductive approach.*

The psychometric (or normative) approach primarily revolves around the measuring of cognitive deficits (quantifying degrees of deviation from normative values). This approach, which is the prevailing clinical method in many parts of the world (including the United States and many countries across Europe), utilises standardised test scores that have been derived from normally distributed populations. The central aim of psychometric testing is to demonstrate statistically how a patient's test performance compares to that of a standardised population – individuals tested in order to gather normative data (Lezak et al., 2012). Numerical data are used to identify *if* deficits in cognitive function are present, and to what quantifiable degree.

With psychometrics, '[p]redictions about the site of the lesion and its nature (diffuse or focal, static or changing) are based on statistically identified relationships between test scores' (Luria & Majovski, 1977, p. 961). One reason why psychometric testing has widespread popularity is that it allows for a patient's individual test performances to be compared directly and precisely to other performances achieved by that particular patient, as well as to the performances of other patients (Lezak et al., 2012). Some of the key aspects of this approach are described below. The central approach outlined in this chapter (and the previous chapter) is to some extent a hybrid of the psychometric and hypothetico-deductive approaches, and is now being increasingly used in certain settings.

The second paradigm practitioners need to be aware of is the hypothetico-deductive approach, which rests largely on Luria's theory of brain functioning (see Chapter 6). An understanding of the neuroanatomical correlates of normal mental functions, and how these relate to the specific deficits observed in the patient, is key to this approach. *Qualitative observation* and the need to *generate hypotheses* in order to test neurocognitive functions are of fundamental importance. This approach essentially involves investigating *multiple possible determinants of failure* with respect to the patient's neurocognitive performance, and then eliminating as many explanations for the observed deficits as possible (Walsh & Darby, 1999). This principle of *multiple determination* is central. Here, '[b]ehavioural deficits are defined in terms of impaired test performance. But impaired test performance may be a final common pathway for expression of quite diverse types of impairment' (Walsh & Darby, 1999, p. 388).

The hypothetico-deductive approach dictates that the key role of psychologists is to 'qualify the symptom' through the generation and testing of hypotheses about the complex underlying functional nature of patients' deficits (Luria, 1973). 'Qualifying the symptom' refers to focusing on *how* the patient failed on a particular test, rather than merely on *whether* s/he was able to pass (Luria & Majovski, 1977). Psychologists therefore require good theoretical knowledge of the brain's functional organisation (and of various aspects of other medical disciplines, for example, neurology) in order to generate appropriate hypotheses. The testing of these hypotheses through the history-taking process and neuropsychological testing then leads to the identification of a collectively meaningful group of symptoms that point to a hypothesised underlying lesion-site (Luria & Majovski, 1977). The hypothetico-deductive paradigm of dynamic neuropsychology provides an efficient and cost-effective clinical tool through which a comprehensive neurocognitive assessment can be performed. This approach is important for developing countries, where resources (and infrastructure) are often scarce. It also lends itself well to the conducting of assessments at the bedside, which is sometimes the only option in acute-care settings. Such assessments are therefore often somewhat similar to the bedside clinical assessment outlined in the previous chapter.

The psychometric approach remains dominant in many parts of the world. One reason for this is that the psychometric tradition has been the cornerstone of clinical practice and teaching, especially in clinical psychology, for many decades. This should come as no surprise given that neuropsychology is taught and practised secondary to clinical psychology in many countries. It is also an approach that lends itself to the application of technology, such as computer-based assessment, although the associated costs can be prohibitive in underfunded settings. Nevertheless, opportunities are now becoming available for the hypothetico-deductive approach to become much more widely used, especially in developing countries where the practice-framework of psychology is typically less established and therefore represents something of a blank slate.

Another reason why the hypothetico-deductive approach in its true sense is not always practised is the amount of medical knowledge from disciplines such as neurology and radiology that is required in order to practise competently. For many, it is simply easier to stick to the pure quantitative psychology associated with the psychometric tradition – although, with the advancements in the neurosciences, this is becoming increasingly difficult to do in view of the increasing integration and collaboration of various neuroscientific disciplines. In many of these disciplines a foundation level of knowledge in neuropsychology is required. Unsurprisingly, in the practice of neuropsychology in South Africa, for example, the hypothetico-deductive approach is becoming increasingly popular.

The hypothetico-deductive approach in practice

In the hypothetico-deductive assessment, history-taking plays the fundamental role, taking up perhaps two-thirds of the assessment time. During history-taking, and also beforehand, when neuropsychological testing is being planned, the key is to generate *hypotheses* regarding the patient. These hypotheses are based on linking knowledge of the underlying pathology with knowledge of the clinical symptoms and signs observed in the patient. The assessment itself then provides the structure within which to test these hypotheses by gaining information from the patient. Tests merely serve to confirm or reject the hypotheses (you are the master of the tests, not the other way around). The process followed is akin to detective work, and is consistent with how clinical diagnoses are made by medical practitioners.

In contrast to the psychometric approach, a flexible range of individual tests is used to assess specific neurocognitive domains of function, which are then linked to neuroanatomical correlates within the brain. This is similar to bedside cognitive assessment referred to in Chapter 8, although more thorough and flexible. The tests are not always scored in full, using their official scoring procedures; patients' test performances can be judged qualitatively in order to confirm or reject a hypothesis. This is not a static process; as hypotheses are rejected or accepted, they are updated, or new ones may emerge, which are then tested accordingly. These new or modified hypotheses are continually considered within the context of the known history and other clinical data. For example, when using the Rey Complex Figure Test (Rey-Osterrieth Complex Figure), the clinician, rather than simply scoring the Figure out of 36, will instead closely observed the patient completing the task and qualitatively inspect the copy for signs of *neglect*, of *constructional apraxia*, of a disorganised planning strategy or for signs of simplification (the latter two both being signs of executive impairment).

Similarly, given that qualitative observations are key, when using tests such as the Fist/Side/Palm test, the clinician will focus on continuing the task until s/he is convinced that the patient can do it. If the patient is unable to complete the task successfully, the clinician will then explore *why* this is the case. Here, either a possible dorsolateral pre-motor deficit may be to blame, or another confounding factor, such as inattention, where the patient was not paying attention to the instructions. It is through the generation of hypotheses regarding the origin of such test performances that the clinical picture is revealed. For a final example, when using the Red/Green Test of inhibition, the test would be used to confirm a hypothesis that the clinician already had: from my observations and my history-taking, this patient appears disinhibited – let me just confirm this with a quick test. In other words, patients' performances on all tests should always be considered for consistency with other aspects of their presentation.

Practical statistics

How does one decide if test results are within the normal, expected range for an individual patient? Many factors are usually considered, including qualitative observations, the patient's level of cooperation and his/her clinical history, to list but a few. Psychologists ultimately use test *norms* to make informed, statistically based decisions about patients' performances on different tests. There are several very good textbooks specifically devoted to neuropsychological tests and their norms. Wherever possible, such books should always be consulted when interpreting patients' test results. Unfortunately, however, the quality and availability of norms varies substantially across the world.

Most tests and test batteries currently in use originate in Europe or the United States. Before using a particular set of norms, it is important to ascertain the quality of the normative data and whether the norms are applicable to the patient population at hand. This includes the average level (and quality) of education, age range, sample size and the type of population, such as normal controls or patients with a specific brain pathology. Rather unsurprisingly, using different sets of norms can substantially alter the standardised scores obtained, along with their interpretation. The use of inappropriate norms can render psychometric data obsolete.

The problems associated with using (and/or trying to establish) norms are especially pertinent in developing world and cross-cultural settings, where, when used, most tests and psychometric batteries frequently prove to be culturally biased – such settings usually have populations that are far from homogeneous. It must also be remembered that the Western world is fast becoming increasingly multicultural. There are a number of different factors to consider here, including: different cultural understandings, such as lack of exposure to Western conceptual ideas; socio-cultural influences; wide variation in the level and quality of education; varying socio-economic status; and the prevalence of many different languages spoken around the world. All these factors contribute towards the errors that occur when using inappropriate norms.

Cultural, socio-economic and linguistic factors can make it very difficult, if not impossible in some instances, to be able to establish reliable and accurate norms in developing world settings, especially when US- and European-based tests/batteries are used. In fact, there are many parts of the world where norms for certain tests (and/or for lower educational levels) simply do not exist. In many parts of the world, the psychometric approach is not feasible. In such settings, the hypothetico-deductive approach will likely prove a more viable one for assessing and making important decisions about patients. Clinicians working in these contexts (especially in the developing world) should be open to the possibility of adopting alternative approaches and developing culture fair tests and test batteries. For an example of the adaptation of neurocognitive tests for cultural fairness, see the Mosdell, Balchin and Ameen (2010) reference in the 'Selected further reading' at the end of this chapter.

Another crucial factor to consider when interpreting test results is the patient's premorbid general intellectual function. Neuropsychological test performance is always interpreted against the background of an individual's own abilities, and specifically his/her likely premorbid intellectual level of functioning. There are specific neuropsychological tests designed to provide an indication of premorbid ability. However, such tests can be problematic: for example, most are language-based, working from the assumption that language correlates with general intellectual abilities. Under certain conditions, significant difficulties can arise when using the language-based model to retro-predict patients' general intellectual ability. In patients whose neurological conditions involve the language areas of the brain, results on these tests may underestimate their premorbid levels of functioning. As a knock-on effect, this will almost certainly contaminate the statistical interpretation of results from other areas of the neuropsychological assessment, as the generic comparison norm used to compare their performance against is incorrect. And again, with reference to cross-cultural factors, many patients from poorer backgrounds, who have been educationally deprived, will most likely struggle with this approach to testing.

Neuropsychology uses relatively simple *statistical* methods to consider individual patients' performance against normative data. The *normal distribution curve* is the comparison benchmark; a test performance is considered to be in the 'impaired' range when it is *two standard score deviations* below the average of normative data and the patient's 'own' normative performance with regard to his/her general intellectual ability. One standard deviation below the expected score will still be within the normal range, but below the expected performance for the particular individual. How do we communicate impaired test performance? Generally speaking, *z-scores* or percentiles are used. A z-score is obtained by subtracting the average score (from the test's norms) from the score the patient obtains, and then dividing the difference by the standard deviation (again obtained from the norms). Almost all other standard scores (scores based on a standard deviation) can be calculated from z-scores. *Non-standard scores* include *percentiles* and *IQ equivalent scores*. These can be estimated from z-scores, provided that the norms used have been derived from a normally distributed population. There are, however, other non-statistical principles (outlined below) that are also fundamental to test administration and interpretation.

Clinical strategies

In addition to statistical methods, certain clinical principles are also fundamental to test administration and interpretation: for example, *ethics*, and the *pragmatics* of the situation. With regard to pragmatics, in a system where a constant patient throughput is required, clinicians simply cannot have the luxury of routinely administering very lengthy neuropsychological testing sessions. However, this has to be balanced with the ethics of clinical practice. Testing that contributes nothing is unethical. But this cuts both ways. It is not good practice to prematurely abandon testing due to time or cost pressures. And, one should not test patients unnecessarily: for example, where it is absolutely clear from the bedside examination that there is obvious and significant cognitive impairment. In a way, it is unethical to put patients through testing that is most likely to negatively influence their mood if you already know the answer to the referral question.

Another area requiring careful judgement is patient fatigue. Psychologists should give patients regular breaks during testing; failing to do so can artificially decrease scores and provide a false picture of patients' cognitive strengths and limitations. This may in turn result in failures during the diagnosis, formulation and rehabilitation phases of patients' care.

It is important to fully engage patients during neuropsychological testing. For the most part it would be a false economy to test during the first consultation (assuming that there is time for this once the initial clinical assessment has been completed!). A more productive strategy is to allow enough time for patients to 'warm' to the situation of seeing a psychologist. Anxiety can be a real problem during testing and may badly distort results. Psychologists need to constantly remind themselves that they are intending to test cognition and not emotion. Anybody can be tested in such a way that they underperform, most notably because of being made to feel anxious.

There are things that can be done to limit (but probably not completely exclude) the effects of anxiety during neuropsychological testing. First, always reassure patients. Engage them in the process of testing by packing away test equipment as you move to the next sub-test. Lay out test materials in an uncluttered way so that there is enough space for you to work and for patients to take part in the procedure. Position yourself so that it is easy to handle test materials while also having to make notes. Always clearly explain what you are doing, inviting questions if the patient is puzzled or curious. Reassure patients that they can only do their best and that nothing else is expected of them. Wherever possible, prebook a quiet and distraction-free environment for assessments. Always remember to switch off mobile phones.

The following are some other, more technical considerations that relate to test administration. First, consider patients' *inputs* (via vision or hearing, for example) and their *outputs* (through speech or arm movement, for example) in relation to cognitive function, and then adjust test administration accordingly. This is particularly relevant for patients with perceptual or motor impairments. For example, if patients cannot hear, use visual input as an alternative, or if they have motor impairment of the dominant hand, then use outputs that do not require handwriting or drawing in order to elicit a reliable response. Always test and probe the limits of patients' performances. This means that psychologists should sometimes persevere beyond the termination rules of tests, especially when, despite a succession of failures, there is still a sense that the patient is probably capable of completing some of the more difficult items/trials. This is important, as information about premorbid ability, for example, may be revealed this way. Being able to do a task, but requiring more time, has a completely different meaning from not being able to perform a task at all. This distinction is hidden by an 'impaired' score that was derived due to time limits being strictly adhered to. Psychologists sometimes 'bend' or modify test instructions to obtain richer qualitative information in order to 'illuminate' numerical data.

Under certain circumstances we should also consider using other compensatory strategies to eliminate the influence of specific cognitive deficits that are not the focus of a particular sub-test. For example, providing multiple-choice options where it is suspected that executive dysfunction is the underlying cause of an apparent memory problem.

Interpretation

How are test performances interpreted? This can sometimes be a real minefield of uncertainty, and often a source of worry. First, an important general point: always consider all of the factors that may contribute to poor test performance; that is, not only the possible organic factors, such as acquired brain injury or neurological illness, but also factors such as education level/quality, language and possible cultural biases. Let us now return to the points made about limiting patient anxiety and the provision of a distraction-free environment. Is this not wrong? Should we not test patients under conditions that mirror the 'real world' out there? This is, after all, where they have to live their daily lives. A fundamental issue (and potential source of uncertainty) is whether our interpretation of test performance is not in fact contaminated by test results obtained under more 'ideal' conditions. This is indeed a powerful argument. However, the position advocated in this book is that if one considers the imperfections of norms and statistical methods, and the significant effects of emotion and other factors, then we should also consider strategies that help to ensure optimal test performance. If patients still underperform under these circumstances, we can perhaps then be more confident that we are dealing with true neurocognitive impairment. Additionally, from a humane perspective, given that suffering neuropsychological impairment is a devastating life experience, is it not right to reduce patients' discomfort when they are being subjected to testing that may serve to highlight their impairments?

The final point about the interpretation of test performance is possibly the most important. At its heart it concerns the importance of avoiding 'seduction by numbers'. Numerical values can sometimes make even the most experienced practitioners believe that they have unequivocally identified the 'truth'. This point concerns the question of *how* a patient has failed a particular test, rather than *if* s/he has a test performance that is indicative of cognitive impairment. It is about making *qualitative observations* during testing. Naturally, one has to be very au fait with the testing procedure to be 'free' to observe. Before looking at test scores, try to identify which factor is most relevant to the patient's underperformance. This is the key philosophy behind the hypothetico-deductive approach. The case vignette below illustrates this point.

Abraham, a 60-year-old man from a very disadvantaged background, was referred to neuropsychology for reported cognitive decline following a head injury two years previously. His daughter accompanied him to his appointment. He appeared confused and distractible for much of his assessment, and upon testing, performed poorly on a range of tests administered to him, particularly on more complex tasks and when executive functions were tested. Given Abraham's poor performance on tests of executive functioning and his poor attention, a diagnosis of a severe dysexecutive syndrome might appear the most likely. However, during the consultation, it emerged that Abraham had a long-standing history of alcohol abuse. Importantly, the *qualitative* observations of confusion and distractibility made during his assessment pointed towards an acute confusion state (ACS), possibly due to metabolic deficiency, rather than a dysexecutive picture attributable to a structural lesion. Based on this new information obtained during the assessment, a subsequently metabolic screening was performed, confirming liver dysfunction. The qualitative observations in this case are more compatible with the presentation of an ACS than the numerical results are when viewed in isolation (as these were indicative of executive dysfunction).

This case illustrates two key points. First, that numerical values can sometimes 'seduce' us into thinking that we know something definitive about a patient when in reality we do not. And second, neuropsychologists must always remember to consider that a patient's clinical presentation may be due to a non-localising syndrome and not a structural lesion.

Another issue relates to 'internal norming'. It is a real perennial nettle that tests/ batteries are constantly being updated. New tests are frequently published – often with rather spectacular claims regarding their sensitivity and specificity. Practitioners are regularly faced with the task of getting up to speed with new tests. When learning to administer new tests, first 'test yourself'; practise administering the test until you become less reliant on the test manual – one should be completely au fait with a test/battery before administering it to patients. The next step is crucial: test a 'normal' control, for example, a colleague or student. The key point is that it is very important to *observe a normal performance* on a given test, before trying to interpret the performance of patients with suspected or confirmed brain injury – *abnormality is difficult to detect if one does not know what constitutes normality*. In addition to the use of norms and the calculation of percentiles or z-scores, clinical intuition is developed through repeated observations that are subconsciously compared to one's internal baseline. This skill is difficult to develop without having previously observed what constitutes a 'normal' performance.

Cognitive functions

Many neuropsychologists would probably start, in the majority of cases, with the intention of covering all the main areas of neurocognitive functioning. Inevitably though, as testing progresses, based on the patient's history and so forth, *hypotheses* are formed, tested, updated and then accepted or discarded. What this means is that during assessments, there may be subtle (or more blatant) signs that difficulties exist in a neurocognitive domain other than the one being assessed at the time. No test is 'pure' in the sense that it assesses only one specific cognitive function. Therefore, it is possible to become aware of potential impairments in other domains of function while administering a particular test. As is the case with the bedside assessment, the hierarchical nature of neurocognitive functions needs to be kept in mind when deciding which tests to administer, both before and during the assessment. This is similar metaphorically to having an adaptable recipe for preparing a meal – different quantities of the same group of ingredients might be used to prepare different meals.

Formal testing mirrors the domains covered during bedside testing: *orientation, attention, language, memory, motor functions, praxis, visual perception, spatial cognition* and *executive function*. However, formal testing often includes the assessment of *general intellectual ability*. Table 9.1 summarises the neurocognitive domains tested, along with their associated anatomical regions. While attention is normally the first port

TABLE 9.1 Neurocognitive functions and associated anatomical regions

Neurocognitive function tested	Sub-components constituting neurocognitive function	Likely anatomical regions involved
General intellectual ability	General knowledge; language; mathematical ability; executive function; motor skill; memory, etc.	Distributed; cortical
Information processing	Processing speed; attention; short-term memory; orientation, etc.	Parietal lobes; reticular formation; frontal lobes; frontal connections to basal ganglia
Language	Speech production; comprehension; naming; repetition; reading; writing	Left temporal lobe
Praxis	Ideomotor, ideational, limb kinetic and oral (buccofacial) praxis	Parietal and temporal lobe; occipital-parietal; frontal lobe
Memory	Verbal long-term memory; visual long-term memory	Temporal lobes; hippocampi; limbic system (Papez circuit)
Visuospatial function	Perception; construction; spatial integration, etc.	Parietal lobe; temporal lobe
Motor function and constructional ability	Dexterity; motor speed; constructional ability, etc.	Motor areas of cortex (frontal lobe); cerebellum; parietal lobe
Visual perception	Visual perception; visual recognition (apperception and association)	Occipital lobe; parietal lobe
Mathematical ability	Simple calculation; complex mathematical ability; information processing, etc.	Parietal, temporal and frontal lobes
Executive function	Problem solving; planning; generativity; inhibition; motor fluency; working memory; abstract thought; set-shifting; organisation of memory, etc.	Frontal lobes and frontal-basal connective pathways

of call during the bedside cognitive assessment, in formal neuropsychological testing, psychologists often begin by testing general intellectual ability. This helps to form an impression of general ability, which can be adopted as a standard or 'individual norm' that is then used to compare to the patient's performance in the various neurocognitive domains. In fact, prior to this, many psychologists might administer specific tests designed to gauge premorbid intellectual ability. Realistically, in a busy everyday clinical practice, the 'best performance method', as described by Lezak et al. (2012), is probably the most pragmatic approach to gauging premorbid intellectual ability.

The best performance method assumes that ability in one domain provides evidence of competence in other domains of function; different sources of information are thus drawn upon to form an impression of the patient's likely premorbid ability. Such information includes: selecting the best scores on sub-tests; demographic data, such as level of education; and other samples of achievements that do not lend themselves to scoring. For example, it can be reasonably safely assumed in a person with a doctoral degree and a successful career that significant general underperformance on testing due to severe impairment of information processing does not accurately represent his/her premorbid intellectual ability. A realistic judgement of the patient's premorbid ability provides the essential context for the interpretation of the remainder of the neuropsychological testing, sometimes viewed as the testing 'proper'.

Testing tends to follow the following algorithm (similar to bedside assessment) in order to successively test neurocognitive functioning. Orientation to *person, place* and *time* is always assessed. Next, *attention* should be examined, including *speed of information processing, sustained attention, short-term memory* and *working memory*. Next test *language*, including: comprehension, speech production, repetition, naming ability, writing and reading (including comprehension of what was read). Where available, colleagues from speech and language therapy perform additional comprehensive and useful assessments of this area. Language assessment is sensitive to cultural factors, including the patient's first/home language.

Memory (new learning), or *retention and recall*, should be tested through both the visual and auditory spheres (that is, both the right and left hippocampi assessed independently). Both immediate and delayed recall and recognition after delay require testing. When assessing memory, it is always important to distinguish between an *encoding* and a *retrieval* problem.

Assessment of *spatial cognition* (right hemisphere functions) includes: *constructional praxis, spatial calculations, dressing praxis, perception of two and three-dimensional space, topographical orientation, anosognosia* (and *anosodiaphoria*) and *unilateral spatial neglect*. Where relevant, try to disentangle any motor and visuospatial abnormalities that may be contributing to underperformance.

When assessing *higher visual functioning*, examine visual gnosis in order to look for disorders such as *apperceptive* or *associative visual agnosia*, and *simultanagnosia*. This examination should include: assessing the ability to recognise a complex visual scene; single object recognition; the ability to copy an object; topographical recognition; and face recognition.

A wide range of *executive functions* may require assessment, such as *problem solving, planning, abstract thought, generativity, cognitive estimation, working memory, set shifting, inhibition* and *memory retrieval*. As with all domains of neurocognitive assessment, qualitative observations regarding test performance and the patient's comportment provide key information about insight, disinhibition or apathy, among other functions. Executive functions can be broadly divided into those mediated by the following frontal lobe regions: ventromesial prefrontal cortex (mesial/medial frontal pre-frontal cortex and orbital/basal pre-frontal cortex), dorsolateral pre-frontal cortex (pre-motor and pre-frontal cortex) and deep white matter (subcortical). The mesial cortex is primarily responsible for the selective application of voluntary arousal; damage can produce clouded consciousness, confabulation and ideational perseveration. The orbital/basal cortex is primarily responsible for inhibition and response suppression; damage results in disinhibition, social inappropriateness, distractibility and impulsiveness.

The dorsolateral cortex governs the subordination of goal-directed behaviour to verbally regulated programmes, for motor tasks in the case of the pre-motor cortex, and for abstract thought and problem solving in the case of the pre-frontal cortex. Damage to the dorsolateral convexity can produce concrete thought, loss of problem-solving ability, inability to shift sets, disorganised thought processes and lack of self-critical awareness. The deep white matter is implicated in the governing of spontaneous initiative and curiosity, with damage resulting in adynamia, aspontaneity and impersistence, and akinetic mutism in severe cases. Working memory is also an executive function, and is the ability to hold information in conscious thought while at the same time actively manipulating (working with) the information – as opposed to short-term/immediate memory, which refers to *passively* holding information in conscious thought.

Feedback of results

Neuropsychological testing would have far less utility if the results were not shared with patients. *Feedback* has various functions. Clinically speaking, one of its most important functions is to discuss patients' relative cognitive strengths and weaknesses with a view to informing rehabilitation strategies and setting mutually agreed goals. Some advocate going over the results test-by-test or function-by-function, before allowing time for patients and their relatives (if present) to ask questions and seek clarification. Another approach that can sometimes be very useful in order to engage with patients – and to obtain qualitative data about their awareness of their performances/impairments – is to ask them to reflect on the testing sessions. Subsequently, as a role-reversal exercise, ask patients to try to provide feedback to you regarding their own performances/impairments. In clinical practice, it is interesting to note that, when this strategy is used, patients sometimes give fairly accurate feedback regarding their performance.

Feedback should always be done in a humane, yet truthful manner. It is useful to keep things simple. We need to bear in mind that receiving feedback can be anxiety provoking for many patients. For this and other reasons (such as a patient's limited attention span or poor memory), it is not helpful to bury the basic findings and the meaning and implications of test results under a mountain of irrelevant detail. Overly long or overly detailed explanations can often have very little impact; this can also leave too little time for a two-way discussion regarding the meaning of the results. Finally, it is unhelpful to avoid giving 'bad' news (such as the presence of certain impairments) to patients by, for example, suggesting that more tests be done, or by repeating tests where there is already robust evidence such that it is unlikely that the results will be substantially different.

Tests

The final topic concerning formal neuropsychological testing cannot be avoided and always 'refuses to go away'. An obvious question in any lecture, paper or chapter on neuropsychological testing is: 'What is your preferred test battery or combination of tests?' Alternatively, if you were forced to choose only three neuropsychological tests to take with you to a remote rural hospital, which would they be? The answer of course depends on many factors, including the availability of appropriate norms and translations; how widely the tests are used; which theoretical approach (psychometric or hypothetico-deductive) is being adopted, and so forth. In under-resourced settings, other factors are also important to consider: for example, the cost and availability of tests/test batteries.

There are a number of options when it comes to test batteries, including the Wechsler Adult Intelligence Scale (Wechsler, 1997a), the Wechsler Memory Scale (Wechsler, 1997b) and the Delis–Kaplan Executive Function System (Delis, Kaplan & Kramer, 2001, or where available, the most recent editions of these tests.). These batteries are used in many countries, cover a fairly wide range of functions, utilise tests that have been around for some time and have comparatively good norms. This probably holds true even when only some of their sub-tests are administered rather than the entire battery. Myriad possible combinations of individual 'bedside' tests also exist, depending on clinicians' preferences. Overall, the golden rule when using any neurocognitive tests is that the clinician is the master of the tests and not slave to them – tests merely serve to answer clinical questions.

Conclusion

Neuropsychological testing is an invaluable tool in many situations/contexts. Two key approaches to neuropsychological assessment are the psychometric approach and the hypothetico-deductive approach – perhaps this is still a slightly controversial point given that much of mainstream psychology may still be dominated by the psychometric approach. However, it is definitely true that on many occasions, it is the patient's observed behaviour, rather than the test scores, that is the most telling. In such cases, the hypothetico-deductive approach is particularly useful. In this light, it is not unusual for psychologists working in this area to adapt test administration procedures in an attempt to identify the outer boundaries of a patient's level of ability in a given cognitive domain when using the psychometric approach. A general assessment strategy is to start by testing a broad range of functions and then to continually refine your hypotheses as the assessment progresses. The ability to administer and interpret tests is very much part of psychologists' core professional identity.

Practical tips

1. Own a stopwatch – those belonging to the clinic/hospital disappear like mist in front of the moon on Monday mornings.
2. Pack out the tests that you are going to use *before* starting your assessment, otherwise you are doomed to experience the 'missing block' phenomenon.
3. Laminate a graph of the normal distribution of percentiles and z-scores – this is a great reminder of just how far outlying a test performance must be in order to represent impairment.

Points for reflective practice

1. Choose your ideal neuropsychological test battery/combination of tests, explaining all the reasons for this selection.
2. What are the strengths and limitations of neuropsychological testing?

Selected further reading

Lezak, M. D., Howieson, D. B., Bigler, E. D., & Tranel, D. (2012). *Neuropsychological assessment* (5th ed.). New York: Oxford University Press.

Luria, A. R., & Majovski, L. V. (1977). Basic approaches used in American and Soviet clinical neuropsychology. *American Psychologist, 32,* 959–968.

Mosdell, J., Balchin, R., & Ameen, O. (2010). Adaptation of aphasia tests for neurocognitive screening in South Africa. *South African Journal of Psychology, 40,* 250–261.

Walsh, K. W., & Darby, D. (1999). *Neuropsychology: A clinical approach* (4th ed.). Edinburgh: Churchill Livingston.

10

FORMULATION

Introduction

Formulation represents the process of describing in greater detail the different factors involved in the evolution, expression and maintenance of a patient's clinical presentation at a given point in time. It is a *dynamic process,* and formulations therefore tend to be refined, updated or even radically changed over time. Formulation has important functions, including improving our (and the clinical team's) understanding of why patients present in a certain way, and how this might aid the planning of their rehabilitation. A diagnosis is not the final stage of an assessment, but instead the beginning of the formulation and, ultimately, the treatment plan.

Diagnosis is metaphorically similar to a chapter title – what is contained in the chapter elucidates the title. In short, *formulation is explaining, diagnosis is labelling –* but they are mutually dependent rather than mutually exclusive. Ultimately, clinicians have to make a professional formulation about *how* a given neuropathology presents in a patient together with the other biological, psychological and social factors involved in triggering and maintaining the patient's unique difficulties. The *biopsychosocial model* is perhaps the most widely used framework for formulations in settings where a large proportion of neuropsychologists work. For many, this model makes at least some practical and theoretical sense. It is also a relatively easy model to use for newly qualified psychologists who work with patients with neuropathology.

Neuropsychologists often think 'brain first, social factors and environment second'. Nevertheless, environmental, cultural, linguistic, educational and social factors are also very important, and can significantly influence clinical presentations. Neuropsychologists, taking into consideration their knowledge base, are frequently expected to straddle the biological, psychological, cultural and social aspects of clinical presentations, rather than focusing exclusively on biological or social factors.

Neuropsychologists therefore aim to make biopsychosocial formulations that integrate how a neuropathological condition (with specific neuropsychological impairments) can, at a certain time, and in various ways, affect a patient who is part of a family, an occupational setting and a social system. Formulation serves to complement diagnosis rather than replace it.

Formulation is a topic that does not lend itself well to an exclusively theoretical coverage. It is much better suited to a problem-based or case-study-based approach to learning. Below follow two amalgams of different clinical cases (to ensure confidentiality) in an attempt to provide clear examples of formulations in clinical practice. The first case is from a developed country context, the second from a multicultural and multilingual developing country perspective.

Case one: Mary, a 27-year-old librarian who lived alone, was walking home one night when she was run over by a drunk driver while crossing the road. She sustained a broken leg and facial cuts and bruises, and was knocked unconscious. On arrival at a nearby trauma centre, her Glasgow Coma Scale (GCS) score was 7/15. A CT brain scan revealed left frontal contusion, generalised oedema and a temporal bone fracture depressing upon the lateral temporal lobe. The fracture was elevated neurosurgically. Mary regained consciousness after three days and made a fairly rapid recovery from her physical injuries. She returned home after five weeks and was seen for weekly follow-ups as an outpatient over the next three months. After four months, she started a phased return to work, with much support from her employer. At this point, things started to go wrong. Mary became increasingly anxious and eventually came to the attention of the hospital psychiatry services; she presented with severe depression after having been off work for a couple of months. She was subsequently referred to a brain-injury rehabilitation unit for a multidisciplinary assessment, including a neuropsychology consultation.

Neuropsychological evaluation revealed the following. Mary presented with anxiety and depression. Her assessment did not reveal any obvious neurocognitive impairment. However, testing did reveal that while Mary scored in the superior range of performance for general intellectual ability (in keeping with her level of education), clear impairments of information processing, memory and executive function were noted. She had no premorbid history of psychiatric problems, no major surgery or other major illnesses, no substance abuse and no family history of any significant medical problems. Mary had a masters degree and had been working at her local library since graduating aged 24. She described herself as always having been shy, and as very conscientious and ambitious regarding her career. She did have a small circle of friends, and pursued hiking and travel as hobbies.

By incorporating this information into a formulation, the neuropsychologist understood that, while Mary did display significant symptoms of depression, it was important to understand the evolution of her presentation. In particular, it was important to note that she presented with anxiety when she returned to work. At that point, when she attempted to perform tasks that were previously routine, her cognitive impairment declared itself. Mary was shocked to discover that she was unable to plan book ordering, keep up to date with the library catalogue, and so forth. She kept becoming distracted and would forget important deadlines. When these episodes failed to go away, she feared that she was losing her mind and became very anxious. This anxiety was perpetuated by her high work standards and her conscientiousness. Given that she lived on her own, Mary also had nobody to talk to. Her shyness and introversion also posed an obstacle for her: for example, when it came to being able to discuss what was worrying her with others.

Due to Mary's ongoing difficulties, her family doctor eventually booked her off work. While at home, Mary started to ruminate excessively about her future and eventually became convinced that she would never work again, and that she would soon lose her apartment and become reliant on social security. These thoughts became entrenched and, in a vicious cycle, also prevented her from taking action to try to overcome these perceived obstacles. At this point, she became very depressed and did not leave her apartment much. Consequently, the social isolation she experienced served to further potentiate her already low mood. It was at this point that Mary came to the attention of the hospital psychiatrist and subsequently the brain-injury service.

It is most likely that Mary's presentation satisfies most of the *DSM-IV* (American Psychiatric Association, 1994) diagnostic criteria for a 'Major Depressive Disorder' (and a 'Cognitive Disorder Not Otherwise Specified') following a severe traumatic brain injury. And, it is almost entirely certain that a biological factor (traumatic brain injury) resulted in her neurocognitive impairment. However, her depression appears to be less directly associated with a biological factor – Mary's low mood evolved over time, in response to neurocognitive impairment. It was not necessarily directly and exclusively *caused* by the anatomical and physiological damage resulting from her brain injury. She had no premorbid vulnerability to anxiety or depression. Quite clearly, the neurocognitive impairment resulting from Mary's brain injury was more likely to have caused her anxiety, and this ultimately resulted in her being away from work. Other factors, such as her isolation (social/environmental) and her introversion (psychological) also further contributed to the evolution and maintenance of her depression. Additional psychological factors, her personal ambition and her conscientiousness, all helped to further maintain and accentuate her depression.

In considering this initial biopsychosocial formulation, a multidisciplinary rehabilitation team may have considered incorporating the following treatment strategies. Psychopharmacological approaches may have needed to be considered. This is relevant in light of Mary meeting the diagnostic criteria for depression, and due to the intensity and duration of her *dysphoria*. Psychological approaches, including cognitive behavioural therapy (in view of her constant rumination), the provision of psycho-education (Mary seemed to have been given very little information about traumatic brain injury and its consequences) and cognitive rehabilitation (most likely memory compensation strategies) could all be considered. A referral to social work colleagues to assist with her mounting bills and her eviction fears would prove helpful in reducing Mary's anxiety and depression. Finally, at a later stage, input from occupational therapy regarding a possible return-to-work initiative could also be considered. This formulation, while incorporating biological and social and environmental factors, has emphasised psychological factors – specifically the role of neurocognitive function in this patient's presentation.

Case two: Sizwe, a 54-year-old male, with a grade 5 education (roughly six to seven years of formal schooling), sustained head trauma when a taxi struck him when he was crossing the road with his daughter while returning from a local store. The head injury resulted in an immediate loss of consciousness. Sizwe had a retrograde amnesia for two minutes or so prior to his accident and a period of posttraumatic amnesia (PTA) for approximately one week. His home/first language was isiXhosa, with English his second language. In the weeks following the accident Sizwe reported experiencing memory problems (including everyday forgetfulness, such as forgetting where he put things in his dwelling) and complained of feeling frustrated. He also mentioned in passing that he had trouble controlling his anger. Subjectively, Sizwe felt his memory problems were worsening, and said that in the months following the accident his wife had written basic things down on pieces of paper in an attempt to enable him to remember them.

Sizwe's wife agreed that he was having problems controlling his anger and mood, especially when frustrated. She believed his memory was not deteriorating, but that the level of impairment was remaining constant. Sizwe said during his initial assessment that he had not worked much as a gardener since his accident, as he had problems with his memory when dealing with his employers and did not want to disappoint them or let them down. However, he did state that he would not mind it if he was able to work again. Sizwe, who was from an extremely disadvantaged background, with a very low socio-economic status, was worried about his family's financial situation since his accident, especially given that his wife only had part-time work as a domestic worker (a charwoman).

Although he was reasonably aware of his injuries, he seemed more concerned about his financial circumstances. The hardship already experienced as a family prior to the accident was now a fight for financial survival. Sizwe and his wife also worried about their daughter who was also injured in the accident, and had been left with bad scarring to her legs. Following the accident, Sizwe lost interest in most things that he previously enjoyed; however, he stated that he was not feeling depressed. He also said that he had been getting very tired since the accident, which was especially noticeable in the late afternoon. He did not report any problems with his sleep or appetite and denied any weight loss – his wife corroborated this. Overall, Sizwe gave an adequate history, but it lacked any in-depth detail.

Sizwe was seen by neuropsychology 13 months after his accident. Upon assessment, Sizwe was found to be fully oriented to person, place and time. He appeared distracted and inattentive at times during the assessment. With respect to memory, he was able to encode new information and did not have an axial amnesia, despite his performance being imperfect. For language, confrontation-naming performance was normal and no word-finding difficulties were noted in his spontaneous speech. With regard to spatial cognition, there was no evidence of constructional apraxia or neglect. When executive functions were assessed, his performance indicated a dysexecutive syndrome; he displayed deficits of attention and mental control. Sizwe's short-term memory span was five digits forwards, and only two backwards for working memory.

Sizwe's digit span performance was overshadowed by his apparent inability to grasp the task's instructions. He said that he 'did not do numbers at school'. This almost certainly in part reflected his limited educational opportunities as a child. His phonemic generativity was poor, with a slight improvement in semantic generativity. There was tentative evidence of deficits in functions associated with the pre-motor frontal cortex; despite continuous teaching and practice he struggled to learn and perform a simple motor sequence accurately. He struggled with simple calculations, although this could also be explained by his fluctuating attention and level of education. Sizwe had difficulty solving even very basic problems put to him and appeared slow and concrete in his thought processes.

When incorporating this information from the assessment into a formulation, the neuropsychologist's first task was to recognise the combination of deficits present, in conjunction with the presenting pathology (head trauma), and decide if this was consistent with executive dysfunction. This formulation took place in a developing world, cross-cultural setting, with a poor (very low socio-economic status) patient who had very little formal education and who spoke English only as a second language. Extreme variables such as these are frequently encountered by psychologists working in such settings. Given these factors, a key component of this formulation was to determine which aspects, if any, of Sizwe's poor test performances might be explained by (1) possible cultural biases in the tests, (2) English being his second language, and (3) Sizwe's level of education, all of which were contributing factors.

To determine the most relevant factors involved in Sizwe's performance, the neuropsychologist needed to consider whether the pattern of deficits observed was consistent with executive impairment, or whether there were features of the presentation attributable to these additional factors. It was decided that the telling frontal sign of pre-motor deficits and the difficulties with sustaining focused attention, in combination, along with the other qualitative observations from the testing and the remaining test performances, were indeed all consistent with executive dysfunction. Another key aspect to this formulation was to identify that this type of neurocognitive presentation is typical of head trauma pathology, and that the onset of the deficits coincides with the time of the injury.

When considering psychological factors, it was felt that Sizwe rather unsurprisingly felt frustrated and angry as a result of all that had happened to him. Furthermore, the fact that he was now stuck at home (inactive all day), with little to do, was possibly maintaining these difficulties – although it could also be explained by his frontal disinhibition. Adding to the clinical picture was his lack of insight into the severity and implications of his deficits, due to both his lesion and, possibly, his lack of education (likewise, his wife also struggled to accurately appraise the situation). Given this, along with his very impoverished circumstances and his obvious lack of job security or an employer to offer support, Sizwe was left in a very difficult situation in terms of trying to adequately cope with his problems. This situation would be extremely difficult for a multidisciplinary team to address. There is very limited community support where Sizwe lived and, given that it is a very impoverished township area, it is also difficult for an occupational therapist and social worker to gain access. This lack of resources is an important aspect of Sizwe's formulation. Unfortunately, in many developing world settings, such resources are simply not always available or accessible to patients (see the 'Formulation: who and when?' section, below).

From a social action perspective, in the multitude of cases such as Sizwe's, psychologists need to give careful consideration as to how to spend their time when it comes to providing further support and care for patients. Here, it is important to determine what resources are available within patients' communities, and to always keep the concept of 'transferable technology' in mind (Nell, 2000) – neuropsychologists can train colleagues from other disciplines who might be working in communities, such as social workers and occupational therapists, or others, such as church members. Such training can, for example, include information about: (1) what to expect following brain injury; (2) how to deal with certain behaviours; (3) what to look out for in terms of symptoms; and (4) how to compensate for cognitive impairments, such as memory problems. Training materials, such as information booklets and questionnaires (translated into local languages, where applicable), can be developed to augment this process.

Opportunities to start outsourced community-based support initiatives should always be taken by psychologists whenever possible. For example, in disadvantaged communities in Cape Town, South Africa, a programme called HeadsUP! has been developed by the non-profit organisation ComaCARE with the help of one of this book's authors. This programme helps to reintegrate brain-injury survivors back into their families and communities. Using a prefabricated office space in the township of Khayelitsha as a hub, families are trained by social workers and lay counsellors (who have been first trained themselves) to cope with disruptive brain-injury behaviours and are offered ongoing support groups in the townships. Such initiatives can make a significant difference to patients' lives post brain injury, with the help of relatively minimal funding and volunteers working around a handful of permanent staff. Psychologists, where available, can play key supervisory and educational roles in such initiatives.

Factors to consider in formulation

We now turn to a brief overview of some of the important factors/areas to consider during case formulations. First, *never underestimate the importance of premorbid personality factors* – each individual brings a unique history that will influence the clinical presentation. Premorbid personality characteristics have potentially important implications for recovery and rehabilitation. For example, the individual who has always been able to see the brighter side of things, who has overcome previous adversity, perhaps through stoicism, who generally tends to worry less about the future and who has always worked hard to achieve personal goals may have a different presentation and outcome from someone with a very similar type and severity of brain injury, but who has a history of not accepting personal responsibility, who has been plagued by chronic worry and self-doubt and who has never really set personal goals or achieved any significant personal success. Always explore premorbid personality factors and try to incorporate these into formulations. While brains may be similar neuroanatomically, people (individual personalities) are not.

The second factor is systemic in nature: wherever possible, always consider the role of patients' families. This is especially relevant where family support is available, and where families have the desire to be closely involved in patients' rehabilitation and care (where appropriate). If we neglect to try to understand the role of families in the amelioration or accentuation of brain-injured patients' disabilities, we do so at our peril. Formulation should always incorporate the very significant contribution – or obstacles – that families can potentially make to patient rehabilitation and care. Similarly, consider the possible effect of role changes: for example, where one partner of a married couple has sustained brain injury – think about how this might be incorporated into a case formulation. In some cultures, it is an important value for families and the community to look after the vulnerable, the elderly and the poorly, while in other cultures this is not the case.

A third point is to consider general demographic factors during case formulations. These can be important under some, but clearly not all circumstances. Education, age, socio-economic status, sex/gender, access to medical services (or lack of access), employment status, employment opportunities within a particular area and access to transport are some of the factors that require consideration. There is a fundamental need for psychologists (and other professionals within the multidisciplinary team) to be sensitive towards cultural factors that may affect the clinical presentation and outcome, and to then incorporate all relevant factors into any formulation.

Practitioners can attempt to identify potentially useful generic skills that can be capitalised upon to help with mobilising the rehabilitation programme, so that it can be directed towards goals that are personally relevant to patients. These skills are often identified by re-examining the patient's social, educational, employment and recreational history pre-dating his/her neurological condition. For example, a male writer may be much more amenable to engaging in interventions where the formulation of his treatment plan incorporates his interest and preference for tasks requiring writing skills. In this hypothetical case, let us say that the main cognitive impairment resulting from *hypoxia* was memory impairment. By acknowledging this patient's premorbid skills and preferences, the use of a written memory book or diary to provide reminders and timetables may potentially be much more likely to meet his approval than would the use of other compensatory technologies, such as a Dictaphone or mobile telephone. One could even consider an ecologically valid assignment, such as him helping to write a patient-information booklet about memory problems.

Formulation: who and when?

Formulations often take place within multidisciplinary teams. Is case formulation the exclusive domain of psychologists? Who makes the first formulation for a new patient? Who endorses the formulation as being one that is useful and accurate? These questions can lead to some confusion and possible misunderstandings. The initial formulation is probably most often the responsibility of the lead clinician for the specific patient. Often this is the person who saw the patient initially and who has some responsibility for coordinating his/her care. This is not necessarily profession-specific either; formulation is in most cases a 'team sport'. Psychologists should enthusiastically contribute to this process, without becoming precious about 'owning' the formulation. The important contributions made by other professions – doctors, nurses, social workers and occupational therapists – really should bring this point home.

Ultimately, most if not all members of the team should contribute to the case formulation, irrespective of who is the 'scribe' responsible for integrating the various perspectives. The only two criteria for the inclusion of information are: (1) whether the point made increases understanding of the patient's presentation; and (2) if it can usefully inform any treatment/rehabilitation strategies. In some settings where neuropsychologists work, formulation as part of a team can be difficult at times. This can be because neuropsychology is often a minority profession, and professionals from other disciplines may be unaware of the contributions that it can make, therefore not considering to ask for neuropsychological input. In such instances, neuropsychologists can try to improve this situation by helping colleagues from other disciplines to understand what neuropsychology can offer both patients and the clinical team.

A second reason why formulation as part of a team can be difficult to implement has to do with working in under-developed healthcare settings. In such settings, there is frequently a lack of infrastructure, and therefore often no opportunity for more organised or systematic delivery of long-term rehabilitation for patients with neurocognitive impairments. In such instances, patients are often seen only once for a diagnostic assessment by psychologists based at hospitals/clinics – this makes it almost impossible to produce an accurate, comprehensive case formulation, which requires utilising clinical observations accumulated over time. Nevertheless, sometimes a very basic, provisional formulation can potentially be helpful for other professionals (for example, nurses, social workers, occupational therapists and healthcare support workers), who may be providing limited clinical reviews and support through home visits, for example.

Case formulations are unlikely to be completely accurate in the first instance, and they are even more unlikely to remain up to date indefinitely. It is very important to remember that *formulations are frequently updated* as new information becomes available or as developments evolve. For example, patients may show progress in response to rehabilitation and/or spontaneous recovery following encephalitis, and may thereby reach a stage where they are ready for an initial attempt at returning to work. At this point, certain pre-injury factors may dominate the formulation – for example, identifying and making use of the support of a colleague from the workplace who is particularly trusted, and who can possibly function as 'buddy' or source of support when the patient first returns to work. Furthermore, as the planned first return visit to work approaches, new factors may emerge: for example, the patient may experience an escalation in anxiety, or an increase in awareness of his/her acquired limitations. These, and similar developments, would need to be incorporated into an updated formulation for it to remain useful.

Naturally occurring life-events may sometimes radically alter an existing case presentation. Acquired brain injury or neurological illnesses do not necessarily prevent other events from occurring in patients' lives. A family member may become ill, or die. A partner may decide to leave. A new baby may be due. There may be significant positive or negative developments with a compensation claim. The care staff at a residential unit or nursing home may change; these staff may have had a trusting and close relationship with a patient with a degenerative neurological condition, nurtured over time, which allowed for effective management of the initial presentation of the patient's aggressive behaviour. This aggressive behaviour may then re-emerge and a new formulation would have to incorporate care approaches that appear to have worked in the past, as well as acknowledging the role of confusion and the loss of the familiar staff in contributing to the patient's presentation. All these considerations – and many other events – are beyond the clinical team's control, but may in many cases have a profound effect on the patient and, by default, on his/her ability or willingness to engage with the previously formulated rehabilitation plan.

Conclusion

Case formulation is acknowledged throughout the health professions to require a fair amount of technical knowledge, clinical skill and perceptiveness. This is no different in neuropsychology. Formulation helps us to think about patients in a more in-depth manner. The aim is to attempt to understand why and how patients function or present in a particular way following brain injury, at a particular point in their lives. Case formulation draws together clinical assessment, special investigations, diagnosis and other sources of information. There are many factors for the clinical team to consider when preparing a case formulation. Some of the most important factors that psychologists should be aware of, and therefore incorporate into their formulations, include: the cultural and language aspects of patients; their premorbid personality characteristics; the level (and quality) of their education; the availability of community support systems; and patients' family dynamics. Case formulation is not intended to be cross-sectional – it has a distinctly longitudinal course and therefore requires regular updating by the multidisciplinary team in order for it to remain effective and contemporary.

Practical tips

1. Be mindful that overly long formulations can put a drain on the time resources of the multidisciplinary team – therefore, always try to be concise.
2. Try to specifically incorporate neurocognitive factors into your formulations, rather than only 'psychological' factors. This will add 'neuropsychological value' to formulations.
3. Read published case reports in the relevant neuropsychological journals to get a feel for how various colleagues prepare case presentations.

Points for reflective practice

1. In your opinion, what are the most important factors to consider when doing a case formulation?
2. Why can we not just make more economical use of time by skipping the formulation process altogether, instead sticking to the diagnosis as a way to communicate about patients?

Selected further reading

Wilson, B. A., Gracey, F., Evans, J. J., & Bateman, A. (2009). *Neuropsychological rehabilitation: Theory, models, therapy and outcome.* Cambridge: Cambridge University Press.

11

NEUROPSYCHOLOGICAL REHABILITATION

Introduction

This chapter provides a brief introduction to neuropsychological rehabilitation. Neuropsychological rehabilitation draws on different theoretical approaches (see Chapter 6) with a view to finding individualised strategies to help patients with cognitive, emotional and behavioural difficulties as identified by neuropsychological assessment (see Chapters 8 and 9). Readers interested in an up-to-date overview of the theories and approaches that have shaped neuropsychological rehabilitation should consult Cicerone (2012); see 'Selected further reading' at the end of this chapter. The cognitive, emotional and behavioural difficulties associated with brain injury are not always neatly separable. Considerable overlap exists: for example, a stroke patient who presents with cognitive impairment may experience some of his/her cognitive difficulties in response to the lack of attention that one might receive as a result of having a low mood. And, a depressed mood may also affect subsequent behaviours too, most notably initiation and general activity levels. These are the types of clinical issues that are often faced during the rehabilitation process.

Formulations (see Chapter 10) can be used to incorporate the factors contributing to patients' problems, and the interactions between these factors. It is the understanding that can be achieved through formulation that should be reflected in the rehabilitation goals set for patients. The goals for neuropsychological rehabilitation should ideally be identified collaboratively. Neuropsychological rehabilitation, given the diverse areas it attempts to address, encompasses several approaches, including: *cognitive rehabilitation, behavioural programmes* and *psychotherapy strategies* (see Chapter 12 for an overview of some of the psychotherapeutic approaches used in brain-injury rehabilitation). While often neuropsychology-led, various professions (such as speech therapy, clinical psychology and occupational therapy) are usually involved in neuropsychological rehabilitation programmes. Unfortunately, in many parts of the world where neuropsychology is not as developed a field, or where resources are scarce, there is simply no infrastructure available to allow for neuropsychological rehabilitation to take place.

In under-resourced healthcare settings, the primary role of neuropsychologists is to diagnose patients' cognitive deficits (often in a one-off assessment); frequently, the neuropsychologist then never encounters the patient again. This situation, apart from the obvious consequences for patients, can also leave psychologists with a sense of 'helplessness' and frustration, feeling as though they have not contributed positively towards helping patients. This subjective experience is common among psychologists who are not able to work in the area of patient rehabilitation. Clinicians who find themselves in this situation may miss out on seeing potentially positive outcomes – instead seeing patients' impairments only when working at the diagnostic 'coalface'. This can be especially depressing for some. Another obvious problem this situation may pose is how one then goes about acquiring the knowledge required to effectively rehabilitate patients following brain injury, when learning opportunities are simply not there. This chapter focuses mainly on the broad principles of cognitive rehabilitation and behavioural strategies, which are often used in conjunction with one another.

Cognitive rehabilitation

Mateer (2005) provides a useful overview of some of the general principles that underpin cognitive rehabilitation, along with some of the popular strategies used for interventions, including *environmental modifications, the use of compensatory strategies or technologies, activities for restoring underlying cognitive impairment, direct instruction, errorless instruction* and *procedural learning*. The following are clinical examples of these generic strategies. Environmental modifications may involve: changing the layout of a house and decreasing clutter in order to reduce the potential for distraction; using laminated signs to indicate the steps to be followed during a task; or displaying a daily programme. Another example might be to include the use of signs or lines on the floor to indicate a route, thereby preventing a patient from getting lost. Many of the environmental adaptations are used to keep patients safe, especially where cognitive impairment and behavioural difficulties substantially increase their vulnerability. Other modifications are designed to prevent perceptual over-stimulation: for example, by ensuring noise levels are within reasonable limits, or avoiding the use of excessively bright lights.

Activities used for helping with neurocognitive difficulties work on the assumption that practice will improve cognitive performance within the target area. These strategies often target *attention*, but are also utilised in other cognitive domains. *Computer-based tasks* are often employed, especially for targeting problems with attention. Some clinicians who use these strategies sometimes employ more naturalistic or ecologically valid technologies, such as computer games, which can be particularly useful when rehabilitating younger patients. Computer games may have a much greater chance of ensuring successful participation in a rehabilitation programme. As a general guideline, it is very important to use strategies and technologies that have high credibility and face validity with the patients concerned.

In contrast to restorative strategies, *compensatory strategies* work from the presumption that cognitive deficits cannot be improved through practice. Here it is speculated that practice without any noticeable benefit may actually run the risk of increasing patients' despondency and/or anxiety. In contrast, compensatory strategies attempt to find ways to overcome the detrimental effects of neurocognitive impairment. Memory impairment is one function where compensatory strategies have made a significant contribution. Wilson (1999) describes a few cases where successful strategies have been employed to overcome some of the effects of memory impairment. The technologies utilised to compensate for poor memory vary from the extremely simple (such as notepads, diaries, notice boards and Dictaphones) to the highly sophisticated (such as electronic devices that can be programmed to remind patients of their personal schedules and tasks, or capture their day visually on computer).

As with many other neuropsychological rehabilitation strategies, there has been a trend towards using technologies that are more ecologically valid and naturalistic in order to increase the chances of rehabilitation gains being generalisable to everyday environments. Some of the most promising examples of such technologies are the memory compensatory strategies that have been used in clinical practice over recent years, including the following examples. There is a great deal to be said for the humble pen-and-paper diary, especially if very small and portable. Patients report that they feel reassured by using such diaries, specifically because they are so simple and , unlike a handheld computer, they cannot fail (and there are no batteries that might fail at a crucial moment!). Sadly, however, a diary can of course be lost or left at home. Whiteboards (especially used in the kitchen) are still popular for helping patients to remember their to-do lists, while at the same time not attracting undue attention to their memory problems (as many people utilise whiteboards anyway).

The following are some of the newer technologies being utilised. Satellite navigation is promising for assisting patients who cannot remember or learn routes. Furthermore, modern mobile/cell phones have been shown to have great potential in serving as effective memory-compensatory tools. A few functions, which exist even on a very basic mobile/cell phone and which patients report finding useful are the calendar/diary program, camera, address book and text messaging (for example, receiving text reminders). The potential of phone apps is an exciting new possibility, along with free Internet programs (such as diaries). These are low-cost but high-tech tools with great potential for use in cognitive rehabilitation. In summary, memory compensatory strategies do not cure memory problems, but they can increase patients' independence, and most importantly, they can reduce anxiety and increase confidence.

Compensatory strategies, while most commonly used for memory rehabilitation, are also used for difficulties related to executive dysfunction. These strategies may have an important role to play, especially where disorders of planning are concerned. Templates that guide patients through the steps of problem solving are sometimes used to good effect. Templates usually include steps such as *identifying the problem*, the *generating of alternatives/options*, *rating each option before selecting a course of action* and, finally, *assessing the outcome/s of the action/s taken*. Structured daily programmes can counteract, in some instances, the effects of loss of initiative or ineffective planning of schedules, while limiting the potential for impulsive or unhelpful perusal of activities that are counter-productive to the patient's rehabilitation programme. However, there is the risk of relying too heavily on these programmes and the potential consequence of experiencing spectacular failure on an important occasion. A significant limitation is that some of the compensatory (and instructional) strategies that are on offer for executive dysfunction can fail to generalise to patients' everyday lives.

Instructional techniques comprise approaches used to facilitate new learning in patients with difficulties in this area; examples include: *breaking up tasks into their basic components*; *using repetition, with instructions with good potential for many immediately correct responses*; and *using revision techniques*, among many others. One very important instructional technique is called *errorless learning* (see Wilson, 1999). The central idea behind errorless learning is to prevent patients from making confusing mistakes that can have a detrimental effect on their ability to memorise new material: for example, avoiding patients guessing, which, if done, would then lead to the wrong answers being learned through incorrect repetition. In essence, patients are actually either given the correct answers (before they give incorrect answers and learn the wrong response), or they are provided with such potent cueing that they cannot make mistakes. Both strategies are used until patients have consolidated the target information. Finally, *procedural memory* (as opposed to declarative memory, which is the recall of facts, biographical details, and so forth) sometimes provides an alternative mechanism to use for new learning.

Behavioural approaches

Patients with neuropathology frequently present with problematic behaviours, such as aggression, poor inhibition and/or inappropriate behaviour. *Behaviour therapy* has a fairly long history – especially in inpatient settings – and is potentially useful for treating such difficulties. For example, *token economies* are used in some inpatient settings to manage and alter undesirable behaviours. Token economies work as follows. First, a baseline measure of the frequency of undesirable behaviours is performed, and the activating and maintaining factors of the behaviours are identified. It is also often useful to try to ascertain what the psychological function of the behaviour is: for example, it may be the only way for a patient to express his/her frustration and anxiety, or it may serve as a guaranteed way of getting attention. Once the baseline frequency has been determined and the behaviours contextually analysed, the clinical team may then set the desired frequency (or the desired levels) for reducing the target behaviours, before agreeing the number of tokens to be earned by the patient when s/he meets the targets. It is also made clear to the patient how many tokens can be exchanged for particular rewards (reinforcers).

There are a few important general points to consider when using reinforcement programmes. One crucial task is to identify a powerful reinforcement that is relevant to the patient. Moreover, one must initially (at least) ensure that it is easy for the patient to meet the change in behaviour that leads to earning a reward. If standards are set too high, patients may not engage with the programme. It is also important to ensure that patients who may have significant cognitive impairment remember what is required of them, as well as what the rewards for compliance are. This is often achieved by the prominent display of: (1) the programme outline (or 'rules'); (2) the levels of performance achieved; and (3) the rewards that have been earned and/or those that it is still possible to earn.

A potential downfall of some reinforcement programmes is the problem of lack of consistency among the staff who are directly involved in patients' daily rehabilitation and who are responsible for applying the programme. This may be particularly problematic in environments with a higher turnover of staff, such as in nursing homes or smaller, less well-staffed slow-stream rehabilitation units. Watson, Rutterford, Shortland, Williamson and Alderman (2001) – see 'Selected further reading' at the end of this chapter – describe an approach designed to overcome some of the difficulties encountered when clinicians try to replicate reinforcement programmes in such environments. Reinforcement programmes – in their different guises – represent the most widely used behavioural approaches in brain-injury rehabilitation settings. These programmes are mostly used to increase desirable behaviours or reduce undesirable behaviours.

A major challenge to the overall utility of some of these programmes is to ensure their generalisation to non-clinical environments. Patient relapses post-discharge are not uncommon unless this issue has been specifically planned for in the design of the reinforcement programme. While tangible reinforcements are mostly used in these programmes, there are also other potential rewards for desirable behaviours. *Social reward* has a potentially important application – even if only used as a subtle strategy – and is perhaps one of the strongest natural reinforcements. For example, if social reward is used in individual psychotherapy as a way of trying to increase appropriate interpersonal behaviours (such as asking questions to show interest, listening to another person or giving a compliment to another person), then hopefully some gains may generalise to other interpersonal interactions post-discharge. Social reinforcement can be a potent force for increasing certain types of behaviours, and is potentially more useful in a brain-injury rehabilitation context than are principles, such as *extinction*, for reducing undesirable behaviours. For example, ignoring excessive swearing in patients who are *impulsive* with a view to extinguishing this behaviour is going to be, in many cases, potentially less effective than reinforcing other, desirable social skills.

Behaviour modification programmes are all well and good as medium-term strategies for the rehabilitation of certain behaviours, but what about the more disruptive behaviours that occur in the moment and that have to be managed more immediately? *Distraction* is a fairly widely used behavioural technique for managing behaviours as they occur, such as verbal aggression or agitation. Or perhaps this is not completely true – the effectiveness of distraction depends somewhat on identifying the early signs of agitation and then distracting the patient *before* escalation occurs. While this approach can work quite well, perhaps in part because it 'utilises' one of the common cognitive impairments associated with brain injury, namely *distractibility*, it is not always effective. To its credit, distraction is a very simple technique that is easily understood and that can be taught with minimal input to staff in nursing homes, or family members, for example. Another example of a behavioural technique that is used to manage aggressive or inappropriate behaviours on the spot is *time out*. There are various modifications of this technique in use in brain-injury rehabilitation.

Other rehabilitation techniques and strategies

With many rehabilitation techniques, the relationship between clinician and patient is a huge source of variance. Generally speaking, clinicians who have better relationships with their patients may be more likely to succeed in achieving favourable outcomes, irrespective of technique. There are additional approaches to brain-injury rehabilitation programmes other than cognitive rehabilitation and behaviour modification techniques. These are almost always integral to more comprehensive programmes, on either an inpatient or outpatient basis, and may place more emphasis on the therapeutic relationship. For example, *behavioural activation* is sometimes used as a strategy in its own right, but is also often used to augment other approaches, such as cognitive behavioural therapy. Only a few additional approaches are listed here.

One of the more useful interventions for a service to offer is the provision of *group therapy*, including *rehabilitation groups for patients* and *carer support groups*. In addition, *educational groups* are common to many rehabilitation programmes, where patients (and often family members) are provided with fairly detailed information regarding the nature of their conditions. Some of the general aims of these groups are to increase patients' and their relatives' understanding of common symptoms, to teach simple compensatory strategies and to increase awareness about the conditions affecting patients. Although not a primary focus of most of these types of psycho-educational groups, some of the additional positive outcomes reported include a reduction in anxiety, demystification of the diagnosis and the emotional support obtained from speaking to others who are in the same situation. Sometimes other rehabilitation interventions are provided in groups, such as cognitive rehabilitation through a *memory group*.

Group work done solely with carers or relatives is another important intervention to be offered. There are two very useful reasons to provide *family support groups*, both of which make good clinical sense. First, much of the rehabilitation input that is provided directly to patients needs monitoring and/or prompting in their home environments. For this reason, a collaborative approach with families is vital to ensure the generalisation of therapeutic gains beyond the hospital/clinic. Second, relatives who are emotionally well, and who feel supported, are in a better position to care for their loved ones. Clinicians have to ultimately acknowledge that, long after they have ceased to be involved in patients' rehabilitation, it is the relatives, partners and carers who have to look after them. *Help the family to cope and you have increased the chances of a better long-term outcome for the patient.*

In acknowledging the obvious fact that patients' family members also suffer terribly as a result of patients' brain injuries, one needs to be aware that there is a key role for psychologists to play in working with relatives and in providing potential support in the context of patient rehabilitation. Helping families to adapt to patients' impairments and helping to work through changes in relationships following brain injury are issues that psychologists can address. For example, for further information on such issues, see the Bowen, Yeates and Palmer (2010) reference in the 'Selected further reading' list at the end of this chapter.

Sometimes, more formal *family therapy* or *couples therapy* may be necessary to augment, on a more systemic level, the overall programme of rehabilitation offered to patients. Where patients are receiving individual psychological therapy (and if resources allow for it), it is perhaps sensible to have another psychologist provide couples or family therapy in order to prevent the potential for the blurring of roles, while also ensuring that there is the best possible chance for the development of robust therapeutic relationships within these different settings. This is a more resource-hungry (and therefore costly) option than group work when it comes to providing family support. In fact, of particular relevance in under-resourced environments is the fact that almost any rehabilitation intervention offered in a group format is more cost-effective and has the potential to reach larger numbers of patients who would otherwise not have been seen.

Return-to-work initiatives represent another core aspect of many rehabilitation programmes. These are usually led by occupational therapists, with some input from psychologists and other colleagues. For those patients with the desire and a realistic chance to return to employment (be it voluntary, part-time, or pre-injury level employment), such initiatives often have high face validity. There are many good reasons why return-to-work rehabilitation can have an excellent effect on outcome, including: a reduction in financial burden; opportunities to socialise; increasing patient confidence; reducing family stress; opportunities for deriving a sense of purpose; and potential reduction in inappropriate long-term reliance on health and social care providers. This is especially crucial in developing countries, where funding for support of chronic disability may be limited or even non-existent.

The following are some general points to consider when working towards the patient returning to employment, studying or a meaningful activity. Psychologists should work collaboratively with patients, employers and other relevant parties in order to identify the optimal time for returning to work. Attempting to return too soon may result in failure and loss of confidence, while returning too late may reduce the chances of success. A good clinical 'guideline' is to '*start low, go slow, and aim high'*; pace a return to work to match the patient's strengths and weaknesses at that particular point in time. Work closely with employers. If possible, try to co-opt someone in the workplace who the patient gets on well with, and who is willing to provide on-the-job support. Always review the patient's progress regularly. Make sure (with the patient's permission of course) that the employer understands the difficulties that arise from the patient's neurocognitive impairment.

Under-resourced areas

There are many countries and contexts (in both the developing and developed world) where there are few, if any, psychologists and where there is a lack of the resources and infrastructure required to conduct patient rehabilitation (including provision of psychotherapy), which necessitates creative adaptations to practice (Coetzer, 2013a). So, what strategies can be adopted here? In such situations, patients and their families quickly find themselves back in what are often very impoverished and disadvantaged circumstances, far from physical access to services.

Many patients cannot afford rehabilitation services, or these services are not appropriate for the patient's specific cultural background. Often this results in severe socio-economic deprivation, and can be associated with many other adverse outcomes, such as having to turn to crime simply to survive. Consequently, communities as a whole may be negatively affected.

Despite the magnitude of these problems, there are strategies that can be tried in order to extend service delivery to such patients. The first of these is to initiate community projects and the training of volunteers who live within communities in order to empower them with some basic skills (such as behavioural management). The World Health Organization (WHO) has encouraged the use of community health workers (CHWs) around the world in the fight to improve healthcare services in impoverished and disadvantaged settings. The idea is that (1) these CHWs are from the local communities and cultures, allowing them to be properly integrated rather than alienated, and (2) they have been taught at least a crash-course in the skills that they need to provide in a given area (Swartz, 1998). Neuropsychology needs to consider this general strategy in many areas around the globe. This can help empower individuals in the community with confidence in the very basic neuropsychological rehabilitation principles: for example, the role of reinforcement in managing behaviour. Furthermore, offering support and supervision from registered professional psychologists, where available, may facilitate ongoing skills development and help to ensure that basic standards of care are met.

On a practical level, with respect to implementation, psychologists need to do the following things to augment the above-mentioned strategies: (1) develop culturally appropriate methods for identifying problem areas within communities; (2) help to empower communities and individual families to be able to help patients themselves; (3) provide resources, such as workshops, in order to distribute knowledge and skills among community members; and (4) target individuals within the community who are leaders and who can tell their community about the benefits of rehabilitation (Edwards & Louw, 1998). Individuals living within a community often have better information regarding potential opportunities for volunteering or informal employment openings. Ideally, voluntary or informal community employment projects can have wider utility or benefit to communities: for example, creating open spaces for recreation and informal sport in inner-city areas, or increasing access to clean water in deprived rural areas. Finally, key to the success of such strategies is the need to have community members and CHWs who are fluent in the local language/s so that they can serve the vital role of interpreters. Language proficiency is crucial to the processes involved in both knowledge transfer and community education.

Conclusion

Rehabilitation in neuropsychology encompasses several different approaches, including *behaviour therapy* and *cognitive rehabilitation*. Other approaches are often used as part of more comprehensive neuropsychological rehabilitation programmes, including *group-based approaches*, such as *psycho-education* and *family support groups*. In clinical practice, neuropsychological rehabilitation primarily targets neurocognitive impairment and behavioural difficulties, although not exclusively. The rehabilitation of these impairments can have a significant positive effect on functional outcomes, most notably with respect to returning to work or studying and increasing independence, while at the same time reducing social isolation. It is often forgotten that effective compensatory strategies can also ameliorate emotional difficulties to some extent, especially anxiety. Unfortunately, in many parts of the world there is simply no infrastructure and resources available to allow for neuropsychological rehabilitation to take place. In these settings, the primary role of neuropsychologists (if available) is to diagnose cognitive deficits in the acute-care setting. Where neuropsychological resources are scarce, appropriate community-based initiatives have to be collaboratively developed.

Practical tips

1. Try to identify some of the commonalities in the difficulties that patients experience, and consider if these problems could be more effectively rehabilitated in a group context.
2. Always determine which technologies patients are already using in their daily lives (such as mobile phones), and then try to match a chosen compensatory strategy to their preference in order to ensure personal ecological validity.
3. Find out as much as you can about the communities where your patients live, and what opportunities might already exist to augment or extend your rehabilitation programmes.

Points for reflective practice

1. What are the strengths and limitations of the behavioural approaches used to manage difficult behaviours in patients with significant neurocognitive impairment (such as poor memory and executive dysfunction)?
2. Is there not a risk that compensatory strategies may make patients too dependent, thereby slowing down their spontaneous recovery or the possibility of finding alternative ways of performing functions?
3. Can psychologists who are based in hospital settings offer anything to patients who are discharged to remote rural areas, or are the logistical barriers simply too difficult to overcome?

Selected further reading

Bowen, C., Yeates, G., & Palmer, S. (2010). *Relational approach to rehabilitation: Thinking about relationships after brain injury.* London: Karnac Books.

Cicerone, K. D. (2012). Facts, theories, values: Shaping the course of neurorehabilitation. The 60th John Stanley Coulter memorial lecture. *Archives of Physical & Medical Rehabilitation, 93,* 188–191.

Mateer, C. A. (2005). Fundamentals of cognitive rehabilitation. In P. W. Halligan & D. T. Wade (Eds.), *Effectiveness of rehabilitation for cognitive deficits* (pp. 21–29). New York: Oxford University Press.

Watson, C., Rutterford, N. A., Shortland, D., Williamson, N., & Alderman, N. (2001). Reduction of chronic aggressive behaviour 10 years after brain injury. *Brain Injury, 15,* 1003–1015.

12

PSYCHOTHERAPY APPROACHES

Introduction

Psychotherapy is sometimes considered to be a very specialist area in settings where neuropsychology is practised. However, the reality is that in clinical practice, it is not an uncommon component of neuropsychologists' daily work. In many rehabilitation settings, psychotherapy is the area of practice that psychologists and other practitioners return to without fail when faced with providing long-term patient care. This assertion makes sense if we acknowledge that most acquired brain injuries and neurological illnesses result in chronic impairment and corresponding disability. It is these difficulties that may also lead to problems for patients when it comes to adjusting emotionally. There are, at present, no 'cures' for these conditions and difficulties. The provision of opportunities for patients to speak about and emotionally adjust to their conditions is one important ingredient in ensuring better long-term outcomes. Patients often report finding solace in being able to voice their fears, anger and the other emotions that stem from having suffered brain injury. Here, psychologists can make a useful and valued contribution to patient care, both in terms of improving emotional outcome and preventing relapse.

In some cultures it is not customary to *talk* about one's problems, and illness and distress are usually not referred to verbally, in psychological terms – this is often believed to be a source of the frequency of somatisation seen in certain cultures around the world. In addition, professional knowledge of psychotherapies is largely understood from a Western perspective, rather than an indigenous one, which often leads to biased views regarding disorders and their treatment. For example, some indigenous African cultures have very different beliefs regarding *healing*. Around the world, there are also varying views regarding the relationship between the individual and society, and differing opinions and beliefs about what constitutes normality versus abnormality (Swartz, 1998).

While specific issues surrounding cultural beliefs about verbalising health concerns and the conceptualisation of treatment create many difficulties for the field of psychology, there are also other potential obstacles. In many healthcare settings, there is very little diversity, if any, among psychologists, which adds to this complexity. There is urgent need in many countries to find and establish viable alternatives to the traditional psychotherapies that have been developed in the Western world, and which are based on Western and European treatment strategies and models of illness and health. Language also poses a potential hurdle in multilingual settings, where clinician and patient frequently do not speak the same first language. In such instances, it may be difficult for effective psychotherapeutic interventions to take place. For example, the psychotherapeutic interaction between clinician and patient would be detrimentally affected if an interpreter were present – the most obvious problem here being the loss (even if only perceived) of confidentiality, which is the ethical cornerstone of psychotherapy.

General strategies

There are limitations and obstacles to working psychotherapeutically with patients with neuropathology – even the most pro-psychotherapy of clinicians recognise this. One cannot get away from the fact that many patients with neuropathology have neurocognitive impairments and behavioural difficulties that seem to contraindicate psychotherapeutic work. For example, one may question if psychotherapy would be beneficial for patients with very severe memory or language impairment. Another obstacle to psychotherapeutic interventions in this population is encountered when working with patients who lack insight and/or self-awareness. There is also the situation that occurs where clinicians who are available to conduct psychotherapy are not trained neuropsychologists and therefore lack knowledge regarding neurocognitive syndromes and presentations. Interestingly, though, psychotherapy may also provide one of the very few clinical strategies that one can use to engage with these more complex patients. Judd and Wilson (2005) provide an overview of some of the difficulties encountered when working psychotherapeutically with this population; see 'Selected further reading' at the end of this chapter.

Despite these not insignificant barriers, psychologists do provide psychological therapy to some patients with brain injury. This often requires some fairly straightforward practical adaptations to be made to the psychologist's practice, some of which compensate for the potential effects related to cognitive impairment. For example, some adaptations include: overcoming memory problems by providing session summaries; counteracting problems with attention by providing shorter sessions; providing fewer and more concise in-session responses; and ensuring an especially quiet clinic environment, free of potentially distracting noise. Coetzer (2010, 2013b) provides further, more detailed information regarding such adaptations; see 'Selected further reading' at the end of this chapter. Table 12.1 provides a brief overview of some common adaptations to psychotherapeutic practice when working with patients with neurocognitive impairments.

TABLE 12.1 Practical general adaptations to psychological interventions in acquired brain injury

Adaptation	Provided by	Consider for
Clinical time provided	Reducing or increasing patient's consultation time; providing short breaks during consultations	Patients presenting with: poor sustained attention; fatigability (reduce time); slowness; poor comprehension; memory problems (increase time)
	Reducing or increasing frequency of consultations; clinician availability	Increasing the chances for therapeutic progress and the generalisation of gains (less frequent); during relapse (more frequent)
Service delivery model	Prioritising long-term follow-up over a short episode of care; not discharging patients, instead providing a self-referral option	For helping with longer-term psychological adjustment to brain injury; relapse prevention; facilitating long-term independence and ability to self-manage potential relapses
Environment where patient is seen	Limiting potential for environmental noise and distractions; decluttering the room; displaying simple signage; providing clear directions/maps to hospital/clinic	Patients who may have poor information processing, or are distractible; reducing the potential for agitation, aggression and non-attendance
Provision of memory aids	Audio recordings; written summaries of sessions; use of diaries; a 'rehab file', which can be referred back to	Patients with severe memory impairment; patients with no social support (including those who live alone)
Engagement with rehabilitation and therapy process	The therapeutic relationship; providing advocacy; the language that therapy is provided in; ease of contact; mobile phone text reminders of appointments to prevent non-attendance; an understanding and sensitivity to cultural factors	Cultural factors; where is there a risk of not participating in rehabilitation; when there is the risk of loss to follow-up
Generalisation strategies	Behavioural experiments to implement and experientially practise therapeutic gains within the patient's home environment; using relatives to help remind about and monitor rehabilitation 'homework' assignments; offering patient self-help groups; voluntary-sector community support groups	Patients with apathy and lack of initiation; patients who are depressed and/or socially isolated

Apathy and *aggression* are frequently encountered. Some psychologists find it difficult to deal with the lengthy silences and lack of participation that are commonly associated with apathy. Indeed, it is probably fairly common for inexperienced psychotherapists to become nervous and to talk more themselves when faced with long silences from patients – a potentially less effective strategy when working with patients with brain injuries! This should be avoided, and counteracted by therapists limiting their responses, while at the same time trying to engage with patients by, for example, questioning them (but leaving them ample time to respond), rather than falling into the trap of asking yet more questions when a response is not forthcoming.

Managing aggressive behaviour in psychotherapy is a daunting task and it would be fair to say that most clinicians find this a fairly difficult obstacle to overcome. It can be a helpful strategy to 'listen patients through' carefully and thoroughly, without interrupting, and only then attempting to identify what they are actually trying to communicate. For example, aggressive behaviour may sometimes represent feelings of frustration, caused by the loss of independence and/or by cognitive impairments, and so forth, or due to the pain and confusion related to loss of identity, lifestyle or role, to name but a few. Physical pain is often a trigger for aggressive behaviour.

Aggression may also serve a function: for example, for drawing attention to a problem that nobody has taken seriously. Alternatively, aggression may represent an exaggeration of premorbid patterns. Try not to convince patients that their behaviour is unhelpful, especially in the heat of the moment. Trying to reason with patients who are agitated will more often than not unintentionally provide 'grist to the mill'. Avoid responding to patients who are in the midst of a spell of heightened emotion. Instead, wait for a calmer window of opportunity to help patients to understand that the observed behaviour represents symptomatology rather than their character. During calmer spells, use reflection on the psychotherapeutic process to try to get patients to engage in conceptualising how others might experience their behaviours, or for them to consider what the effects of their behaviour might be. In the final analysis, when working with aggressive patients it is always important to ensure clinicians' safety. If there is any doubt, leave the situation, inconspicuously, while maintaining a serene facade if at all possible!

Cognitive behavioural therapy

Cognitive behavioural therapy (*CBT*) is potentially well suited to helping manage some of the emotional difficulties experienced by patients with acquired brain injury. For example, Kahn-Bourne and Brown (2003) propose that CBT can be useful in the treatment of depression in patients with traumatic brain injury. They postulate that therapy should: (1) be client-centred; (2) clearly delineate the presenting problems; (3) identify the impact on functioning and activating situations; (4) consider pre-injury factors; and (5) identify the patient's appraisal of the brain injury. Furthermore, the authors reason that CBT should be adapted for patients with brain injuries by using a number of techniques, including: memory aids; shortened consultations; increased frequency of consultations; the involvement of relatives or friends to assist with homework assignments (such as behavioural activation); and, finally, the use of summarising as a strategy to keep patients focused during consultations. These authors point out the relationship between self-awareness and depression, and emphasise the importance of addressing this issue as part of a CBT approach (Kahn-Bourne & Brown, 2003).

CBT can potentially lend itself well to psychotherapeutic work with patients with neuropathology because of the structure it provides. This may be helpful for patients with executive dysfunction, including those with general problem-solving or organisational abilities. It may also be easier to compensate for memory difficulties when using CBT: for example, by doubling up homework assignments to function as additional memory aids. Indeed, experience in clinical practice seems to indicate that exercise sheets, diaries and reading assignments can all be quite effective in counteracting memory impairment. Furthermore, behavioural experiments and homework assignments may be particularly useful for counteracting apathy and lack of initiative. Finally, CBT is an attractive option in under-resourced systems because of its perceived cost-effectiveness and its potential for knowledge and skills transfer to community workers – through the use of manuals for therapy delivery, for example.

There are also limitations to the usefulness of CBT. Some of the likely beliefs encountered following brain injury may be difficult to address with CBT: for example, brain injury represents a catastrophic event for most patients. As such, these beliefs or schemata may, to some extent, reflect reality for the patient. Under these circumstances it can be difficult (and possibly not always productive) to try to change patients' views about their neurological conditions. Other psychotherapies, such as *Acceptance and Commitment Therapy (ACT)*, may be important alternatives to consider in such circumstances; for example, see the Kangas and McDonald (2011) reference in 'Selected further reading' at the end of this chapter. More generally, CBT has been criticised for failing to explicitly address the emotional consequences of patients' difficulties. While it provides fairly effective strategies for reappraising patients' views of their disabilities, it may not be the most effective psychotherapy for helping them to come to terms emotionally with the losses and changes that result from brain injury.

Psychotherapies that address grief and loss

Several general psychotherapeutic and counselling approaches may help patients to work through the potentially numerous losses associated with brain injury. Counselling, along with other *humanistic* approaches, can be helpful in assisting patients to: (1) gain a better understanding of their brain injury; (2) express emotions related to loss and grief; and (3) work towards adjusting to life post-injury. The therapeutic relationship is key to many counselling approaches, and may be particularly suited to manage adjustment problems secondary to brain injury. Counselling is a resource that is possibly more widely available within the community, and may increase access to psychological therapy for some brain-injured patients who live in remote or under-resourced areas. A potential contribution that neuropsychologists may be able to make in order to provide counselling is through the provision of supervision, which can, for example, be provided either directly or through tele-medicine technologies (video links) and freely available technologies.

When psychologists work directly to provide counselling to patients who present with emotional difficulties related to loss, the following considerations might be useful. First, never assume that all patients will experience emotional maladjustment, grief or mourning following brain injury, or that they will go through the 'normal' stages of mourning. Some people do not go through a mourning process. In some cases, this may be (at least partially) due to the result of impaired self-awareness, or related to premorbid personality characteristics, such as stoicism or reticence. It is important to bear in mind that culture can also significantly colour patients' presentations and vary how they view and interact with their disability. In some cultures, 'keeping a stiff upper lip' is the norm, while in others wailing is common in the face of adversity. For patients who appear to experience loss, approaches that incorporate clinical skills and personal clinician variables (such as empathy, the ability to listen, compassion and containment) may prove beneficial. These skills generally prove useful in guiding patients towards expressing their emotions and helping them to better understand their current circumstances within the context of their losses. These are also generic skills that can provide opportunities for the training of community workers who work in remote areas.

Neuropsychoanalysis

Neuropsychoanalysis is an emergent field that can offer further, unique techniques for the rehabilitation of some patients with cognitive impairment. The goal of neuropsychoanalysis is to link the understanding of biological brain functions with a person's psychological functions and behaviour (the psychoanalytically understood concepts) to better understand how the brain (the human being) functions – known as the clinico-anatomical method. In other words, the aim is to study patients' deficits simultaneously from both a neuroscientific and psychoanalytic perspective, drawing on the terminology of both disciplines to best understand what is observed (Solms & Turnbull, 2002). Neuropsychoanalysis offers a different observational perspective from the other psychotherapies.

The challenge for neuropsychoanalysis is to bridge the divide – readily enforced in the neuroscientific community – between the organic (neuronal) aspects of the brain, which can be empirically studied, and the psychological mind of the person, which is the subjective experience. It is by looking at the individual from both these perspectives that one is able to see where the benefits for this type of approach lie. The key is to discern patterns between lesions in the brain and the mental functions, many of which are of interest to psychoanalysts (Solms & Turnbull, 2002). Once these connections are made, patients' deficits can be closely studied and treated. Some deficits are a direct result of the organic brain lesion, while others are part of the patient's reaction to his/her lesion, and can hence possibly be treated through psychoanalytic therapy.

Mindfulness

Recently, the 'third wave' cognitive behaviour therapies have become increasingly popular. While the evidence base is not yet particularly robust, the number of clinicians who report using at least some aspects of these therapies in their work appears to be increasing. Interesting work is now starting to emerge. For example, Aniskiewicz (2007) proposed a mindfulness approach to the management of depression in patients with neurological conditions. The author suggests that psychotherapy should aim to reduce suffering and promote an active engagement with life through the active pursuit of personal goals. This approach resembles aspects of *behavioural activation*, a technique that could be ideal for managing problems related to apathy and lack of motivation. Behavioural activation is also central to CBT. Aniskiewicz (2007) emphasizes the need to help patients during the psychotherapeutic process to accept life as it is following brain injury in order to overcome the emotional difficulties experienced in response to the loss of their pre-injury life. Finally, *mindfulness meditation* can help patients to live life in the moment, facilitating their engagement with life as it is now, while potentially counteracting the emotional distress associated with a focus on one's disability (Aniskiewicz, 2007).

Some meditation techniques may be useful in neurological patients who present with significant anxiety. Becoming more focused on the present moment, and learning to orientate towards an increased awareness of perception and cognition, may increase patients' understandings of the nature of bodily sensations, thoughts and feelings. This skill may help patients to limit the impact of, or prevent rumination and possible fixation on, some of the physical disabilities they experience. These approaches may also have the potential to equip patients with a useful tool for managing everyday anxiety. Again, strategies used to compensate for possible memory difficulties should always be included. Some exercises may be given in printed format for patients to practise at home. Similarly, CDs containing experiential exercises can be provided as a reminder of the work covered during a session, while doubling as homework assignments. Dairies used for documenting and reflecting on experiences during exercises also serve as helpful memory aids, while ensuring the generalisation of meditation techniques beyond the consultation room. These are low-cost strategies for increasing the potential for the dissemination of psychological self-management skills. While meditation may be useful for some patients, this is not an approach that will be suitable for all. Careful assessment should, as always, guide the choice of psychological therapy offered to patients.

A general overview

A general overview of the psychotherapeutic processes used with patients with neuropathology may help the reader to form a more pragmatic understanding of some of the relevant issues. There appears to be considerably more overlap between the general components or stages of the different psychological therapies than has been conventionally thought. There is possibly more similarity between the different psychotherapies, especially with regard to what may account for therapeutic change, than is generally acknowledged. For example, the *therapeutic relationship* is of universal importance to all psychotherapeutic endeavours, not only counselling approaches. While clearly some-what of an over-generalisation and over-simplification, several psychotherapies used with patients with neuropathology tend to start off by assessing patients' subjectively reported difficulties, along with their general expectations of psychotherapy.

In many cases, therapists may also provide general information about psycho-therapy and 'how it might work'. The provision of information regarding the patient's pathology is fairly universal. The emotions associated with the experience of impairments and corresponding disabilities are also explored. Some therapies provide skills (such as CBT) to manage some of the difficult emotions (or thoughts), others emphasise finding meaning (psychodynamic), while some focus on provid-ing strategies for living in the present (mindfulness approaches). The unifying theme is the pursuit of the resolution of emotional distress, along with the nurturing of the skills required to achieve this often-elusive goal.

In summary, the following stages may constitute the overall psychotherapeutic process:

- assessment of the clinical presentation and presenting problems;
- feedback from the initial findings, and the options for rehabilitation;
- provision of information regarding psychotherapy; ascertaining the patient's preference for psychotherapy and his/her willingness to engage in it;
- defining the psychotherapeutic goals with the patient using a collaborative approach;
- clarifying practicalities, such as the frequency and duration of sessions, and when reviews of progress will take place;
- provision of information regarding brain pathologies;
- exploration of emotions;
- working towards skills that will help the patient to manage troublesome emo-tions, behaviour and thoughts;
- regular review of progress and the achievement of goals.

While it is clear that this outline will not necessarily represent the stages of psycho-logical therapy in many situations, it is still a useful framework for clinicians to keep in mind when starting off in this area. This outline does not by any means represent all of the complexities and nuances involved in the overall psychological manage-ment of patients (such as systemic interventions that also include work with fam-ilies). The following case study (an amalgam of clinical cases) further illuminates some of concepts discussed thus far.

Case illustration

Frances was in her second year at university studying fine art, when she was injured in a road traffic accident. She was a mature student, aged 42. After having been a secretary at a legal firm for many years, she decided to study 'community development', as she had a long-standing desire to work in the community and make a 'meaningful contribution to the wellbeing' of the local rural population. Frances was a passenger in a car that was struck from the side by a car jumping a red light. She was on the side opposite the impact, but sustained a traumatic brain injury (but no orthopaedic injuries). This was evidenced by a Glasgow Coma Scale (GCS) score of 7/15 on admission to hospital, with loss of consciousness for five days and post-traumatic amnesia for approximately two weeks after the incident and approximately three minutes prior to it. A CT brain scan revealed bilateral frontal contusions, and contusion of the anterior pole of the left temporal lobe. Frances's doctor referred her for a psychological assessment one year after the accident.

Upon initial assessment, Frances was found to be well presented, friendly and cooperative. She was slightly impulsive at times, and appeared somewhat slow, possibly related to difficulties of information processing. Frances described herself as being 'in a constant state of befuddlement'. She said she struggled to make sense of things and that her main goal for therapy was to work specifically on this. Formal neuropsychological testing revealed that Frances had superior general intellectual ability, excellent language skills, good constructional abilities, but some memory impairment (on delayed recall). In contrast, her recall of line sketches was above average. Frances showed signs of executive dysfunction, with difficulty with set shifting, problem solving and planning. During a follow-up session Frances was asked, in a role-reversal exercise, to provide the psychologist with the feedback that she was expecting. In doing so, Frances showed some awareness of her cognitive difficulties, but did not provide an effective 'translation' of where these impairments came from or how they were affecting her everyday life.

The next stage of Frances's care was fairly didactic, with the psychologist taking the lead during the sessions. The aim was to provide Frances with as much information as needed regarding traumatic brain injury and its consequences. The use of the phrase 'as much information as needed' is used in a particular context here: Frances was not given a huge amount of information to start off with, to prevent cognitive overload, and was instead gradually provided with information that she could assimilate in small chunks. More importantly, information was provided in this fashion to prevent her from becoming emotionally overwhelmed. Metaphorically speaking, Frances proceeded through a journey of discovery in a new country, first learning the main geography and cities, before starting to fit everything together in an attempt to obtain an understanding beyond that of a tourist's perspective – a resident's perspective, if you like. This metaphor resonated with Frances, and after a few sessions she spontaneously developed the metaphor further by reporting that her goal for the treatment had evolved to one of trying to discover how to become a citizen of this new country. She also explained that while it was an uncertain journey, she felt as though she had to do it, as her pining to live in her 'country of origin' was extremely painful.

During the next stage, which lasted several sessions spread over six months, Frances explored this 'country of origin' metaphor. It became clearer over time that this seemed to represent core aspects of her personality and identity that pre-dated her accident. Some of the most painful losses for her included: her own view of herself having changed from that of ability, potential and opportunity to that of disability (she was unable to return to college); the loss of her self-esteem (she thought she was not good enough to make a meaningful contribution to society); and the stagnation that she experienced (she could not see her life ever becoming purposeful again). During this stage, the psychologist was much less didactic and instead facilitated the process of defining and expressing the emotions that Frances had become aware of during the course of psychotherapy. These emotions included anger (directed at the driver), grief ('My life has been lost') and confusion ('Who on earth have I become?'). Some of these emotions were expressed intensely, revealing the depth of the grief that she was suffering. The uncertainty and perplexity that she experienced in relating to herself provided the clinical 'signpost' for the next stage of the therapeutic process.

During the following stage of psychotherapy, much time was spent exploring how Frances's life had changed, how she was now living and how she was trying to make sense of her brain injury. This took place on many levels: for example, at a philosophical level ('Why did this ever happen to me?'), at a religious level ('Why was this allowed to happen to me? I have been a good person my whole life') and at an existential level ('What will become of me?'). During this stage, experiential techniques and strategies were employed to help Frances to form a new sense of who she now was (her identity), and help her to identify what the meaning and purpose of her life were, incorporating her accident as a life event. She reported during this stage that she still felt 'befuddled' when attempting to make sense of things, and that she had started to write things down to try to help. Frances's writing project progressed to the point where she started to write her life story, but she found the later chapters (the post-accident period) quite anxiety provoking.

Conclusion

To some patients with neuropathology, the addition of psychotherapy to their overall rehabilitation plan can make an important difference (despite this not being the rehabilitation approach of choice for all). Psychotherapy may be especially relevant for the management of the more chronic emotional difficulties that can hamper some patients' adjustment, often many years after brain injury. In fact, for such patients, there is sometimes very little on offer other than psychological therapy for their further rehabilitation and care. There are of course several caveats to this assertion, including awareness on the part of psychologists of the potential problems associated with the severe cognitive impairment and poor insight that can result from brain injury. Hence, there should be strategies in place to compensate for some of the cognitive impairments that can negatively affect patients' ability to derive benefit from psychological therapy, along with some work to address poor insight and understanding. Finally, strategies to ensure opportunities for the generalisation of therapeutic gains beyond the clinic environment are key to the success of psychotherapy in this clinical population.

Practical tips

1. Do not hesitate to provide written session summaries for patients – recollections of what was covered during psychotherapy sessions may be very different without the aid of summaries.
2. Always remind yourself that not everyone with brain injury will benefit from psychotherapy, and do not be afraid to point this out when you receive an inappropriate referral.
3. Consider the possibility that 'less may be more' when providing 'talking therapies' for patients who have information-processing difficulties.
4. It is possible that simple skills, such as effective listening, refraining from providing complex explanations or interventions and being compassionate may be much more important than perhaps previously thought.

Points for reflective practice

1. Brain injury often results in permanent impairment and associated disability. Is psychotherapy not powerless to overcome this reality?
2. Describe and discuss the adaptations that may be needed in order to conduct more effective psychotherapeutic interventions with brain-injured patients.
3. What are the potential strengths and weaknesses of cognitive behavioural therapy (CBT) when used with patients with neuropathology?

Selected further reading

Block, C. K., & West, S. E. (2013). Psychotherapeutic treatment of survivors of traumatic brain injury: Review of the literature and special considerations. *Brain Injury, 27,* 775–788.

Coetzer, R. (2010). *Anxiety and mood disorders following traumatic brain injury: Clinical assessment and psychotherapy.* London: Karnac Books.

Coetzer, R. (2013a). Psychotherapy after acquired brain injury: Is less more? *Rev. Chil. Neuropsicol, 8,* 36–41.

Judd, D., & Wilson, S. L. (2005). Psychotherapy with brain injury survivors: An investigation of the challenges encountered by clinicians and their modifications to therapeutic practice. *Brain Injury, 19,* 437–449.

Kangas, M., & McDonald, S. (2011). Is it time to act? The potential of acceptance and commitment therapy for psychological problems following acquired brain injury. *Neuropsychological Rehabilitation, 21,* 250–276.

13

RECORD KEEPING

Introduction

Although clinical *record keeping* is very much part of our professional practice (see Chapter 15), it is such a routine activity for most psychologists that it is dealt with here in its own right. Clinical records have various functions, of which only a few are listed here. Notes document the important epochs in a patient's care, while at the same time serving as an aide-memoire for the psychologist. Notes allow psychologists to communicate with colleagues who are also involved in patients' care – and help to facilitate our evolving diagnostic formulations. Writing clinical notes requires considerable skill – it is definitely a skill to be able to capture your clinical observations in writing. Part of this skill is not only to hone one's clinical observations in writing, but also to develop the ability to distinguish between what is objective and what is subjective during consultations.

A corollary to good record keeping is that it may also be the practitioner's (only) 'insurance policy' when s/he is asked at a later stage (often many years later) to comment on the assessment or rehabilitation of a patient who was previously seen. Patients may change in terms of their presentations and this is important to acknowledge when reading over previous notes – notes represent what happened on a particular occasion, which may be different from what was observed during subsequent visits. It can be anxiety provoking if one's notes are unexpectedly subjected to scrutiny. It is therefore invaluable to write clinical notes meticulously, focusing as much as possible on what was objectively observed, while using neutral, non-judgemental language throughout. If time permits, always read over your notes once they have been completed to check for errors and to see whether what has been written will make sense to colleagues involved in the patient's care.

Since 2009, the Health Professions Council (currently the Health and Care Professions Council, HCPC) has regulated psychologists in the United Kingdom. The

HCPC has published *Standards of Conduct*, some of which pertain to clinical record keeping. The HCPC standards make it clear that psychologists should always keep records of all patients they have assessed/treated. Furthermore, it is specified that notes must be made promptly, be legible and be signed and dated. Notes must always be protected against being lost and being accessed by unauthorised individuals, and should never under any circumstances be tampered with. These standards are very similar to the professional guidelines and requirements for record keeping in psychology in many other countries. Indeed, these requirements almost certainly mirror those of most other healthcare professions too, irrespective of country.

In South Africa, for example, the Health Professions Council of South Africa (HPCSA) – of which the Professional Board for Psychology that regulates the clinical practice of psychologists is a part – has published rules and guidelines entitled *Guidelines for Good Practice in the Health Care Professions*, including *Guidelines on the Keeping of Patient Records*. These guidelines cover, among others, instructions on: *What constitutes a health record*; *Compulsory keeping of records*; *Accountability*; *Certificates and reports*; *Altering of records*; and *Access to records*.

Besides formal rules and policies, there are other 'rules of thumb' passed down by generations of supervisors in psychology, most of which would be seen as common sense, but which remain invaluable nonetheless. This is relevant to newly qualified psychologists, for whom some of the following advice is frequently given: (1) always write notes in such a way that you would be happy for patients to read them; (2) if it is not written down, it was not done; (3) more is not always better; (4) stick to facts and steer clear of opinions; and (5) never write derogatory statements about patients or colleagues. These are fairly general points. Are there any more specific rules, guidelines and policies on clinical note writing in the field of neuropsychology?

Writing notes in neuropsychology

Unfortunately, while there is fairly extensive guidance on record keeping in clinical psychology, provided by the various professional organisations in different countries (for example, the American Psychological Association, the British Psychological Society and the HCPC), there is much less pertaining specifically to clinical neuropsychology. In fact, very few training programmes in psychology are likely to provide direct and substantial teaching on this important aspect of professional practice. Generally speaking, note writing is seen as a skill that is picked up during clinical practice, initially while in a training position, and perhaps subsequently as a function of doing case reviews during supervision. A reality of professional life is that newly qualified practitioners are increasingly exposed to requests for reports (or indeed complete clinical files), typically from a law firm or other external organisation. These requests frequently relate to patients' claims for compensation, or to matters pertaining to social or welfare services following brain injury. However, they sometimes relate to criminal proceedings or other matters, where it may be important to consider the fact that the patient has a history of brain injury and has had contact with rehabilitation or diagnostic services. Whatever the reason, one thing is certain: these requests focus our minds on how we write clinical notes!

While many colleagues may beg to differ, the practice of clinical neuropsychology is arguably the most structured of the applied psychologies. It is possible that the central role played by formal neuropsychological testing/assessment has something to do with this perception. Clinical neuropsychology appears to lend itself more to structure, diagnostics, objectivity and the application of algorithms than most of the other specialities within psychology. Some people reason that this is the case because neuropsychology is very much rooted within the brain and behavioural science. Accordingly, should our writing of notes not then reflect this 'objectivity' gained from having a robust 'scientific basis'? Unfortunately, this ideal is not universally applied, and there is huge variation in note-writing technique and style among practitioners. Much of this variation may be explained by differences in pre-qualification training curricula, or the amount of practice with note writing during placements or internships. Perhaps this is not entirely surprising if one considers that only very limited guidance has been published relating specifically to the issues surrounding record keeping in clinical neuropsychology.

Harel, Steinberg and Snyder (2006) provide one of the very few sources of information pertaining to note writing in clinical neuropsychology. The following are some of the authors' points. Clinical notes should always be signed and dated. The reason for seeing the patient should always be stated. Notes should be contemporaneous and written as soon as possible after the patient has been seen. Always document a refusal on the patient's part to be seen and, conversely, an agreement to be seen, or an agreement to take part in an intervention or assessment. Assess risk, especially with regard to self-harm, and document your findings. Write down the findings from cognitive assessments. Document the findings from the mental status examination, including notes reporting the patient's mood and affect. Never make substantial changes to previously written notes. Ensure that the confidentially of notes is maintained (Harel et al., 2006). In addition to these guidelines, it is important to make two further points. First, notes should report the assessment's findings, or the input and outcome during an intervention, rather than merely offering a purely 'journalistic' reflection of what the patient said. Second, notes should be clear enough to make it possible for someone else to pick up your work in your absence.

General points

A few additional general points relating to writing clinical notes are highlighted here. This is by no means an exhaustive list, but merely a starting point for learning about the practical issues surrounding this important professional activity. As mentioned previously, clinical notes should ideally be written as soon as possible in order to ensure that they are contemporaneous. Some psychologists prefer to write notes during sessions. This has a few advantages, including that it overcomes the inevitable problems of variable recall and interference that occur if notes are written at the end of the session or, worse, at the end of the day. Another potential benefit, especially in brain-injury rehabilitation settings, is that the notes can then be shared with patients 'in the moment', thereby serving as a memory aid, while at the same time keeping them fully informed regarding the content of their clinical records. A downside to this technique is that writing notes during sessions can be distracting, and can potentially convey the message to the patient that you are uninterested.

Always write notes clearly and legibly, try to keep them concise and always sign and print your name and your profession and/or qualifications (preferably using an ink stamp for the latter). Always: date (and where relevant record the time) all entries in the clinical record; indicate who was present at the consultation, especially if relatives or other professionals attended; document when consent was obtained from the patient and, most importantly, specify what the consent was for. Always record when clinical risk was assessed, what the findings were and what actions were taken. With regard to the last point, this is one of the many situations where a printed risk assessment form can be completed and filed in the patient's clinical notes or folder. Pre-printed documentation is increasingly being used to facilitate documentation that adheres to professional standards. Furthermore, in the future, computer-based note making and record keeping is likely to further decrease, or even eliminate, the use of handwritten clinical records. However, the same principles that pertain to the maintenance of confidentiality, for example, still apply, irrespective of whether a paper or digital record is kept, while others such as the legibility of handwriting do not apply.

With regard to general writing style, a useful rule of thumb is to make your clinical notes in such a manner that you would be happy for your patients to read them. To achieve this, the following advice helps. Avoid jargon or technical terms that contribute very little to actually explaining the clinical phenomena being reported. Only use abbreviations that are recognisable to most people. Always be very clear as to what is objective and what is subjective (narrative), making this distinction obvious in your notes. For example, a patient's narrative is subjective, while observations relating to his/her gait are objective. Refrain from writing down as fact reports about third parties that are unsubstantiated: for example, the quality (or lack of it) of treatment that the patient supposedly received from other clinicians.

Many patients with neurocognitive impairment are involved in legal processes at some point (such as insurance claims or court proceedings), which greatly increases the likelihood that your notes will be subpoenaed. Thus, always remember that clinical notes have an uncanny tendency to 'come back to haunt you'. Sod's Law would suggest that this is especially true under certain circumstances, for example when notes are: (1) written in haste; (2) written without careful formulation; (3) overly long and/or contain vast amounts of non-clinical, potentially irrelevant information.

The point has been made a few times already that there is limited guidance available regarding note writing in clinical neuropsychology. One strategy to compensate for this lack of information is for psychologists to be more formal in assessing and reviewing how they document patient contact by systematically reviewing their adherence to existing local policies and procedures. This can help to determine the usefulness and quality of existing record keeping protocols and identify potentially helpful changes to practice. This type of structured approach to practice improvement is usually pursued as part of an *internal clinical audit* or through *practice improvement initiatives*. Below follows an example of such an initiative, along with its outcomes.

An example of a clinical audit

An in-service clinical audit can be helpful where there are potential gaps in defining more explicitly what the content of clinical notes should include, as well as when considering whether this is a skill that can be addressed with practice-based learning approaches (Coetzer, 2009). For example, the following standards for follow-up clinical notes in neuropsychology were identified through a clinical audit (Coetzer, 2009):

1. Clinical notes should clearly state where and when the patient was seen and who was present.
2. Document the patient's subjective report of any changes since s/he was last seen, including progress made and any obstacles encountered.
3. Specify the purpose of the consultation: for example, follow-up psychotherapy, cognitive rehabilitation, clinical review or feedback on the results of neuro-psychological testing.
4. Document the main points pertaining to any intervention provided (for example, work on memory strategies as part of cognitive rehabilitation) so that it is possible to review these strategies during the next session.
5. The important areas of the mental status examination (including the bedside cognitive assessment) should always be reviewed and the findings documented, including if there are no changes.
6. When documenting the findings from the mental status examination, make it clear in the notes what is subjective, as opposed to what is objective. The mental status examination sometimes also functions as the clinical risk assessment, or at least part thereof.
7. Note all the tests used, all the outcome measures and the questionnaires administered, along with all the scores obtained.
8. The clinical notes should conclude with a management plan. For example, when/if the patient will be next seen, and for what purpose; whether there are other things that need arranging (such as a referral to neurology, or arranging a visit to work); or if repeat testing is planned.

These eight in-service standards for clinical neuropsychological notes were subsequently audited, and then training was provided before a re-audit took place.

The following hypothetical case vignette provides an example of what clinical notes in neuropsychology would look like in practice when loosely conforming to the above-mentioned guidelines.

30–11–2010: Follow-up @ outpatients, for cog rehab & review.

Mr J attended on his own.

Reviewed previous psychotherapy session notes with Mr J.

Current difficulties: Mr J reported that he had been managing a bit better since he was last seen 2 weeks ago. Reported finding the strategies we discussed useful. In particular, keeping a notebook by the phone as well as using the diary function on his mobile phone. Mr J reported that this had reduced his anxiety about missing appointments. We reviewed these memory compensatory strategies again. I provided general information about traumatic brain injury & potential long-term outcome. Emphasised that outcome is impossible to predict with complete accuracy.

Discussed goals:
1. To discuss with employer a graded return to work, starting with mornings only
2. Mr J to contact DVLA about returning to driving

Clinical presentation:
R-handed
Neat, friendly and cooperative
Orientated for Time, Place & Person
Walks with a limp, uses a stick
Slight ataxia R arm
Attention and concentration: distractible
Speech: subtle word finding difficulties noted
Difficulties with ST memory
Executive function: modestly impulsive at times
Mood: objective observation: not depressed. Reported no thoughts or plans to harm self or others. Retains a good sense of future. Enjoys some activities. Appropriate expression of affect. Subjective: 'I feel fine. Life is OK at the moment'.
Anxiety: mild. Reported some somatic symptoms of anxiety, e.g. palpitations
Sleep: mild initial insomnia, no terminal insomnia
Appetite: constant, 'good'
Weight: possibly reduced
Energy: reduced, feels tired a lot of the time, fatigues easily
Thought processes & perceptual functions: Normal

Plan:
1. Follow-up in 2 weeks or as requested to review clinically and continue cognitive rehabilitation
2. Update General Practitioner with short report
3. Contact employer – patient consented to this
4. Consider referral to Occupational Therapist

Signed
[Clinical Neuropsychologist]

An example of clinical notes

There are a few points to consider regarding this example. First, there are essentially four generic components: (1) the patient report-back or narrative; (2) a description of the main points pertaining to the intervention; (3) a review of the patient's mental status and cognition; and (4) a plan of action. In essence, it is the last component that would enable a colleague to provide a review and follow-up if the treating psychologist is unavailable. Second, the risk assessment is contained in the mental status examination in this example, but may well, at other times, be much more comprehensive. Third, the patient's consent is documented. Despite abbreviations being used, these should ideally be avoided or limited to those where there is no ambiguity regarding their meaning. Many of these points also apply to other areas of clinical documentation, a couple of examples of which are briefly discussed below.

Report writing

Reports on neuropsychological testing do not have to be excessively voluminous. On the contrary, there are many good reasons for traditionally longer reports to be edited down and made more concise. This can help to avoid reports becoming nebulous, while making them more useful for patients and other readers. Another consideration is of course cost. In areas where resources, and particularly neuropsychology, are limited, writing very long, detailed reports reduces the time available for direct patient contact. This can result in the limited time that does exist for neuropsychology being used to provide a comprehensive service to only a very few patients, with many then missing out on the opportunity to be assessed – an unrealistically long waiting list soon develops. Report writing is also influenced by culture and language. In multilingual environments, reports may have to be translated in order to be useful to patients, especially if used for feedback on neuropsychological testing. For example, without a report written in the patient's first/home language, s/he cannot use a copy of the report to refer back to when results and compensatory strategies have been forgotten.

There are various types of report written by neuropsychologists, including: reports conveying the results and interpretation of neuropsychological testing; those outlining the findings from an initial clinical assessment to a referring party; and short reports that provide periodic updates for a patient's general practitioner. There are also other types of report, including, for example, those written when neuropsychologists make referrals to other colleagues, and those written for medico-legal purposes or as letters to advocates on the behalf of patients (for example, reports addressed to social or welfare departments). Whatever the purpose of a report, a few suggestions may be helpful to consider. As previously mentioned, always write reports in such a way that you are happy for patients to read them. Always define your target audience. This will determine the report's length and style, the use of technical terms and which content should be prioritised for inclusion. For example, a report about neuropsychological test results, intended for another neuropsychologist, would most likely differ from one being sent to a general practitioner.

The value of summaries at the end of reports cannot be overstated (especially for those who take over the management of patients after you). However, summaries should not simply be a repetition of what has been documented elsewhere in the report. In order to be useful, summaries should focus on outlining only the most important findings or observations, while containing recommendations or plans of action, along with a formulation. Most psychologists struggle with this part of a report. Aim to write a formulation that explains the findings that have been briefly summarised and which covers potential psychological, social and biological factors. Use the combined summary of the findings and the short formulation to inform the recommendations and the plan of action. If these three aspects of the summary component of the report 'communicate' or flow logically, the report will be more clinically useful. A well-written report, especially one outlining neuropsychology test results, may have additional benefits and functionality: summaries are often invaluable to patients with memory problems, who may wish to have a short record that they can refer to later.

Patient summaries

In addition to copies of neuropsychological test reports, some patients also request *summaries of clinical sessions*. These summaries are most often seen as a memory aid, and can also be useful for: (1) maintaining a focus on the themes covered in psychotherapy; (2) helping to facilitate a sense of continuity; and (3) preventing any misunderstanding between psychologist and patient. Again, there are different styles for doing summaries, including, for example, a letter format, or simply a page with a list of points that were covered and an outline of any actions to be followed up. Irrespective of style, summaries should ideally: contain no overly long sentences; avoid technical jargon or terms that can be misinterpreted; and be one page long (or no more than *two pages*). Where possible, try to incorporate a reminder of any homework assignments – for example, as might be the case where a patient is seen for cognitive behavioural therapy and behavioural experiments were agreed upon. Always review the previous summary with patients when they attend follow-up appointments, and invite feedback or questions in order to facilitate understanding and maintain focus on the rehabilitation goals.

Other documentation

Certain documents used in healthcare environments lend themselves particularly well to the use of printed, standardised formats. This is usually the case where the intervention or assessment provided to the majority of patients varies little, or where a printed form might serve as a reminder to the practitioner to perform an important task. With regard to the latter, assessment of clinical risk is a good example of where standardised formats can function as reminders, and serve to homogenise practitioners' approaches to certain crucial duties. Forms may also be useful in providing a framework for interns or trainees, facilitating learning by helping to capture important clinical information within a predetermined format. Examples of these documents include: standardised summaries of psychometric results; referral pro formas; consent forms; bedside cognitive assessment; a matrix for agreed rehabilitation goals; and longitudinal charting of scores on outcome measures.

The initial clinical assessment also lends itself, to some extent, to a standardised format, although many practitioners prefer a more flexible approach for documenting this clinical activity. Some brain-injury rehabilitation services use a standardised format to capture discharge summaries. In certain circumstances, such documents can help to clarify some of the components of a clinical pathway. Standardised, printed documentation used to augment written notes and reports may have the additional function of potentially increasing clinician uptake and adherence to other routine tasks, such as outcome measurement. Printed documents also lend themselves well to translation into other languages and can improve cost-effectiveness. Ultimately, though, there is likely to be a gradual transition from handwritten notes and individualised reports to standardised, printed documentation, and eventually fully (or almost) digitised healthcare records. The ever-increasing use of modern technology may have many benefits when it comes to simplifying the record keeping and correspondence associated with patient care.

Conclusion

Writing clinical notes is a constant, mandatory professional activity for all practitioners who work with patients. While seen by some as merely the administrative aspect of clinical practice, this is a complex activity that is much more integrated with patient care than meets the eye. Clinical record keeping and report writing do not lend themselves all that well to direct, didactic training, and should always be complemented with practice-based learning and supervision. This is essential in order to help newly qualified practitioners to avoid some of the pitfalls associated with performing these important tasks. In under-resourced healthcare environments, it is important to first consider carefully what the essential purposes of neuropsychological reports are, and then to develop skills to ensure optimum efficiency and reduce potentially unnecessary (or less essential) time being spent on activities that are not directly related to patients. The use of pre-printed templates and information technology may also be helpful strategies in such environments, ensuring adherence to minimum standards of care in a more cost-effective manner.

Practical tips

1. Always write/dictate reports as soon as possible after seeing patients.
2. Learn to do more than just 'listen and write' – observe patients, and then practise how to capture your objective observations in your clinical notes.
3. Perhaps the real skill is to write reports that will keep psychologists out of court. Write reports that provide enough relevant information to make it redundant for you to appear in court to provide evidence (this is of course different if the reason for writing the report in the first place is for medico-legal purposes).

Points for reflective practice

1. Why are psychologists expected to write notes?
2. List some of the functions of written reports in neuropsychology.
3. Devise your own pro forma to document the bedside mental status and cognitive examination.

Selected further reading

Harel, B. T., Steinberg, B. A., & Snyder, P. J. (2006). The medical chart: Efficient information-gathering strategies and proper chart noting. In P. J. Snyder, P. D. Nussbaum, & D. L. Robins (Eds.), *Clinical neuropsychology: A pocket handbook for assessment* (pp. 9–16). Washington, DC: American Psychological Association.

Health Professions Council of South Africa. (2008). *Guidelines for Good Practice in the Health Care Professions: Booklet 14 – Guidelines on the Keeping of Patient Records.* www.hpcsa.co.za/downloads/conduct_ethics/rules/generic_ethical_rules/booklet_14_keeping_of_patience_records.pdf.

PART III

Professional issues

14
ETHICS

Introduction

Ethical principles are guidelines that should be omnipresent in the background of all decisions that clinicians make. Metaphorically speaking, ethics provide the compass for professional practice, whereas professional codes of conduct are perhaps more akin to the actual bearings on the map. There are many universal moral principles that have influenced and determined the ethical principles of healthcare professionals. It should come as no surprise then that there is substantial similarity between the ethical principles and codes of conduct of many different countries. For example, some of the key elements or concepts underpinning ethical conduct in some of these professional codes include *autonomy*, *non-maleficence* and *truthfulness*. Most of the principles are of course more directly linked to the provision of clinical interventions for patients, but some relate to fitness to practise clinically – the obvious one being *competence*. However, some principles relate to areas other than the practitioner's skills and knowledge. One should ensure that one is mentally and physically fit to practise. For example, know when you need a holiday – and be aware of when the subtle signs of professional lassitude are creeping in.

This chapter draws primarily on the published models of ethical principles and codes of conduct from the United Kingdom, the United States (as examples from developed countries) and South Africa (representing an example from the developing world). Given that these ethical principles and codes of conduct are based on very similar values and principles, common to many other countries' codes, the emphasis is on more generic ethical considerations than the specifics of the relevant codes of practice. It is these broader ethical principles that should ideally guide decision-making in psychology. Furthermore, they should also serve to inspire practitioners to function at the highest professional level in order to benefit the public. Psychologists need to continually study developments within the field, always staying up to date with the specific rules contained in the relevant codes of conduct – which ethical principles ultimately translate into in practice.

General ethical principles

The American Psychological Association's *Ethical Principles of Psychologists and Code of Conduct* (2002) includes the following information. First, *beneficence* and *non-maleficence* essentially mean that practitioners should, in the first instance, do no harm, and then try to do good for those for whose care they are responsible. This principle pertains very clearly and transparently to the direct clinical interventions that psychologists provide. This is perhaps one of the most universal moral foundations on which healthcare is based, and serves to inform many of the daily decisions made about patient care. Second, *fidelity* and *responsibility* are also central. These terms essentially mean the forging of relationships of trust with those who psychologists work with. The third principle is *integrity*: psychologists should always be *truthful* and *accurate* – this pertains to both clinical and non-clinical activities (for example, research and management). The fourth principle *justice* is elaborated on below.

Besides the obvious informative power of the principle of *justice* for clinical practice, it also has more strategic relevance to models of service delivery. Justice refers to the encouragement of fairness and equal access for all people to the potential benefits psychology offers. In everyday clinical practice, justice means seeing all referrals, irrespective of the clinician's personal preference or academic interest. At a more strategic level, it is also about access to healthcare. This is indeed one of the foundations of publicly funded healthcare systems, such as the National Health Service in the United Kingdom and state-funded hospitals in many other countries, which are free at the point of service delivery. In practice, it is often the case that because of the vast amounts of money needed to provide a fully funded state healthcare system, patients may sadly not have access to everything that may be available in either a patient- or medical-aid-funded system.

The fifth ethical principle encapsulates the need to *respect people's dignity and their rights*. This includes an awareness and acknowledgement of the worth of patients and their potential for self-determination. All these ethical principles can be particularly relevant in settings where patients with neuropathology are seen in which a balance has to be found between protecting vulnerable individuals while at the same time facilitating their independence. Often the process of clinical reasoning and reflective practice helps psychologists and their colleagues to identify the best decisions for patients at a given time, under particular circumstances. One strategy that is always considered in order to try to ensure patients' potential for self-determination is to include them (as closely as possible) in discussions about their rehabilitation plans. Obviously, many factors need to be considered: for example, patients' level of self-awareness or insight, which may have a direct bearing on their ability to make sound decisions for themselves.

The British Psychological Society's *Code of Ethics and Conduct* (2009) embraces very similar values to those contained in the American Psychological Association's code. The fundamental philosophical approach can be described as the 'British eclectic tradition', which contains the moral principles that inform practitioners' decisions. Important functions of the 'code' are to protect the public and to promote professional standards of practice. This code is based on four principles: respect, competence, responsibility and integrity. Each principle is described in terms of a statement of values and then subsequently defined by means of a set of standards of conduct. These essentially represent the more specific professional rules for practising psychologists, based on the four underlying ethical principles.

The first ethical principle in the British code, respect, pertains to patients' right to self-determination, the valuing of their dignity and being mindful of potential power differentials between patients and psychologists. Clearly this is a very important ethical principle for psychologists who work with patients with neuropathology, as one must be sensitive towards the high incidence of associated disability in this population in order to avoid potential discrimination. The second principle is competence, which relates to professional knowledge and skills, including the knowledge of ethical principles. Responsibility means that psychologists should always avoid harming their patients, and also relates to avoiding tainting the profession through personal misconduct. Integrity refers to the need for psychologists to be truthful, accurate and fair in conducting professional activities – including both clinical and non-clinical activities (such as research conduct and interactions with colleagues).

From a developing world perspective, the 13 core values and standards of the South African code are outlined by the Health Professions Council of South Africa (HPCSA) in their Core Ethical Values and Standards for Good Practice (2008), part of their Guidelines for Good Practice in the Health Care Professions. Again, many of these values and standards are similar to those of the United Kingdom and the United States. The first of these is respect for persons, communicating the fact that practitioners should respect patients as human beings, while acknowledging their dignity, worth and value. The second ethical value, best interests or well-being (non-maleficence), refers to the assertion that practitioners 'should not harm or act against the best interests of patients, even when the interests of the latter conflict with their own self-interest' (HPCSA, 2008c, p. 2). In other words, practitioners should always try to do good to those for whose care they are responsible – this also applies to situations where the patient's interests are in conflict with those of the self-interest of the practitioner (beneficence). The value of human rights is the recognition of the human rights of all patients by healthcare professionals. The principle of autonomy communicates that '[h]ealth care practitioners should honour the right of patients to self-determination or to make their own informed choices, and to live their lives by their own beliefs, values and preferences' (HPCSA, 2008c, p. 2).

The sixth principle, integrity, means that practitioners should include all these values and standards in their daily work and be truthful, accurate and fair in conducting their work. As the term suggests, truthfulness means that practitioners should always be honest with patients and remain professional. The eighth principle, confidentiality, is elaborated on below. The value of compassion communicates that healthcare practitioners should be sensitive to (and show empathy towards) the individual and social needs of patients, while seeking to create mechanisms for providing comfort and support where appropriate and possible. The principle of *tolerance* dictates that '[h]ealth care practitioners should respect the rights of people to have different ethical beliefs as these may arise from deeply held personal, religious or cultural convictions' (HPCSA, 2008c, p. 2). *Justice* refers to the need for healthcare professionals to treat patients fairly and impartially. The 12th core value, termed *professional competence and self-improvement*, highlights the need for practitioners to constantly strive to improve their skills and knowledge to the highest possible level. Finally, *community* refers to the call for healthcare professionals to strive to improve society through their work.

In the codes of the United Kingdom, the United States and South Africa, general ethical principles culminate in rules or standards of professional practice. These standards are more objective and measureable than the principles upon which they are based. The first rule is *confidentiality*, which is closely related to informed consent. Psychologists have a duty to keep appropriate records of their interactions with patients, while ensuring that these are kept confidential at all times – unless, as is stated in the South African values and standards, that 'overriding reasons confer a moral or legal right to disclosure' (HPCSA, 2008c, p. 2). In multicultural, multilingual settings, where interpreters are relied upon in order to conduct assessments, confidentiality can be a problematic area to govern. Often, especially in under-resourced settings, practitioners do not speak the patients' language. In this case, a third party has to be relied upon to do the interpreting. Apart from the other obvious problems that relying upon an interpreter poses, this situation results in patients having to disclose personal information to someone other than the psychologist – thereby breaking what is supposed to be an intimate and private relationship between clinician and patient. This unfortunate reality is not uncommon, especially in a country such as South Africa where 11 official languages are spoken.

Psychologists have a duty to explain the limitations to confidentiality to patients. For example, where there is a civil duty, where a risk of harm to self or others outweighs this professional practice rule, or when an interpreter has to be used. It is essential that informed consent is obtained *before* releasing confidential information about patients to third parties who are not directly involved in their care. Practitioners working with brain injury need to consider that patients will most likely have neurocognitive difficulties, making it more difficult to ensure that consent is actually based on the patient being fully informed and aware of his/her own circumstances and able to weigh up the relative pros and cons. For example, extra time, or repetition and memory aids, may need to be employed to ensure that vulnerable patients are given a genuine opportunity to consider matters before they consent (such as agreeing to the release of neuropsychology reports, accepting an intervention or agreeing to be a research participant).

Another common area of professional practice concerns the conflicts and tensions that arise from *dual relationships*: for example, treating a friend or family member; personal relationships with patients; and supervising an intern to whom the practitioner is married, which should all be avoided. Sometimes boundaries can be subtler than in these few scenarios. Should a psychologist who is directly and continually involved in the long-term rehabilitation of a patient with a brain injury be willing to perform a medico-legal assessment? What are the potential ethical tensions here? As a clinician involved in the care of the patient, the primary allegiance would be to 'do good' and to avoid 'doing harm' by providing appropriate rehabilitation interventions. However, another duty would be to advocate for the patient. Hence, would providing a medico-legal assessment actually help in this regard? The clinician performing an independent medico-legal assessment has a primary duty to the court, whereas one of the foundations of providing psychological therapy relates to the therapeutic relationship with patients. Any activities that may pose a threat to this relationship should be considered by the psychologist and avoided where deemed appropriate. However, compromises are sometimes possible. For example, in this particular scenario, the psychologist may consider agreeing to do a report based on the clinical records and then declare that this represents a perspective on the patient's ongoing difficulties and care, as opposed to doing a cross-sectional, independent diagnostic assessment. In this way, the psychologist can possibly avoid the inevitable problems associated with the dual relationship of being a therapist and an independent assessor, while at the same time being an effective advocate for the patient.

We now turn to professional practice issues that have wider organisational implications. For example, the service within which the neuropsychologist works may provide the vast majority of its psychological therapy within a group context. This service then receives a referral of a young male with cognitive impairment, severe social anxiety and physical disability following surgery for a left temporal lobe brain tumour. Neuropsychological assessment reveals that in addition to cognitive factors, physical disfigurement associated with the surgery is possibly an additional source of his anxiety, especially in social situations. As a result, the patient has become socially avoidant and isolated, negatively affecting his functional outcomes. In this hypothetical case, the neuropsychologist has to consider what is available within the service, along with the individual needs of the patient. The neuropsychologist also has to consider the potential harm that might be caused by exposing the patient to an anxiety-provoking group situation, while at the same time considering the need to work towards anxiety reduction and better functional outcomes. The psychologist may, in collaboration with the patient, explore and define the rehabilitation goals, and it may then transpire that what he needs cannot be provided by the service, given its existing configuration. In addition to the obvious professional practice issues, there are also more fundamental ethical issues regarding equal access to appropriate evidence-based interventions, which need to be addressed at an organisational or service development level.

There are many other professional practice issues that relate very potently to clinical neuropsychology, including: *always practising within your competence* and, in neuropsychology in particular, *the need to stay up to date with developments and advancements in assessment instruments.* Neuropsychological tests are continually being developed and updated, and psychologists should ensure that they receive training (or perform self-directed study, where appropriate) in order to keep abreast of the latest methods for assessing neuropsychological functions. This need is not only limited to testing, as there is also the continual development of rehabilitation interventions that psychologists need to maintain knowledge of. These developmental needs should ideally be identified and planned for as part of supervision and individual performance appraisal processes. Report writing is another area that sometimes proves troublesome. Neuropsychological assessments are time-consuming, as is the scoring of tests and the writing of reports that communicate findings. To avoid delaying the completion of reports beyond what would be a reasonable expectation on the behalf of the referrer (and the patient), it is essential to plan patients' assessments to allow enough time to score tests and write up reports. It is ideal to write reports shortly after having administered tests.

Conclusion

Ethical principles guide psychologists' decisions on a daily basis. These principles are the philosophical foundations upon which all aspects of practice should be based. While professional rules are much more clear and objective, it is the ethical principles that should more permanently – and almost subconsciously – shape and determine psychologists' attitudes, views and approaches to clinical work and other areas of practice. To ensure the development of this crucial area of practice, psychologists should regularly revisit their relevant ethical codes as part of ongoing reflective practice, as part of clinical supervision and in complex patient-related situations. In many respects – particularly for newly qualified psychologists or those new to neuropsychology – this would form part of problem-based learning. The following question is an example of the type that might be considered as part of reflective practice. If one were asked, in some perverse academic exercise, to provide a one-line summary of all of the ethics of a clinical neuropsychologist, what might the answer be? This is an impossibly difficult task. Nevertheless, perhaps the following should be considered as a possible answer: *do no harm, and practise within your professional competence.*

Practical tips

1. Always know how to contact your supervisor.
2. Do not be afraid to buy time before making an important decision.
3. Always try to involve patients in decision-making, however difficult the decision might be.
4. Realise the importance of sometimes being open to admitting that one is agnostic.

Points for reflective practice

1. Which one of the generic ethical principles stands out as the most important for patient care?
2. Can tensions develop between the ethical codes of psychologists and the organisational policies derived from the models of service delivery that are provided by their employers?

Selected further reading

Bush, S. S. (2005). *A casebook of ethical challenges in neuropsychology.* Hove, UK: Psychology Press.

15

PROFESSIONAL PRACTICE

Introduction

Training and professional regulation in clinical neuropsychology vary fairly widely across the world. The main general distinction is between stand-alone clinical neuropsychology training programmes/schemes and those that offer clinical neuropsychology training post-qualification in another area of psychology (typically clinical psychology). With the latter, qualification as a psychologist is in essence an entry requirement for further professional training in clinical neuropsychology. Another distinction is the level at which the training is provided. This generally tends to be at doctoral degree or postdoctoral level, but in some countries programmes are offered at masters degree level (such as in South Africa and Australia) or at diploma level. In most countries, the completion of the training requirements in clinical neuropsychology results in formal accreditation as an acknowledged specialist within the field. In addition, in many countries, clinical psychologists (and other types of psychologist) work in settings where they provide neuropsychological assessment and rehabilitation to patients. An overview of a few approaches to professional training in clinical neuropsychology is now provided to illustrate some of the differences that exist around the world.

International training programmes

In the United States, specialisation in clinical neuropsychology starts at doctoral level at accredited institutions and includes an internship. The *Houston Policy Statement* (after the Houston Conference) defines what a clinical neuropsychologist is, along with the knowledge and skills required for competency. Division 40 of the American Psychological Association (APA) serves clinical neuropsychology, but does not accredit training programmes – this function is performed by the *American*

Board of Professional Neuropsychology, which grants board certification and diplomate status in neuropsychology to candidates who successfully complete an accredited two-year postdoctoral programme. Similarly, in Australia, clinical neuropsychology is generally a speciality training provided at either masters or doctoral level; however, as in many other countries, psychologists from other disciplines can also provide neuropsychological services to patients – such individuals would have received some training in clinical neuropsychology prior to qualification as a psychologist. In Canada, specialist doctoral-level training programmes in clinical neuropsychology are probably less well developed than those in the United Sates, but many psychologists do provide neuropsychological services to patients and have received training in this area.

In Britain, training in clinical neuropsychology is a post-qualification specialist training regulated by the *Division of Neuropsychology of the British Psychological Society*. Qualification as a psychologist, in most cases as a clinical psychologist (but not exclusively so), is an entry requirement for this training. Psychologists in Britain who have completed accredited training programmes then register with, and are regulated by, the *Health and Care Professions Council*. Psychologists wishing to undertake further training in clinical neuropsychology can attend approved university programmes in order to acquire the knowledge base that underpins the qualification or, alternatively, they can proceed through the Division of Neuropsychology assessment process independently. In addition, there is an assessment process that candidates have to go through with the Division of Neuropsychology before they can qualify. This process includes written examinations (if the candidate has not attended a university programme), an extensive case portfolio, a research project (only for a minority of candidates, usually a doctoral thesis suffices), extended case reports and a viva (oral examination). Successful completion of this process results in inclusion on the *Specialist Register of the Division of Neuropsychology*.

Formal training in clinical neuropsychology varies widely across Continental Europe. Many Continental countries have professional organisations supporting clinical neuropsychology as a profession, but there has not been a consistent or uniform development of formal training programmes in clinical neuropsychology. In some countries there is almost no (or hardly any) support for, or training in, clinical neuropsychology. During 2007, an overarching organisation called the *Federation of European Societies of Neuropsychology* was formed, bringing these organisations together. Some member organisations include the *Nederlandse Vereniging voor Neuropsigologie* (Netherlands), *Gesellschaft für Neuropsigologie* (Germany) and the *Federation of Spanish Societies of Neuropsychology* (Spain). A potential stumbling block to developing and providing standardised training in clinical neuropsychology across Continental Europe relates to the number of different languages spoken in the member countries.

With regard to some other countries around the world, in South Africa, for example, the *Health Professions Council of South Africa* (*HPCSA*) registers and regulates psychologists. There are several divisions for psychologists. Neuropsychology has recently been promulgated, and is now officially recognised as a distinct professional category, under the auspices of the *Professional Board for Psychology*, which is part of the HPCSA. Formal training in neuropsychology in South Africa (at masters level) is now offered at a handful of universities, and the infrastructure required for the discipline to function – such as internship posts at state hospitals – will need to begin to be established. The *South African Clinical Neuropsychology Association* (*SACNA*) has traditionally been involved in training and accreditation issues pertaining to clinical neuropsychology.

Professional practice in clinical settings

Most psychologists, including clinical neuropsychologists, are guided by ethical principles (see Chapter 14), which are often formalised by their respective national professional or regulatory organisations. While there are substantial differences across the world, some of these principles are fairly universal with respect to the majority of the ethical rules and codes of conduct of psychology. Such principles include: respect for patient autonomy and freedom; doing no harm in the first instance and, if possible, some good; only practising within your own areas of competence; preserving confidentially, but also knowing its limits; standards of communication with colleagues; and always being truthful. While these ethical guidelines are invariably embedded in the rules and regulations of professional bodies, their more important function is the constant influence that they should have on psychologists' everyday clinical work. In essence, professional practice tends to reflect, on a practical level, how ethical principles translate into the everyday work of clinical neuropsychologists.

A few general examples of approaches to professional practice now follow, before a few more specific areas, including risk assessment, are briefly discussed. The first area relates to receiving referrals. Needless to say, this is an inescapable reality of being a neuropsychologist. It is mostly the case in neurology and brain-injury rehabilitation settings that the diagnosis (including aetiology) or suspected diagnosis is backed up by more objective evidence than is generally the case in mental health settings, for example. There is very little scope for psychologists working in these settings to refuse referrals and not engage in assessing and rehabilitating patients with neurocognitive impairment. In fact, some might suggest that it is akin to committing professional suicide if psychologists fail, for whatever reason, to at least provide an initial clinical assessment before declining to accept a patient with either confirmed or suspected brain injury. A robust rule is to first see and assess the patient before deciding to accept or reject a referral – unless this course of action is very obvious from the referral letter. It is easier to make a decision once a patient is seen, and it is much more acceptable to the referring party if the patient is not accepted for specific reasons. This approach also helps to ensure the relevance and credibility of neuropsychology as a profession.

The importance of *respecting colleagues* and their opinions is also related to the issue of psychologists working within a wider healthcare context with other professionals, and is central to building long-term professional relationships. Respect should go beyond the normal social niceties of communication that are mandatory in any work environment. Of much greater relevance is the importance of having a genuine openness to others' opinions and ways of doing things. It is unprofessional to make potentially derogatory or inflammatory statements about colleagues. If one has a genuine concern about an issue relating to a colleague, the correct professional course of action is to first talk *directly* with the individual concerned – this way, misunderstandings can be avoided before becoming troublesome.

There are other ways of behaving unprofessionally in one's working relationships with colleagues: for example, by becoming embroiled in office politics, undermining colleagues or being overly Machiavellian. Sometimes unprofessional behaviour can be subtler: for example, doing nothing when gossip or rumours about a colleague that are obviously untrue are doing the rounds. It is vitally important to treat all colleagues with the utmost respect. Always remember to question what are objective facts, as opposed to what represents subjective opinion. Being perceptive enough to see narrative for what it is should help steer practitioners away from potentially murky waters. Avoiding team dynamics, while maintaining an awareness of what is happening, is also particularly important under two circumstances: when a newly qualified practitioner joins an established team, and when a practitioner (newly qualified or not) joins an established team working in an unfamiliar cultural (and/or language) context.

Confidentiality is an area of professional practice that may appear very simple when viewed superficially. The mantra is simple: *the doctor–patient relationship is sacred.* Or is it? The answer is that yes, it mostly is, but not in every situation. Maintaining confidentiality is hugely important. Failure to do so is possibly one of the most significant sources of complaints received regarding professional practice. Always declare to patients during their first consultations that there are exceptions to maintaining confidentiality. These exceptions essentially relate to situations where psychologists have a duty to protect the public and, in particular, where there is a risk to children or vulnerable adults. These limits to confidentiality need to be made clear to patients, and usually pertain to issues such as the potential risk of patients harming themselves (or others); a history of serious, previously unreported, criminal behaviour; or the intention to engage in illegal behaviour, among others. One should seriously consider breaking confidentiality if there is risk that involves children. Here, countries have differing rules when it comes to children being at risk; in some, it is the legal duty of psychologists to disclose such risks, even if this requires confidentiality to be broken.

How does the rule of informed consent affect confidentiality, or more specifically, the breaking of confidentiality? Under the very difficult circumstances where it becomes clear, after careful consideration, that psychologists will definitely need to break confidentiality, patients should still ideally be informed of the course of action, if at all possible, unless this further increases risk. It is important to approach this very difficult situation in a truthful, open manner, to ensure that the therapeutic relationship is preserved (wherever possible). Maintaining a good relationship with a high-risk patient may make managing the risks easier. High-risk patients who are not attending appointments, or who are not being open enough to discuss (or disclose) their potentially risky behaviours, lead to psychologists not having enough information upon which to base decisions. This has the potential to make the risk management far more difficult, with errors of judgement due to unreliable information – either too lenient a decision, or too coercive a decision. Below follow more specific issues and examples related to professional practice and management of clinical risk.

Risk assessment

Risk assessment, or the potential for adverse events that stem from the management of patients, is integral to the work of most clinicians, including psychologists. Risk can pertain to either patients or clinicians. Risk to clinicians concerns anything that will affect their ability to perform their jobs safely and effectively. For example, working in a clinic without panic buttons or the presence of other members of staff, while seeing an agitated patient with a history of violence, poses an unacceptable risk to the clinician. Risk to patients concerns anything that may negatively affect them, as well as the effects that their behaviours or actions might have on others. The most important risk here is probably the potential to commit homicide. Assessment of risk can be a specific, isolated activity in its own right, or it can form part of another assessment. The latter occurs during the first assessment or routine follow-up of patients. Specialised, focused risk assessments usually follow a particular structure and format, and may be used in defined populations known to present with high levels of clinical risks – such as forensic groups. Neuropsychologists assess risk every time they perform a patient assessment, but also if a specific situation requires a more extensive, specialist risk assessment. Potential clinical risks can exist within many areas of patients' functioning: for example, risk of suicide; the potential for violence; vulnerability to abuse; an inability to fend for themselves (including financially); and an inability to perform activities of daily living (such as driving a motor vehicle safely).

Neurocognitive impairment (especially executive dysfunction) can make patients less capable of thinking through problems. The following are some high-risk areas commonly encountered when working with patients with neurocognitive impairment. First, the potential for violence and aggression, most notably following traumatic brain injury, can be a concern. Second, rates of suicide are elevated in some patients with neurocognitive impairment. Practitioners need to be constantly on the lookout for suicide risk (although this is actually very difficult to identify and predict). Third, paranoia, while not necessarily common in neurological populations, should always be a cause for serious concern. This is especially true where there is the potential for patients to respond to firmly held delusions associated with violence. As is the case with the potential for suicide, the accurate prediction of the actual occurrence of violence in this situation is complex – and is a great source of anxiety for practitioners. Professional practice in these situations probably necessitates a conservative approach (more so than is usual), where prevention of a potential disaster outweighs other factors, such as the therapeutic relationship.

There are sometimes practical steps to be taken in attempting to minimise the potential risks clinicians may face. For example, home visits where only the patient and psychologist are present should be avoided where possible – or should only be agreed to where there will be a 'chaperone' present (for example, a colleague or family member). It is probably safer to only agree to home visits where there is an obvious clinical reason why patients cannot attend the hospital/clinic (for example, if they are wheelchair bound with no access to public transport, or they have severe *agoraphobia*). Other strategies include the use of technology (such as portable panic and transmission devices incorporated with identity badges), and a 'buddy system' for phoning an identified colleague upon arrival and immediately after home visits. Home visits carry the risk, however small, of practitioners being attacked and then being unable to request assistance. They also pose the risk of receiving complaints and then being unable to disprove beyond doubt what happened during a consultation. While such outcomes are usually extremely uncommon, the rule of 'low frequency but disastrous consequences' may very well apply.

When working in a new or unfamiliar clinical setting, practitioners should: (1) ascertain where panic buttons are located prior to seeing patients; (2) learn what the departmental procedure is in a crisis, for example, where the assembly point is located in the event of a fire; and (3) learn whom to contact in the event of a crisis. Some basic strategies used to minimise clinician risk include: positioning oneself closer to the door of a room to prevent being blocked from escaping by an aggressive patient; being prepared to leave the room before agitation escalates; the fitting of peepholes in consultation rooms; and avoiding getting into debates about 'acceptable behaviours' or 'departmental policies' with agitated patients. Trying to convince an agitated patient to 'see the error of their ways' once a certain threshold has been passed increases the risk for further escalation rather than reducing it. Other strategies can sometimes be more helpful under these circumstances, such as *distraction* or *deflection*. When working away from the hospital/clinic, clinicians should carry a mobile phone and an inconspicuous portable alarm wherever possible.

Risk can be present when patients struggle to 'think things through'. Neuropsychologists are often asked to opine on a patient's ability to make decisions. In particular, if patients have neurocognitive impairments that interfere with their ability to make decisions, then this becomes a different scenario from determining whether someone is making a good versus a bad decision. The question in such cases always pertains to the patient's ability – from a neurocognitive perspective – to make decisions, irrespective of whether these are good or bad decisions. Although not immediately apparent, the inability to make decisions may pose considerable clinical risk in many situations. Generally speaking, from a neurocognitive perspective, the steps required of the patient can be broken down into the following: the ability to process the question under consideration; the ability to hold this information in memory; the ability to weigh up the pros and cons involved, and then come to a decision; and, finally, the ability to communicate the decision that has been made. Sometimes these processes are formalised in law and associated legal tests.

In the United Kingdom, the steps that form the basic legal test that is deemed necessary for making decisions are contained in the *Mental Capacity Act* (2005). However, this act does not exist in a vacuum. Psychologists working in the United Kingdom also need to be aware of several other laws that have potential bearing on their practice. Some of these laws include the *Mental Health Act*, the *Human Rights Act* and the *Freedom of Information Act*, among several others. It is not uncommon for psychologists to have to provide reports outlining their opinions on these matters. In South Africa, *Chapter Five* of the *Mental Health Care Act* (No. 17 of 2002) sets guidelines, procedures and requirements for working with and assisting vulnerable patients (with Section 26 referring to patients who are unable to make decisions for themselves). An important consideration in the South African context (and in other multicultural environments) when determining patients' ability to make decisions is what language/s they are able to speak. Finally, besides the obvious professional issues around clinical accuracy pertaining to patients' capacity for decision-making, there is also the practical demand of providing timely reports, which is an issue of professional administration.

Professional administration

If truth be told, some clinicians, including psychologists, find administrative tasks an arduous extra burden, given their busy schedules. Administration forms part of *practice management*. Practice management refers to an area of professional activity that relates to: organising clinical schedules; creating an environment conducive to patient care; communication; leadership; and planning, among many other tasks. Colleagues (perhaps the more cynical ones) sometimes assert that if a clinician wants to be treated like a professional then s/he has to behave like one – this is perhaps a rather flippant and somewhat harsh statement. However, we do have to consider whether it actually contains a modicum of truth. Do clinicians who have persistently chaotic schedules inspire confidence? What about clinicians who spend a disproportionate amount of time in meetings and reading policies, but who have waiting lists of patients extending to over a year? Conversely, clinicians who see patients from 'sunrise to sunset', but who are totally uninvolved in the non-clinical activities that are essential to delivering services, also fail to inspire confidence. Possibly one of the most important administrative skills to develop is the ability to briefly review lists of tasks, and then prioritise the implementation of these tasks within what will inevitably be a tight time schedule in the world of clinical practice. Much of this skill is about achieving and maintaining a sensible balance.

The crucial point is how to prioritise tasks in order to achieve at least some semblance of balance. The question then is: on which principles should the process of prioritisation be based? A possible answer is that they should be based on *patient needs*. Activities that delay patient care should generally be given a lower priority in a tight clinical time schedule. Likewise, activities that facilitate patient care should be prioritised, and actual patient contact should have the highest priority under almost all circumstances. Do not cancel clinics in order to attend meetings; instead, cancel low-priority meetings in order to attend clinics. Activities that have no direct relevance to, or significant influence on, patient care should be avoided. This is an important component of clinical leadership. Once issues related to patient care have been effectively dealt with, other things generally tend to fall into place. However, to return to the question of what this prioritisation should be based on, we can see here, without too much deliberation, that the underlying guiding principle for decision-making and prioritisation is one of psychology's core ethical values: *in the first instance, do no harm, and if possible, do some good*. There are fortunately some practical steps to consider in order to facilitate smooth patient throughput within a hospital/clinic.

Sometimes very simple administrative strategies can really make a big difference and help to ensure as high professional standards of care as are reasonably achievable. For example, having one 'dummy' appointment (available slot) per week in your diary can make such a difference if there is a crisis, or if a patient has to be seen at short notice. If there happens to be no crisis during a particular week, then this appointment hour can be productively spent writing reports, writing up research, doing supervision or undertaking various other professional activities. Always make sure that secretarial members of staff are aware of where you are and how to contact you. Always return telephone calls as soon as possible. Never go on holiday without arranging with a colleague to provide cover for your patients – and make sure that patients know who to contact in the event of a crisis. Always try to write reports before you start to struggle to formulate due to the length of time that has elapsed since you saw a patient. It is also important to think about your audience when writing reports. Apart from the courts, does anybody actually need a 'thesis' when a short, clear and concise report can communicate, in simple language, the findings of a neuropsychological assessment or the outline of a rehabilitation intervention? To avoid making a really poor professional impression, send out short reports in good time, rather than voluminous documents several weeks or even months too late – by which time most will probably have little practical value anyway. A backlog of reports poses one of the main obstacles to effective administration and is a common source of complaints regarding professional practice.

A final example of practice management concerns the provision of clarity around what a clinical service does and does not provide. Always make your criteria for accepting referrals very clear, and if possible, make these criteria available within the public domain. Never try to evaluate the appropriateness of referrals in isolation from either an accepted diagnostic system and/or clinical guidelines. Creating self-generated 'diagnostic entities' may propel the service into irrelevance in the eyes of referring parties. For example, the term 'patients with serious mental illness secondary to biological factors' is meaningless for the purposes of making it clear to referrers which of their patients are eligible for referral. In this context, what constitutes serious mental illness? Rather use recognised diagnostic systems and make it clear which patients can be seen. 'Biological factors' is a term that is so vague that many interpretations are possible – does this mean brain injury acquired in adulthood, such as a stroke or traumatic brain injury? Or does it refer to developmental disorders? What about learning disabilities, progressive genetic disorders or dementias, perhaps? And what about the 'everything has at least some biological determinant' point of view? So, instead, *be very clear about your criteria for accepting referrals*. Clinicians who give very quick and explicit rejections of referrals, based on vague referral criteria, can frustrate referring parties. Finally, do not forget about the patients and their relatives who use the service – ensure that good information about the service is available to them, in the form of leaflets and an Internet site, for example.

Conclusion

Professional practice represents, to a large extent, the 'translation' of ethical principles into practitioners' daily activities. If in doubt, psychologists can in most instances refer back to these core ethical principles when making decisions regarding professional practice. Generally speaking, patient care and its prioritisation direct the daily practice of psychologists in many situations. It is important to remember what the core skills of a neuropsychologist entail, and what tasks are not to be dealt with by neuropsychologists. For example, advocating for homeless patients is a task for neuropsychologists, whereas physically organising patients' accommodation is not. The latter is within the professional domain of other colleagues, such as social workers. There are other important factors pertaining to professional practice that need to be kept in mind. For example, where there is a duty to society (specifically in protecting the public), additional consideration should be given to the decision-making process as it relates to professional practice. Finally, while it is a rather mundane topic to some, the oil that keeps the machinery of professional practice turning is the ability to embrace and pursue effective practice management. At the heart of this lies effective administration. Dysfunctional administrative processes can badly sabotage even the most diligent and conscientious practitioner's efforts to maintain high standards in everyday professional practice.

Practical tips

1. Try not to reject a referral without first having made a clinical assessment through seeing the patient (unless of course it is blatantly obvious that a referral is not appropriate: for example, if it falls outside your catchment area).
2. Read the Houston Conference, which is available on the APA website.
3. Give administrative members of staff a thorough induction as to how you wish to manage your everyday professional activities, and then give them complete control over your diary. Perhaps this is counter-intuitive, but if done correctly, it can pay rich dividends.

Points for reflective practice

1. What in your opinion are the three most important areas of professional practice for psychologists?
2. Design and describe your preferred administration system for a busy out-patient neuropsychology clinic based at a hospital.

Selected further reading

Division of Neuropsychology (2004). *Professional practice guidelines.* Leicester: British Psychological Society.

16

SUPERVISION

Introduction

Supervision is a core pillar of *continuing professional development* for clinicians, and has an additional function pertaining to managing clinical risks. However, the contribution of supervision towards ongoing skills development has always been the most pertinent and relevant function of this professional activity. Supervision is not unique to psychology. Most (if not all) healthcare professions have some form of supervision or clinical mentoring in order to provide opportunities for professional development. Besides professional development and support, supervision ensures that the important checks and balances necessary for safe evidence-based patient care take place. Professional regulatory bodies in most countries require evidence of ongoing professional development, which includes regular supervision as a requirement for continued registration. This chapter provides an overview of both the receiving and the provision of supervision, highlighting some logistical issues surrounding the process.

Receiving supervision

Patient care tends to take priority over all other activities within hospital/clinic environments, and rightly so. Consequently, non-clinical activities can sometimes be seen as less urgent. Under certain conditions, these activities may decrease; for example, if they are cancelled more and more frequently in order to meet the ever-increasing clinical demands that are so typical of many clinical environments – a state of affairs that is clearly less than optimal. Finding a balance in this quagmire of demands is essential for maintaining standards of care and ensuring professional development. All psychologists providing a service to patients should receive supervision in one form or another. However, it must be acknowledged that this should be counterbalanced by clinical duties, and some flexibility should always be retained for decision-making when schedules are planned or changed. It is important that consideration be given to the overall purpose and goals of supervision. Furthermore, it can be very helpful to identify strategies that make supervision a satisfying, interesting and meaningful experience. This is of course important not only for the supervisee, but also for the supervisor too!

Effective supervision should have important links with ethics, codes of conduct and professional practice. One of the most protective ethical principles (for both the practitioner and the public) is for psychologists to work within their areas of competence. To develop competency, practitioners need guidance, support and monitoring, which all occur during supervision. These key aspects to supervision have a few important objectives, including the development of new clinical skills, the refinement of case formulations, the development of report writing technique and the acquisition of new knowledge. At the same time, supervision provides the checks and balances necessary to protect the public. For these and many other reasons, psychologists who are new to training (or who are currently undergoing training) in clinical neuropsychology are expected to work under the supervision of a fully qualified (preferably experienced) clinical neuropsychologist. For example, in the United Kingdom, this expectation is made explicit in the *Professional practice guidelines of the division of neuropsychology* (British Psychological Society, 2003) – this translates to supervisors being on the *Specialist Register of the Division of Neuropsychology* (and for certain purposes, also a BPS registered supervisor).

One of the main purposes of clinical supervision is to develop professional skills. Two strategies to achieve this goal include *reflective practice* and *career planning*. Reflective practice can be particularly complementary to problem-based learning. It demands an openness and willingness to examine and consider approaches to patient management other than one's own, and requires well-thought-through formulation. A thoughtful approach to case formulation will facilitate more considered weighing up of alternative diagnoses and treatments. During case reviews and reflections, new areas for skills development may be identified. For example, during a case review it may be decided that the patient did not derive benefit from cognitive behavioural therapy, whereas a mindfulness approach might yield positive results. To address this, a goal may be set for the psychologist under supervision to access mindfulness training. Supervision can also be an ideal forum for discussing issues related to transference and counter-transference. For supervision to be effective, feedback should be fairly immediate to allow for adjustments to one's practice to be made in response.

Career planning

Career planning focuses much more on longer-term aims/goals (individual and organisational) and ambitions, and is often done in collaboration with supervisors – but not exclusively so. Career planning works best when the supervisee's ambitions for professional development are congruent with both his/her areas for skills development (as identified collaboratively with the supervisor) and with the organisation's plans for service development. Areas identified might include both clinical and non-clinical skills. The most common non-clinical area is probably *management skills*. Kapur (2009) provides an overview of some generic skills that consultant-grade neuropsychologists will require to function effectively. These include technical, personal and planning (future-orientated) skills (Kapur, 2009). Clinical knowledge and skills identified by supervisee and supervisor – which also potentially tie in with future organisational plans for service development – can be pursued through the attendance of training courses and conferences, by obtaining further qualifications through studying, and/or through receiving specialist external supervision. However, these are definitely not the only options. An important factor to consider is whether there is funding available to sponsor practitioners for further training. Unfortunately, it is a harsh reality that financial support is often very limited, especially in under-resourced/developing world settings.

Other vehicles for the development of skills and knowledge include *secondments* (transfers to other areas of work) and *projects*, which can both prove very rewarding. These are, to some extent, similar to problem-based learning in that individuals are exposed, from day one, to dealing with real and practical issues that require new skills. There is also the invaluable experience of working with new people and within different settings. Besides learning about working with new clinical populations, there are opportunities to develop and forge new professional contacts, and to become involved in different clinical networks. Examples of such opportunities include: working in another clinical area or unit; piloting a new service; doing a substantial clinical research project; or accepting management or supervision responsibilities for a new staff member. Clearly, projects and secondments provide the opportunity to develop substantial amounts of transferable clinical and non-clinical skills and knowledge. This acquired knowledge can then be utilised more broadly, to the benefit of both psychologists and the field.

The imparting of expertise from specialists in a particular field to others lacking training or expertise in that particular domain has been called 'transferable technology' (Nell, 2000). The need for such transfers is especially dire in developing countries, such as South Africa, where neuropsychology is a fledgling field, where there is a large population in need of clinical services and where specialist expertise is scarce. Such transfers are invaluable to the growth and development of psychology (and psychological services) around the world, especially in developing world contexts. These opportunities can, in many cases – especially over the longer term – facilitate psychologists' career development far more effectively than can attendance at conferences or the pursuit of additional qualifications. Furthermore, at times there may be less obvious forms of training that can facilitate the provision of patient care and the transference of neuropsychological skills to a much wider audience (including professionals in other fields). Perhaps most notable here is the opportunity to learn a new language, which is particularly relevant in multilingual societies.

Mentoring is another important tool for career development. Mentoring can be applied to the clinical and non-clinical aspects of career development, but is perhaps traditionally more associated with management development. Some might even argue that all good clinical supervisors should also be good mentors! Mentoring can be an ideal way to develop skills in management development, which is an area that is almost always somewhat foreign to newly qualified clinicians. While there has been an increase over recent years in the availability of management training courses specifically tailored to healthcare environments, such courses may not always address the skills and knowledge that are relevant to specialist clinical areas (such as neuropsychology and brain-injury rehabilitation services). When psychologists accept new management and/or service development responsibilities as part of their career development, having regular access to someone with a proven track record in these specific areas is as valuable as pursuing further (often generic) management training. In the final analysis though, mentoring and structured management training should complement each other. Through these processes, newly qualified psychologists become equipped to take the lead in important roles, including service development, departmental management and becoming experienced supervisors.

Providing supervision

Exhortations to make supervision meaningful abound, but how do we actually work towards achieving this goal? There are probably as many views on making supervision a worthwhile endeavour as there are supervisors! Some colleagues emphasise the importance of the personal qualities of the supervisor, while others give more weight to the supervisor's technical skills and knowledge. Many would probably agree that a balance between technical skill and personal qualities is required. Some might even argue that a good supervisor is 'born' rather than trained. Others emphasise the role of training in the development of the skills and qualities required to be a good clinical supervisor. Experience and ongoing clinical activity in the specialism are also likely to be important factors. Clearly, there are many factors that are likely to play a role in the quality of a supervisor. In attempting to bring some clarity and direction to the field, Milne (2009) argues that the provision of supervision should be primarily based on evidence. Furthermore, supervision should always be considered from the perspective of the cultural context within which it is being delivered.

Who are psychologists likely to supervise? Requests to supervise staff usually start much earlier than expected. Newly qualified psychologists are usually expected, almost from the word go, to supervise (at least partially, or for specific, circumscribed tasks) assistant psychologists (graduates or technicians). Recently qualified psychologists also soon find themselves in a situation where they supervise the newly qualified ones! It is prudent then to start preparing for these changes in one's professional role as early as possible. The first step is to identify in your own supervision the skills that are particular to your own stage of development and which require further input. The typical first port of call for acquiring initial technical skills is to attend a university-based workshop. This is a helpful strategy for obtaining some of the fundamental knowledge required before beginning to supervise others. At the same time, in addition to formal training, at least *some* implicit and explicit learning is taking place as a result of observation and experience during one's own supervision. These early experiences may also provide some of the grounding for later career supervision responsibilities.

How can psychologists who are starting to supervise others for the first time try to make strategic sense of the process? It is crucial to know what the developmental needs of new supervisees are. To learn this, one should initially spend time finding out the person's level of skill, what his/her developmental areas are and what his/her short-term career aspirations are. Thereafter, set initial goals, and then discuss the process involved in providing and receiving supervision. Make it clear how you are going to organise the pragmatics of supervision sessions. Try to understand what works with regard to your supervisee's learning style. Supervisors should never underestimate the importance of timely feedback. This is especially relevant when feedback can be used to reinforce desirable behaviours, but also when it is used to raise difficult issues, such as underperformance. Always consider the dynamic nature of supervision – a few factors affect the process over time. Some of your supervisees may vacillate between needing supervision and desiring more professional independence. Create opportunities for independence as part of skills development. Allow dependence if this ultimately helps with developing the skills that will increase confidence. Be aware that many newly qualified psychologists and trainees may prefer more structure and provision of information, before gradually prioritising the non-technical aspects of their work as their confidence in their knowledge grows. In some ways, this reflects the transition from 'training' to 'development'. Supervision can be prone to becoming moribund, usually due to clinical demands and time constraints. Being mindful of some of the aforementioned dynamic processes can help to counteract the 'dwindling effect' associated with always 'doing things the same way'.

We now turn to some of the more 'hands-on' aspects of being a supervisor. Again, there will almost certainly be as many 'rules of thumb' as there are supervisors, but here are a few suggestions that have, in the authors' view, worked well in providing supervision. First, create opportunities for 'showing, doing and teaching'. There are two key aspects to showing supervisees how to perform specific clinical tasks. The first relates to technique: it is invaluable to let your supervisees sit in with you and observe directly how (with all its likely imperfections) you apply technical clinical skills to patient care. The second aspect of modelling is more about professional development than about teaching technical skills and, as such, it is similar to *leading by example*. It provides opportunities for supervisees to observe the more hidden aspects of professional practice, such as bedside manner, interacting with other colleagues, clinical reasoning and professionalism. Leading by example is more important than we think. Put simply, if you want others to see patients every day, then see patients every day yourself. Supervisees will then hopefully do the same, and will in turn teach the next generation – whom they will eventually be responsible for supervising.

Other functions of supervision

Supervision may serve other functions too: for example, it sometimes has a *pastoral function*. This role entails being aware of, and supporting where required, colleagues who may be experiencing stress, or who may be at risk of professional burnout. However, this supervisory role definitely does not constitute personal psychotherapy, nor should it be seen as a substitute for psychotherapy. Psychotherapy, if required by a supervisee, should be sought and pursued outside the work environment. Some might opine differently, but to separate out these roles is likely to be a wise strategy. Blurring the boundaries between psychotherapy and supervision is likely to result in conflicts of interest, and may make it very difficult to address issues such as underperformance. Similarly, supervision, under ideal circumstances, should be removed from line management. However, in reality, low staff numbers sometimes dictate that the same person often performs these potentially quite different functions. Strategies to overcome this problem include in-service peer-group supervision sessions and the arrangement of external (to the service) individual supervision. Opportunities for offering external supervision (from a distance) for remote areas may be available by using technologies such as video conferencing. In under-resourced areas where more costly technologies are unviable, telephone access may partially substitute for face-to-face contact.

Supervisors may also perform other tasks. It is not unusual for one to be asked to provide references or confirmation of supervised experience; for example, when supervisees are pursuing further training or registration with a professional body. Colleagues may ask you to help to arrange clinical cover for their supervisees while they are away – be prepared to provide cover yourself if required. The supervision setting can provide a useful forum to develop the skills needed to disseminate neuropsychological knowledge to other professionals. Two increasingly valuable skills for neuropsychologists to possess are the ability to raise awareness about the work involved in neuropsychology and the ability to teach basic psychological techniques and simple interventions to the clinical team or community-based volunteers, especially where resources are scarce. The development of these skills can be achieved through various means in supervision, including, for example, through modelling and direct discussion about the value of knowledge dissemination.

A potentially difficult topic sometimes raised during supervision concerns professional relationships with other staff. Supervisors would be wise to tread carefully here. Avoid taking sides, being 'sucked in' and/or judging prematurely. It is useful to listen and observe for a good while, thereafter identifying difficulties, and only then discussing and mutually agreeing on the course of action that the supervisee should take. It is important to stress that it is the supervisee who needs to take action, rather than the supervisor. The role of supervisors is to review progress.

Supervisees may sometimes request 'career counselling'. Do not automatically interpret this as representing potential professional frustration, general unhappiness or a strategy to improve remuneration and/or working conditions. It may actually represent a positive reflection of your credibility as a supervisor. Supervisees may trust and respect your opinion enough to venture a genuine request for advice about how to progress with their careers. As is the case with our provision of care to patients, we have a professional duty to always give supervisees the best available (under the circumstances) support and advice, based on our expertise and experience.

Documentation

The question of whether a record of supervision should be kept is sometimes a contentious one. Moreover, if a record *is* kept, then what level of detail should be captured? Alternatively, the keeping of supervision records may be viewed by supervisees as being potentially stifling to their openness and full disclosure with regard to either perceived or actual mistakes made. However, records may actually be required for the purpose of the annual renewal of professional registration, for example. Having at least some evidence that practitioners were not working unsupervised may actually be protective – this may be particularly important if litigation takes place. Under these circumstances, objective, measurable evidence of supervision received may help to prove that the colleague's practice complied with minimum professional standards. Perhaps, then, the question is more about what level of detail should be captured and where this captured information should be recorded, rather than if some form of record should be kept in the first place. The following suggestions may be useful in some, but clearly not all, clinical situations.

In many situations, a note in the clinical file, signed by either the supervisor or supervisee (and sometimes both), which states that supervision was received, probably represents the minimum professional standard required to document that supervision took place. In addition, supervisees should at least keep a record of which cases were discussed – when, with whom and what the duration of the supervision session was. In some cases, suggestions for patients' management may be captured to function as an aide-memoire for supervisees. As far as the level of detail to be captured in records is concerned, in addition to the anxiety that might be caused if too much detail is provided – thereby inhibiting the supervisee from being open and disclosing everything fully – there can also be anxiety on the part of the supervisor. Here, supervisors may think that very detailed notes represent documented proof that they prescriptively told supervisees what to do with regard to changes in patient management. This may cause supervisors to worry that adverse outcomes related to patient care may be interpreted as a direct consequence of their suggestions provided during supervision – whereas they are ultimately due to the interventions of the supervisee. In almost all situations, *documentation should be agreed upon between the supervisor and supervisee*, and must always comply with the relevant organisational policies and professional regulations.

Practicalities

Supervision generally works better when the logistics of the process are well managed. If you are the supervisee, make sure you are always on time. To make full use of the often-limited supervision time, make sure you identify priority cases that require discussion in advance. If possible, have a look at the last inscription or most recent summary in the case file in order to refresh your memory. Make sure to update data pertaining to total active caseload, 'Did Not Attends' (DNA-rates), the time required for report writing, and so forth. Make a summary of what you would like to cover during supervision and have a copy for your supervisor if possible. Always be clear as to what the specific management questions are for your cases, whenever guidance, or a second opinion, is required. Without this, supervision can easily degenerate into an updating session, without any opportunities to learn. Providing specific management/diagnostic questions helps to stimulate case formulation and supervision. Finally, present new cases in a format that is conducive to formulation, diagnostics and management planning – if this is not done, then very few cases will be covered within the inevitably limited time available to both you and your supervisor.

If you are the supervisor, always be punctual. Newly qualified practitioners and trainees tend to carry heavy caseloads and have very busy schedules. There will inevitably be lots of cases to go over and other matters requiring discussion. Divert telephone calls and other non-essential disturbances. Always ensure that you are familiar with supervisees' cases – it does not inspire confidence if a supervisor cannot remember a case that has already been discussed several times. Be flexible – sometimes supervisees have experienced a crisis and would prefer to discuss it, rather than sticking to a pre-determined agenda. Try to ascertain, from an early stage, what style of supervision works best for your supervisee, and adapt your style if this facilitates skills development. Empathy is also important: always try to recall how you experienced being newly qualified/in a training position. Empathy can be, in many situations, the skill that unblocks resistance and facilitates the development of a professional relationship between supervisor and supervisee. This is certain to facilitate the development of openness towards the acquisition of knowledge and skills during the supervision process. It also models a skill that is likely to one day be very valuable to supervisees during their transition to becoming supervisors.

Conclusion

Psychologists new to brain-injury rehabilitation and diagnostic settings must work under the supervision of a fully qualified clinical neuropsychologist. This is not always easy to achieve in under-resourced healthcare systems (encountered in both the developing and developed world). Clinical supervision has many benefits, including the provision of a systematic and gradual development of skills and experience, and the assurance that clinicians always work within their competence – thereby helping to protect patients. There are many practical strategies that can make supervision more satisfying and conducive to learning for both supervisee and supervisor, many of which centre on preparation and a commitment to hands-on learning through regular patient contact. An important component of this process is a commitment to a problem-based approach within supervision. Supervisees should attempt to learn in an experiential way from the process of receiving supervision, in addition to developing their clinical skills related to patient care. Supervisees will become supervisors before too long, and their early supervision experiences will significantly shape their own supervision skills and style.

Practical tips

1. Ensure that you are familiar with all the supervision-related policies, rules and regulations of your employer and professional body.
2. Keep a notebook with anonymous patient summaries – this is a great repository of clinical activity that you can then later refer back to during supervision. It will also serve as an invaluable memory aid.
3. From an early stage, provide your supervisees with practical opportunities to disseminate knowledge to the clinical team, and allow them to supervise circumscribed psychological components of other professionals' work with patients.

Points for reflective practice

1. List the characteristics of an ideal supervisor.
2. How could a psychologist who is working single-handedly in a remote rural hospital obtain clinical supervision?
3. What constitutes 'bad' supervision?

Selected further reading

Kapur, N. (2009). Advice to a newly appointed consultant neuropsychologist: Aspire for excellence. *The British Psychological Society Division of Neuropsychology Newsletter, 2*, 1–2.

17

RESEARCH, ACADEMIA AND AUDIT

Introduction

Training or recruiting one clinical neuropsychologist is likely to have a greater direct effect on patient care in under-resourced areas than most research endeavours. So why then do we include a chapter on research and academia in a book that, at its heart, advocates for a practice-based learning approach to training in clinical neuropsychology to plug skills gaps in poorly staffed healthcare environments? Are issues related to the training of clinical skills necessarily more important, and should they always be prioritised over our acquisition of knowledge through research-based activities? While most clinical neuropsychologists who provide a service to patients by working in publicly funded hospitals or similar clinical environments will not have a substantial or direct involvement in research, there are nonetheless many reasons why we need a robust understanding of its importance. Research is essential for psychologists in that it allows clinical interventions to be based on sound evidence. For an overview of research within clinical practice in psychology, interested readers can consult the recent Special Issue of *Clinical Psychology Forum* (2013) on this topic; see 'Selected further reading' at the end of this chapter.

Understanding the purpose of research and in particular how to appraise research *evidence* is fundamental to clinical practice. Understanding the limits of the evidence we base our practice upon, and knowing when to provide alternatives when there is no empirical evidence, is equally important knowledge to have in environments where the main activity is providing clinical services to patients. In addition, there are disease processes and clinical syndromes for which modern neuroscience still requires a far greater understanding, and it is here that research plays a vital role in acquiring such knowledge. Without empirical research evidence, it is difficult to advance effective clinical management and rehabilitation for patients. For example, from a developing world perspective, in sub-Saharan Africa HIV/AIDS requires much research in order for its neuropsychological consequences to be properly understood and for appropriate management strategies to be developed.

Healthy *scepticism* is a fundamental cornerstone of science. Scepticism, and the ability to question, are probably the two most important driving forces that propel clinicians into research activities. Scepticism is akin to curiosity; however, it is also different from curiosity on many levels. Scepticism is the healthy questioning of: (1) the current state of affairs; and (2) the teaching that one has received. Sadly, things sometimes fail to progress beyond an initial stage of questioning. Perhaps we should think more clearly about the function of *questioning*. Sometimes there is evidence of phenomena, while at other times there is no evidence of their existence. Nevertheless, the process of questioning does not provide evidence in itself. To contribute to the development of knowledge, we need not only to question, but also to respond by providing potentially credible alternatives, which in turn should be subject to investigation. Without this latter component (especially as a clinician), scepticism runs the risk of being merely perceived as thinly veiled cynicism. Thus, within clinical settings, psychologists can make a valuable contribution to patient care by formulating and investigating research questions that arise from their everyday clinical work.

For hospital-based psychologists, research often entails a lot of work, usually without any protected time available to complete it. Writing protocols, literature reviews, recruiting participants, writing up findings, conference presentations and writing research projects are all very time-consuming. Why on earth then do clinicians ever become involved in research, clinical audits or any academic activity for that matter, if these appear so time-consuming and usually without tangible rewards? There are many reasons why clinicians become involved in research, a few of which are highlighted here. Research (and academic involvement in general) can regenerate clinicians' enthusiasm for taking a different look at how they do things, while at the same time reinvigorating their quest to contribute to knowledge in an ever-expanding field. One might postulate that involvement in academia, even if only peripheral, is the best naturalistic mechanism for facilitating clinicians' ongoing professional development.

Academic activities, be they research- or teaching-related, require the acquisition of a fair amount of in-depth knowledge of the subject matter being researched or taught. Where these activities are thoroughly grounded in clinical practice, the potential benefits for practitioners can be considerable. The scientific landscape in academic clinical neuropsychology tends to evolve quickly, and it is important to stay abreast of the latest trends and developments. Many developments tend to filter down to the level of service provision to patients before too long; for example, some of the latest memory-rehabilitation interventions used today were relatively recently hypotheses being tested in academic neuropsychology. Some developments are also more cost-effective, which is not to be ignored when providing rehabilitation in settings with limited funding. For example, memory-rehabilitation interventions that are simple to deliver under neuropsychologists' supervision, and which increase patients' independence, must surely be preferable.

Neuropsychologists often work with fairly homogeneous populations compared to some clinical populations seen by psychologists in general mental health inpatient units, and those who are part of community mental health teams. Homogeneous populations are sometimes easier to do research with. Neuroscience is a very active field and provides many opportunities for interdisciplinary collaboration. Pilot studies that test models to improve clinical practice can, upon completion, serve as powerful motivators in helping in the release of additional funding to implement new ways of delivering rehabilitation services to patients. These factors, along with a solid grounding with respect to clinical questioning in everyday practice, may be particularly relevant to *outcome studies*.

Outcome studies are important in determining whether clinical interventions are effective at a local level, and inform the development of clinical pathways. They can help to address issues in healthcare systems, where equability is often the strategic aim but is not always being achieved in practice. There are also practical difficulties to consider when planning outcome studies. Such studies are often unable to control for the many variables that occur, which may account for a substantial proportion of the variance observed. For example, the following factors can all limit the clinical utility of research findings: use of different outcome measures; outcome measures that are ecologically invalid; and outcome measures that fail to provide achievements that are relevant to patients. Outcome studies sometimes use retrospective data, which may limit the generalisability of results. If done within a local service, sample sizes may be small, which can make drawing conclusions difficult. Nevertheless, outcome studies do have many potential advantages, including that they can provide a snapshot of how successful a service is in terms of the patient-rehabilitation programmes it provides. Most importantly, outcome studies can serve as a significant stimulus for further service development.

Pitfalls to avoid

Research, audits and other academic activities inevitably take much longer than initially anticipated. There will consequently be a significant impact on the limited time available to psychologists who work clinically. It is therefore important to look for ways of sharing the workload associated with research and related activities. For example, assistance with research may come from trainees, students or temporary staff who work under the supervision of full-time psychologists based in hospitals/clinics. It is often a requirement for these colleagues to complete a small research or clinical audit project as part of their placement or internship. It may be useful for neuropsychologists to have potential research topics (that will contribute to departmental research projects) 'ready' for if/when trainees and interns become available. It is also often a requirement, or at least desirable, for trainees to do some teaching or academic presentations during a placement, which can be very helpful in contributing towards an in-service academic programme. There is perhaps some truth in the saying that is familiar to many clinicians: 'See one, Do one, Teach one.'

In light of its significance, let us return to the point about time commitment. Never underestimate the amount of work involved in writing protocols, proposals and applications. Add to this workload attendance at ethics committee reviews, time to incorporate feedback and time to prepare revisions. After completion, writing up projects can be much more time-consuming than anticipated, especially when factoring in the peer-review process and the re-editing of manuscripts. It may therefore be necessary to plan for this stage more proactively. Many clinicians rely on opportunistic time slots, such as patients' failures to attend appointments or cancelled meetings. However, such slots rarely work very effectively as they are often counterbalanced by unscheduled commitments, such as patients arriving at the hospital/clinic and then having to be seen.

Fragmentation of clinicians' available time slots is perhaps one of the greatest threats to the effective and systematic writing up of research or related projects. Creating a free block of time solely for research purposes is likely to be a more economical use of clinician time. Bits of time snatched here and there from a busy schedule, when summed, usually add up to much more than a single block. There are many reasons for this, but constant interruptions are not conducive to concentrating and getting into intellectual activities that require sustained attention in order to be performed effectively. In addition, each time the process is interrupted, one has to start all over again. The same applies to preparing lectures and academic presentations. Always define the theme and topic of a presentation/lecture as concisely as possible before commencing, then allow enough interruption-free time to systematically work through its individual components.

The most important pitfall to avoid is conducting research that does not comply with the relevant professional code of conduct. For example, the British Psychological Society (2009) provides clear guidance on research in its Code, based on four ethical principles: *respect*, *competence*, *responsibility* and *integrity*. The American Psychological Association (2002) employs very similar ethical principles to guide professional practice, including research, as does the Professional Board for Psychology in South Africa. These principles provide guidance for specific research-related activities, such as informed consent and publishing findings. These are obvious rules that all psychologists are familiar with. However, there are also less explicit ethical issues related to clinical research in psychology that one needs to be aware of. For example, two situations to avoid are: (1) conducting research that has no implication for patient care, or worse; (2) conducting 'research for the sake of research'. Conversely, ethically sound clinical research should, under normal circumstances, directly influence and improve the delivery of patient services.

Evidence-based practice

From a clinical perspective, the primary functions of research, audits and teaching are to answer questions, provide new information and disseminate knowledge that can inform patient care. An important additional function is to facilitate *evidence-based practice*. Even though research findings tend to link clinical practice to existing and emerging evidence of clinical effectiveness in various ways, these ways are not always explicit. Practice-based research may help to confirm or expand psychological treatment alternatives for patients with neurocognitive impairment. Alternatively, a clinical audit may provide the data required to improve models of practice, provide information regarding outcomes or reveal answers pertaining to local service delivery. Hopefully, the end-stage of this whole process is about how research findings ultimately influence clinicians' training. Teaching should provide the next generation of neuropsychologists not only with the latest best-practice models, but also with the 'how' answers regarding the gathering of evidence that is relevant to clinical practice. Familiarity with research and clinical audit processes may prove very helpful in the development of the skills that underpin evidence-based patient care.

The following hypothetical example attempts to illustrate some of these above-mentioned points. In a post-acute brain-injury rehabilitation service providing state-funded healthcare, it gradually transpired through feedback to clinicians that patients and their relatives were generally reporting high levels of satisfaction with the service, as well as perceived increases in their quality of life. However, colleagues also became increasingly aware that many patients were nonetheless being re-referred to the service after an initial period of appearing settled following discharge from the service's rehabilitation programme. A clinical audit of the service's clinical pathways and outcomes was therefore planned to try to determine, in a more systematic way, which factors contributed to these almost diametrically opposed outcomes that had been informally observed. How can patients and their relatives report satisfaction with the rehabilitation received, and report positive outcomes on a fairly consistent basis, only to be re-referred for further rehabilitation months later?

The clinical audit began with a brief literature review, confirming that the majority of patients with acquired brain injury present with chronic difficulties, with longer-term improvement being possible. A survey was conducted of 25 consecutive patients and relatives who attended the service for review following re-referral. These participants took part in a short structured interview to determine their views on strategies for reducing re-referral and relapse rates. The following themes emerged. It appeared that the outcomes that were personally relevant to the patients and their relatives required much longer-term follow-up, even if this was to be at a lower intensity than initially provided. For example, patients may periodically encounter unexpected stressors, such as state-provided financial support being reviewed, volunteer work coming to an end or other setbacks. These themes seemed to suggest that in order to reduce relapse rates, patients ideally needed the 'safety net' provided by having open opportunity to re-access the service if/when the factors associated with subsequent relapse first present. In this way, the chances of the costly process of a formal re-referral to the service being required *after* a relapse has already occurred could be reduced. This change in the clinical pathway was also thought to facilitate patient self-management, but this required a new audit in order to be determined.

There are a few relevant points to consider from this scenario. For example, practice-based questions are often embedded in local issues related to the way patient services are delivered. Take, for example, a service that is based in a remote area, away from the nearest city. Rural areas may have less opportunity for the re-employment of patients following brain injury and, accordingly, occupational therapy may instead focus more on volunteer work and other activities that can serve to contribute to the broader community. Such issues lend themselves particularly well to clinical audits, and are very important to investigate when local alternatives/solutions to potential obstacles to good clinical outcomes are required. Clinical audits (and some research questions) are very much contextual in nature. What this means is that there are so many factors to control for in the real world (for example, the brain-injury rehabilitation setting) that even an increase in large-scale, prospective randomised controlled trials cannot always provide all the answers to local issues. This is one reason why practitioners should not decline opportunities to become involved in smaller-scale research/audit projects within the clinical environment. Such projects can eventually bring tangible benefit to those who use clinical services. Interestingly, with respect to brain-injury rehabilitation research, Cicerone (2013) highlights the importance of striking a balance between methodology and pragmatic relevance to clinical practice.

Potential benefits of academic involvement

If research, audit, teaching and other academic activities are so time-consuming, then are there any reasons why psychologists new to the field of neuropsychology should pursue them? While these activities are clearly not the primary functions of the jobs of clinicians, there are still benefits associated with becoming involved, from both personal and organisational perspectives. From a professional standpoint, the acquisition of research and audit skills gives clinicians more in-depth understanding of the intricacies of providing evidence-based clinical care. Conducting research not only generates new knowledge, but also provides an understanding of the nature of the evidence upon which clinical practice is based. Another potential benefit that practitioners may reap is increased opportunity for continuing professional development (CPD), including through *presentations at conferences* and the chance to *publish in peer-reviewed journals*. These may also bring unique opportunities that allow for *professional networking* to occur.

There are many organisational benefits to be achieved through research, audit and other academic activities, some of which are highlighted here. Possibly the most important benefit relates to *service development*. Research and clinical audits can provide powerful evidence for arguments for the development and funding of specific patient services. This can be achieved through various methods. Original research may provide the evidence of the efficacy of a new treatment that is not yet available through state-provided care, and which can then be adopted by an existing rehabilitation service. A literature review or meta-analysis may provide some of the impetus for developing a new service. A clinical audit may provide the necessary evidence required to begin service improvement initiatives. Furthermore, involvement in more general academic activities, such as university-based teaching of future professionals, or conducting research, often increases kudos from employers. A culture of close collaboration with higher academic institutions may have additional spin-offs, such as making recruitment easier, or helping to secure the retention of clinical staff.

Research around the world: challenges and benefits

Given that there are so many different research areas/topics within psychology around the world, and so many approaches and perspectives from which to conduct research, only a few key issues are addressed here. An extremely important challenge to research is access to funding and resources. For example, in developed world (well-funded) countries in Europe, experimental psychology can tackle a range of fascinating study topics through the use of sophisticated technology, such as advanced imaging techniques and computer-aided programmes and experiments. Apart from the limitations posed by lack of financial resources in many parts of the world, especially the developing world, the use of such an approach to research may not be possible due to the poor education levels of many potential research participants, along with lack of computer literacy. The overall lack of scientific infrastructure and personnel in many countries also makes conducting research (such as that achieved in high-tech European experimental psychology) nearly impossible.

Different perspectives and approaches to research also prevail in certain countries due to historical and political reasons. The reality is that as a consequence of these reasons, research in many countries is restricted by a lack of financial resources, personnel and infrastructure. Clinicians looking to get involved in research need to be aware of such factors. However, this does not necessarily mean that research has a relatively lower importance in poorly resourced settings. In fact, in many developing world contexts, public-health research plays a critical role in policy development and in educating populations about healthier lifestyle practices, among other things. In a positive light, the developing world may, relative to the more established and rigid scientific practices in developed countries, also provide opportunities for discovering novel and ingenious ways of conducting research (along with the development of new methodologies) due to the lack of the constraints associated with relying on highly evolved, costly research infrastructures.

Where research is urgently required, but budgets are extremely limited, emphasis should be placed, wherever possible, on cost-effective methodologies that draw on pre-existing resources. For example, postgraduate students can do data collection for degree purposes, rather than employing research assistants. Expensive technologies (such as test batteries) used for data collection can be avoided in favour of using low-cost alternatives (such as individual bedside tests). Printed materials can hopefully be kept to a minimum, and research designs that require external costs (such as statistical consultants) can be avoided where possible – or kept to an absolute minimum.

Training required for studies might be done by volunteer experts rather than paid consultants. Data collection can hopefully occur in settings that minimise the need to incur transport costs. Of course, these are but a handful of suggestions, and one should always anticipate studies' requirements and have well-planned strategies to ensure cost-effectiveness.

There is potential scope for improving the lives of the underprivileged by conducting research in the developing world, which can offer multicultural perspectives given the diversity of many countries' populations. With large parts of the developed and industrialised world becoming increasingly multicultural, and with the widespread existence of minority groups, there are opportunities for research emanating from the developing world to inform trends in these settings. This is especially true in the example of the development of culturally fair tools for neuropsychological testing, which are being developed in parts of the developing world (such as in South Africa with its multicultural population and 11 official languages). Consequently, there are many exciting opportunities to understand psychology from fresh, multicultural perspectives. The developing world also offers many research avenues for exploring the neurological conditions that are only (or more frequently) encountered in these settings.

Conclusion

Conducting research and related academic activities is not the primary function of psychologists who work clinically with patients on a full-time basis, as their main responsibility lies in patient care. Even in ideal circumstances, involvement in research/academia can be frustrating and time-consuming. Clinicians often have very little time beyond that allocated to direct and indirect patient care. In addition, psychologists' schedules are often unpredictable, where non-scheduled clinical requirements that demand prioritisation often occur unexpectedly. Nevertheless, there are strategies to consider that may help to reduce the obstacles that prevent research from being conducted. There are clear benefits to be achieved if psychologists who work clinically become involved in research/academic activities. The increased opportunity for professional development, including career advancement, the satisfaction derived from being involved in the training of future generations of colleagues and the contribution to employers' kudos all make this a very worthwhile venture. For these reasons, psychologists who work clinically are almost expected to make a contribution to their own development, to the profession, to patients and to the organisation that they work for by partaking in academic work.

Practical tips

1. Research, audits and literature reviews should all result in writing – and writing should be fun. Read Tim Albert's excellent *A–Z of Medical Writing* (BMJ Books, 2000) to discover that you can laugh while you learn!
2. When it comes to the application forms (and other paperwork) that are relevant to your research, first get help/advice from someone who has 'been there, done that', before trying to complete them on your own.
3. If you have the opportunity to develop a service, or the tools for collecting outcome data for your service, decide very carefully what data will be captured. If the service needs to do a retrospective clinical audit at some point in the future, having collected meaningful, accessible data from the onset will save large amounts of time.
4. Read the paper by Powell, Heslin and Greenwood (2002) referred to in 'Selected further reading', and outline how this research might contribute to service development.

Points for reflective practice

1. What are the differences between research, clinical audits and practice-improvement initiatives?
2. What are the real costs of not partaking in research/academia if you are a psychologist who works clinically?

Selected further reading

British Psychological Society, Division of Clinical Psychology. (2013). Special issue: Embedding a research culture in clinical practice. *Clinical Psychology Forum, 241*, 8–44.

Powell, J., Heslin, J., & Greenwood, R. (2002). Community based rehabilitation after severe traumatic brain injury: A randomised controlled trial. *Journal of Neurology, Neurosurgery and Psychiatry, 72*, 193–202.

18
MANAGEMENT

Introduction

Most psychologists who work clinically are likely to have been asked to take on some managerial responsibilities at some point. For those working in under-resourced systems, this request often may have occurred at an early stage in their careers. These responsibilities are usually in addition to providing patient care, and normally pertain to either staff or resources, or both. With regard to staff, responsibility may be for: interns or trainees; assistant psychologists; recently qualified clinical psychologists or neuropsychologists; or, under more unusual circumstances, other professional and/or administrative staff. Management technique is likely to differ in publicly funded healthcare organisations. Some colleagues might even pose the question as to whether extensive investment in management is actually necessary (or a priority) in such environments. Nevertheless, are there any general principles that may be useful as a heuristic aid to guiding management in clinical settings? The answer is that there are probably a multitude of approaches, but a couple of psychotherapeutic principles and philosophical points spring to mind.

In the first instance, always attempt to identify, harness and channel the forces that have the potential to facilitate patient care, rather than trying to resist these organisational 'vectors' head on. Be an effective conduit between clinicians and managers. Acknowledge, and be open to, the fact that individuals who work with you might come from a variety of cultural backgrounds, with beliefs and value systems that may be different to your own. In multilingual environments, always consider the possibility of subtle differences in meaning when communicating with others. Develop an awareness of people's emotions and behaviours and, where possible, reflect on an issue first, rather than trying to offer an immediate response/'solution'. More comment about these principles is provided later. In addition to managerial responsibilities, some psychologists are also involved in providing *strategic leadership*. In healthcare organisations this refers in essence to the concept of *clinical leadership*.

Day-to-day clinical leadership is a specific managerial responsibility, especially where psychologists have to provide guidance about the everyday clinical tasks in a hospital/clinic or rehabilitation unit. Strategic clinical leadership is usually the responsibility of more senior neuropsychologists, and essentially entails tasks related to service development. However, there will always be (certainly in state-provided healthcare) financial realities to be aware of that do not always sit well with clinicians. In some instances, monies may even be taken away, for example, during modernisation – although some more cynical colleagues might view this as a euphemism for 'on the cheap'. The absence of available money for service development should never prevent clinicians from developing plans that can be quickly capitalised upon, once the prevailing financial climate changes and opportunities for improving patient services present themselves.

Opportunities for service development come and go in cycles, often mirroring wider economic conditions. Individuals who are better prepared to capitalise on smaller, opportunistic funding schemes tend to manage to gradually expand existing services for their patients in small increments over the longer term. However, always remember that securing funding is merely a means to an end. In the final analysis, it is always the ability to recruit and retain appropriately qualified professionals – who have the personal characteristics that are appropriate to working with brain-injured patients – that will determine the quality and stability of the service that is delivered to patients and their relatives. There is a strong case to be made for trying to avoid over-managing staff or processes, and instead focusing on recruiting and appointing the correct staff in the first place. Being forced into being involved with less-than-optimal human resources can be time-consuming, and can prove to be more costly in many areas in the long run.

Staff

There is inevitably some overlap between the management of staff and the normal supervision tasks of psychologists (see Chapter 16). With new staff members, be they trainees or otherwise, one of the most important points to consider is how to 'get them going' as soon as possible. This is similar to the process of corporate induction, but represents much more in healthcare settings. The first point to consider is that nobody is done any favours by delaying the inevitable: starting to see patients as soon as possible. It is crucial for new staff to contribute to the unit's functioning from the outset. This is perhaps the most potent vector for acceptance into the clinical team. Some new starters may not have worked in rehabilitation or assessment settings before, but the same general strategy is useful nonetheless. Always provide as much information as is useful. If you do not have an information pack about your service, create one, and include one or two up-to-date review papers on the type of model that is followed. In multilingual and multicultural settings, ensure that this information is provided in all locally spoken languages to help new colleagues to feel welcome, valued, at ease and accepted.

Most clinicians struggle (and/or take time) initially to familiarise themselves with the patient administration system in a new work environment. Therefore, show them how and where patient appointments are made, what is included in a clinical file and where neuropsychology notes are made, how computer systems are accessed and where neuropsychological tests are stored. While disseminating information that is more technical in nature, do not forget about the social aspects of work environments. Many of us have been strangers in a new job and have experienced how embarrassing it can be to unintentionally 'steal the tea' – always formally introduce new colleagues to the whole team and, at the same time, make sure to tell them about the social routines within the service (including, for example, how the 'in-house' tea and coffee system works!). It can really be awkward to learn after a week or two that the tea you have been enjoying requires payment to a person you have never met. Try to be aware and tolerant of other colleagues' customs and practices that are different to your own (for example, dietary habits, or religious practices such as going to Mosque for Friday prayers) in order to avoid potentially embarrassing, awkward and/or offensive situations. This is particularly salient in multicultural environments.

During induction, be sure to provide information about where to park, where lunch or snacks can be bought and after-work social activities (if there are any). Invest a little time in helping colleagues to familiarise themselves with the 'house rules' of their new work environment. This is not only good manners, but can also really speed up the process of settling into what is, for most, usually a bit of an anxiety-provoking situation. The sooner these aspects of the induction process take place, the sooner the inevitable clinical work can commence. Perhaps it is a truism, or perhaps not, but many experienced clinicians would give the following advice: if something is inevitable, do it as soon as possible. Many of us would recognise this mantra, which often has a lot of relevance when starting a new job. One of the best strategies to reduce new colleagues' anxiety is to immerse them almost immediately into clinical work, along with giving them a genuine welcome into the multidisciplinary team.

One of the most important goals for clinician managers to achieve regarding new members of staff is to prevent them from becoming isolated and feeling unsupported. To help to achieve this aim, the African humanist philosophy of *ubuntu* can serve as a useful frame of reference when offering support to new colleagues. *Ubuntu* refers to a set of values that highlight collectiveness and community, whereby all people are interconnected as part of a greater common good. Furthermore, doing positive things for others is part of a greater good that will benefit you as an individual. When an individual suffers, it affects everyone; everyone identifies with himself/herself by identifying with others. Belief in *ubuntu* can, in a positive way, function as a powerful force in developing collective identity and shared ideals within a clinical service. This collective belief/worldview can also serve to boost team morale in challenging healthcare settings. *Ubuntu* can also help support the value of 'goodwill', crucial to many aspects of being a healthcare professional.

Being part of a clinical team is perhaps the most potent counterforce to isolation. It is important to *identify a caseload early*. Try to avoid giving new colleagues existing cases – channelling new referrals to them is a much more productive strategy. Look into practical strategies that can get things going straight away, such as inviting new colleagues to sit in with you when you see patients. This strategy of *immediate immersion* should be counterbalanced by the simultaneous protection of new colleagues. It would be unreasonable to overwhelm someone before they have had an appropriate chance to find their feet. In addition, do not 'forget' about colleagues once you think that they have had enough time to find their feet. Lack of willingness to fully engage in direct patient care can occur for many reasons, including personal stress, poor organisational ability or due to a lack of clarity provided by managers, among many others. It can also be the result of poor management, including ineffective induction and/or a lack of professional support, or due to other, more 'developmental' factors.

Possibly one of the more common reasons for 'slow starting' can be a function of a colleague having received limited basic training in clinical neuropsychology. Unfortunately, this issue can be more time-consuming to address. Some training programmes simply do not have the resources or time to equip their trainees well enough to 'hit the ground running' when it comes to clinical practice in neuropsychology. This does not necessarily reflect on academic standards per se. On the contrary, sometimes very high academic standards actually come at the cost of developing practical pre-qualification clinical skills in specialist fields, such as neuropsychology. A lack of clinical skill can result in considerable anxiety and, perhaps unsurprisingly, an associated avoidance of patient contact because of a lack of confidence. Avoidance of patient contact can be subtle and difficult to identify with certainty. For example, over-enthusiasm for attending endless meetings (many busy clinicians tend to dread these) or for doing substantial amounts of research-related activities, or someone who becomes involved in non-clinical training and other initiatives, may *sometimes* be early signals indicative of an underlying difficulty that needs addressing. When this is definitely the case, introduce a robust plan of practice-based learning before the patterns of avoidance become entrenched – and consequently much more difficult to address. The above-mentioned concept of *ubuntu* can serve as a useful tool in addressing such problems by offering unconfident members of staff a reminder of the humanistic values that are so important in contributing to patient care.

Working in teams

In most working environments, it is the presence of people, rather than technology or technical tasks, that tends to bring complexity. Generally speaking, it is easier to master process than it is to manage people. In order to have a 'long and happy life' in a multidisciplinary team, it is important to avoid team politics. Becoming intimately involved in the 'mechanics' of team politics can often be a sure recipe for disaster. Social interactions in the workplace serve important functions too: for example, as a source of support or for obtaining information on an informal basis (again, the concept of *ubuntu* is useful here, if part of the organisation's belief system). However, when these normal social processes become disturbed, it is perhaps best for 'insiders' not to have the dual role of both participant and 'problem solver'. Psychologists who are in leadership positions should consider the following: if the group needed a group analyst, they would surely have asked for one. More importantly, if psychologists ever have to contribute towards resolving conflict in their own team (where they work) in the future, then their credibility will almost certainly depend to a large degree on their track record. The outcome will be positive for the psychologist if s/he is judged to be a fair and neutral observer, who can be trusted to provide unbiased opinions and feedback. If, however, s/he has been very much part of team politics and/or conflicts in the past, then s/he is more likely to fail this peer judgement.

What other strategies can be helpful for teamwork? Prigatano (1999) provides some suggestions, including the observation that managing brain-injury rehabilitation teams can be more stressful than working with patients, and that different personality styles have to be accommodated in order to achieve a balance. It can also be important to develop the ability to observe team dynamics for a period of time first, before attempting to identify strategies that have the potential to benefit the team as a whole – rather than trying to solve a specific interpersonal problem in isolation. Perhaps it is a bit of a cliché, but it is nevertheless true that *empathy*, and specifically the ability to see a colleague's view during teamwork, is a huge strength to have. Empathy is also a cornerstone in the management of skill and technique. Being able to carefully listen to others can also be extremely facilitative in team environments. A team is a very good learning ground in which to practise being empathetic.

It is easy to forget why empathy is such an important quality when working with complex neurocognitive impairments and disabilities – which usually (but not always) demand several professionals to contribute to different aspects of patients' rehabilitation. This is the case because, generally speaking, no single profession or specific rehabilitation intervention necessarily provides the only solution – 'there are many ways to skin a cat'. To ensure that open debate takes place regarding patients' care, empathy and due consideration are required for others' suggestions. Additional skills and strategies that can prove helpful in cementing teams that work with complex impairments/disability are: being approachable as a team leader; being consistent and flexible; and always being willing to 'go the extra mile'. Remember that an antagonistic team can be a significant obstacle to optimal rehabilitation; therefore, preventing problems from developing is generally better than trying to rectify them once they have already occurred. Conversely, a well-integrated, fully functioning team is often a prerequisite for the further development of existing services. Again, concepts such as *ubuntu* (from the African context) can be utilised in the quest to form an effective and synergised clinical team.

Service development

It is inevitable that most practitioners will at some stage become aware of those aspects of clinical care that their patients are not receiving. This may happen as a result of several factors. Research may report new interventions that are potentially more effective, but unfortunately sometimes also more labour (clinician input) intensive. This might make it financially unviable to provide these treatments in a unit that receives limited public funds to provide a free service to patients. At other times, there are geographical barriers to overcome, such as those that exist in services based in remote rural areas. Similarly, there may not be a large enough population, and by implication insufficient patient numbers, to justify the provision of a tertiary clinical service. Patient advocacy and support groups may call, quite rightly, for better services to be provided to clinical populations that have not previously been catered for, including, for example, those with rare neurological disorders. However, such pleas can often fall on deaf ears. There may simply not be money available to support such initiatives. For various reasons, many patient populations have limited access to input from clinical neuropsychology. Neuropsychology is a scarce and relatively expensive resource if one considers both the time required per intervention and the number of patients that can realistically be seen by one neuropsychologist over a given period of time.

Clear tensions exist between the need for access to healthcare for all versus economic realities and ethical considerations. Accordingly, many government-funded healthcare services probably intend to prioritise what are seen to be the most essential clinical services during the initial development process of a particular system of healthcare provision. Here, many factors are likely to be considered, including: the potential impact of the service on the health of the population; demand for the service; costs; evidence for the effectiveness of treatments; and the volume of patients who present with a given condition, among many other factors. With most government-funded healthcare services, the source of revenue is almost always direct or indirect taxation and, consequently, these monies have to be spent on the areas of greatest need. Natural gaps in service provision or care pathways within these systems may therefore occur, especially in clinical services that are distant from acute care. However, while the need for acute care is absolutely crucial, it is not the only factor on which the health of a population depends.

Long-term care, or lack thereof, can also affect the health of communities and societies, adding to the social burden placed on them as a whole. For example, traumatic brain injuries result in relatively fewer fatalities (in certain populations), compared to other diseases such as cancer. However, the number of survivors of neuropathological conditions should also be considered more closely. Many patients who have suffered an acquired brain injury present with complex impairment that is associated with significant disability. A substantial proportion of these patients have very substantial financial burdens, along with long-term rehabilitation and care needs. Should a publicly funded healthcare system take these patients on board, or would it be better to fund other conditions, such as coronary heart disease or cancer, in order to reduce cross-sectional mortality rates and ensure maximum impact for investments? This is indeed a very difficult question for those who are responsible for making decisions regarding the allocation of healthcare funds. Perhaps it is useful for practitioners in leadership positions, who have responsibility for service development, to have empathy and understanding towards how impossible it must be to make decisions that will please everyone.

Practitioners who understand the realities of publicly funded healthcare systems may recognise some truth in the following metaphor. The real issue in healthcare funding when negotiating with commissioners is mostly about 'how the cake is cut', as opposed to 'having a bigger cake'. Nevertheless, we need to keep up to date with policy changes that may have a significant impact on service development, especially when these have the potential to secure funding. For example, in the United Kingdom, an important policy for highlighting the need for developing services within the NHS is the *National service framework for long term neurological conditions* (Department of Health, 2005). An additional strategy is to contribute, at a local level, to the strategic review of existing services, either through membership of a relevant committee or by becoming involved in relevant outcomes research. The reality is that psychologists may have to stay the course, continuing to see patients day in and day out, while at the same time remaining open to unexpected opportunities. Identify the right people who can influence service development and then work with them. Use outcome data to convince funders. Apply efforts for service development at the micro level (an extra session of psychology), as well as the strategic level (a new service for patients with Parkinson's disease). Ideally though, service development should be driven by only one factor – the improvement of the lives of patients and their families. Always bear in mind that, more often than not, service development is determined by financial realities and political pressures.

Psychologists need to be aware of the role that politics plays, especially when associated with resource shortages. Politics can influence clinical practice from a government level, an institutional level and/or from within the practice framework of psychology itself (for example, rivalry and disagreement between clinical psychology and neuropsychology over which clinicians are most competent to assess patients with neurocognitive impairment). Political agendas can determine who has access/priority to funds and infrastructure (if available), which pathologies are assessed, which research is funded and how many clinicians are required per capita for certain clinical populations. Psychologists need to be cognisant of these realities and always prepared to advocate for patients through active clinical leadership and by adopting ingenuity when it comes to addressing concerns. For example, in lobbying for resources, psychologists may have to align with other colleagues, such as neurologists and neurosurgeons, who work with the same patient populations and understand their requirements, and can therefore throw their weight behind initiatives to make resources available. Psychologists should always be apprised of the pros and cons of health economic arguments for the care and needs of specific patient populations.

Where resources are scarce, there is often a gap between what policies promise versus what is delivered in reality. Psychologists should seek to address this gap by drawing authorities' attention to the most urgent needs of patients, and by developing additional services where needed – this may require training colleagues in related disciplines to offer support. As highlighted in Chapter 1, the profession of neuropsychology may have to be strategically marketed, countering for the effects of politicised histories, and the perceived value and contribution of psychology in relation to brain injury by key stakeholders may have to be addressed. For example, in certain services, physical rehabilitation may be favoured over cognitive rehabilitation, or colleagues such as speech and occupational therapists may operate in complete isolation from neuropsychologists.

When developing services, it is also important for practitioners to understand the perspectives, aspirations and needs of those for whom they are trying to advocate and develop a better clinical service. We can learn much about the needs of others by listening more to patient accounts of their rehabilitation following brain injury. To some extent, this entails having empathy not only for patients' neurocognitive impairments, but also for the obstacles and frustrations that patients encounter when seeking help and support. Anne McDonald, a medical doctor who was diagnosed with a brain tumour, provides one of the most poignant descriptions of the experience of acute treatment and long-term follow-up by a patient with neuropathological illness. In McDonald (2009) she provides an account of the emotional, physical and other difficulties that resulted from being diagnosed with a brain tumour, as well as the significant difficulties encountered in navigating her post-acute support and rehabilitation within a complex healthcare system. This report, and her reflections upon her own experience as a patient, cannot but inspire clinicians to look more closely at the significant gaps in service provision that exist for patients – and perhaps inspire fiercer advocacy on their behalf.

General strategies

Let us now return to some of the general strategies mentioned in this chapter's introduction. Consider the following: the devil is in the detail, but perhaps not always in the way that we may think. Think about a metaphor of an amplifier: when looking through the cooling vents, is it not true that those amplifiers with the fewest visible internal components appear to produce the best musical reproduction? Perhaps the engineering behind this reflects that if the fundamentals of the design are correct and of a high quality, then additional layers of electronics need not be added in order to correct inherent and basic design flaws. This is a useful metaphor on a couple of levels. At an organisational level, it is crucial to identify the core reason for the organisation's existence; put differently, what is the nature of the business? For example, in manufacturing, the core reason might be to produce a reliable piece of equipment. In hospitals, the core function is patient care. In both examples, it is important for leaders to identify irrelevant details in the form of redundant processes, which only serve to slow down 'production' or throughput.

Complexity alone does not automatically equate to quality. This is also important at an individual level. Most clinicians, including psychologists, can benefit from identifying, and then excluding, distracting activities in an endeavour to better manage the limited time that they have to perform their daily tasks.

Arguably one of the most useful skills to develop is the ability to avoid getting distracted by the details that have little or no bearing on patient care. This entails very well-developed prioritisation skills. Most clinicians can list a multitude of meetings, 'task and finish' groups and policy documents that they are expected to contribute to. When conducting your own meetings, use prioritisation in order to define the outcomes to be achieved by the end of the meeting; rather than trawling through repetitive agenda points, set a time limit and stick to it. As mentioned previously, a useful strategy is to identify the initiatives/activities that directly improve, facilitate and/or accelerate patient care, and then throw your weight behind these. Conversely, psychologists should oppose or ignore those activities that clearly detract from patient care.

Perennial requests for data that is either not collected (because it does not have any clinical relevance) or will take considerable investment of time on the part of the clinician to trawl through are particularly deadly drains on clinicians' time. Where there is a clear benefit to patient care, then comply with a request; if not, then question its purpose. However, always remain open to the possibility that there is a benefit, yet unseen, in a request that may at first appear to be counter-productive. If all else fails, remember that there is a simple principle, found in the ethical guidelines of the profession, that is useful in guiding the time-strapped clinician's activity: patient care should always come first – and in the first instance, do no harm. Wasting patient-care resources constitutes doing harm, albeit indirectly.

Let us now return to the first sentence in Chapter 1 of this book: 'Think before you leap.' This links directly with the second general strategy mentioned in the introduction of this chapter, and concerns the ability to identify, and be sensitive towards, the emotional experience of others. It is crucial to be able to read how others feel about plans, suggestions and/or interactions. However, do not be tempted to communicate up front any awareness of perceived discomfort, hostility or anxiety, for example. Instead, rather first wait and see if your observation is actually correct. At the same time, it is a wise strategy to refrain from offering solutions too soon. First judge when an individual or group might be ready/more receptive, before you define the observed issue and open it up for more in-depth discussion. And never, ever manipulate or undermine colleagues who are perceived to be less receptive to strategic (or personal!) goals, in order to ensure that these goals have a better chance of succeeding. Think before you leap into formal processes in order to achieve personal goals, as having an informal, collegial process of involvement instead will do much more good for the team as a whole – this sits at the very heart of the spirit of *ubuntu*. The inevitable toxicity that results from such approaches does more harm than good over the long term, and can badly sabotage the credibility of any practitioner who engages in these Machiavellian strategies. Finally, remember that the opening up of certain issues can do more harm than good – at times you just have to sit on your wisdom and insights.

Conclusion

Management is unfortunately not straightforward in healthcare environments and it does not necessarily lend itself to the direct transfer of skills from other fields. A few general strategies may, under some circumstances, be useful to psychologists who are new to this responsibility. Try to identify and remove redundancy from processes. One should perhaps reflect on the inescapable truth that publicly funded hospitals/clinics are not actually producing products that 'consumers' buy. The 'consumers' (patients) are usually seen under tragic circumstances, and the treatment (the so-called 'product') is not necessarily pleasant, nor are patients actually 'purchasing' the 'product' in the true sense of the word. Compassion is much more useful than a consumer model is with respect to the management of some (but not all) processes within healthcare. The ethos of *ubuntu*, along with appropriate empathy, can be very useful in these environments. Always attempt to nurture and develop a sensitivity and openness towards the feelings of colleagues, their cultural backgrounds and their belief systems, and towards their perspectives and suggestions regarding patient care. It is this sensitivity and openness that can help to make team environments great to work in. Most of all though, psychologists should always remember that there is a great source of management guidance available at their fingertips, so to speak: if in doubt, revisit the profession's codes of ethics. These universal ethical principles will also serve well in guiding management processes.

Practical tips

1. Develop an information pack for your service.
2. Provide enough (useful) information for new employees, and get them going with clinical work as soon as possible, while at the same time protecting them from becoming overwhelmed.
3. Identify the policy documents that may strengthen a service development case and familiarise yourself with them: for example, the British Society of Rehabilitation Medicine's (2009) *Standards for Rehabilitation Services, Mapped on to the National Service Framework for Long-Term Conditions.*
4. Get to know voluntary patient-support advocacy groups, as well as the purchasers/commissioners of clinical services.
5. Early on in your career, familiarise yourself with the format that is required for service development proposals.
6. Always incorporate as much factual numerical data as possible into a service development proposal.

Points for reflective practice

1. If you were a government health minister, how would you fund your country's healthcare system?
2. List then discuss the personal characteristics that, in your opinion, make a good clinician manager.

Selected further reading

British Society of Rehabilitation Medicine. (2009). *BSRM standards for rehabilitation services, mapped on to the National Service Framework for Long-Term Conditions*. London: BSRM.

Division of Neuropsychology. (2003). *Clinical neuropsychology and rehabilitation services for adults with acquired brain injury*. Leicester: British Psychological Society.

McDonald, A. (2009). A patient's journey: Living with a benign brain tumour. *British Medical Journal, 339*, 292–339.

REFERENCES

American Psychiatric Association. (1994). *Diagnostic and statistical manual of mental disorders* (4th ed.). Washington, DC: Author.

American Psychological Association. (2002). *Ethical principles of psychologists and code of conduct.* Washington, DC: Author.

Aniskiewicz, A. S. (2007). *Psychotherapy for neuropsychological challenges.* New York: Jason Aronson.

Bigler, E. D. (2001). The lesion(s) in traumatic brain injury: Implications for clinical neuropsychology. *Archives of Clinical Neuropsychology, 16,* 95–131.

British Psychological Society. (2003). *Professional practice guidelines of the division of neuropsychology.* Retrieved from www.bps.org.uk/sites/default/files/documents/professional_practice_guidelines_-_division_of_neuropsychology.pdf.

British Psychological Society. (2009). *Code of ethics and conduct: Guidance published by the Ethics Committee of the BPS.* Leicester: BPS.

Brown, J., Pengas, G., Dawson, K., Brown, L. A., & Clatworthy, P. (2009). Self administered cognitive screening test (TYM) for detection of Alzheimer's Disease: Cross sectional study. *British Medical Journal, 338,* b2030.

Cicerone, K. D. (2013). Participation after multidisciplinary rehabilitation for moderate to severe traumatic brain injury in adults. *Archives of Physical Medicine and Rehabilitation, 94,* 1421–1423.

Coetzer, R. (2009). An audit of clinical note keeping in neuropsychology. *British Psychological Society Division of Neuropsychology Newsletter, 8,* 1–2.

Coetzer, R. (2013a). Psychotherapy after acquired brain injury: Is less more? *Chilean Journal of Neuropsychology, 8,* 36–41.

Coetzer, R. (2013b). The role of psychotherapy in rehabilitation after traumatic brain injury. In H. Muenchberger, E. Kendall, & J. Wright (Eds.), *Health and healing after traumatic brain injury: Understanding the power of family, friends, community, and other support systems* (pp. 139–152). Santa Barbara, CA: ABC CLIO, Praeger.

Damasio, A. R. (1994). *Descartes' error: Emotion, reason, and the human brain.* London: Picador.

Delis, D., Kaplan, E., & Kramer, J. (2001). *Delis–Kaplan executive function scale.* San Antonio, TX: The Psychological Corporation.

Department of Health. (2005). *National service framework for long term neurological conditions.* London: Department of Health.

Division of Neuropsychology. (2003). *Clinical neuropsychology and rehabilitation services for adults with acquired brain injury.* Leicester: British Psychological Society.

Edwards, D. J. A., & Louw, D. A. (1998). Psychology as a science and a profession. In D. A. Louw & D. J. A. Edwards (Eds.), *Psychology: An introduction for students in southern Africa* (pp. 1–59). Johannesburg: Heinemann.

Fleminger, S. (2008). Long-term psychiatric disorders after traumatic brain injury. *European Journal of Anaesthesiology, 42*, 123–130.

Folstein, M. F., Folstein, S. E. & McHugh, P. R. (1975). Mini-mental state. *Journal of Psychiatric Research, 12*, 189–198.

Harel, B. T., Steinberg, B. A., & Snyder, P. J. (2006). The medical chart: Efficient information-gathering strategies and proper chart noting. In P. J. Snyder, P. D. Nussbaum, & D. L. Robins (Eds.), *Clinical neuropsychology: A pocket handbook for assessment* (pp. 9–16). Washington, DC: American Psychological Association.

Health and Care Professions Council [HCPC]. (2008). *Standards of conduct, performance and ethics.* Retrieved from www.hpc-uk.org/assets/documents/10002367FINALcopyofSCPEJuly2008.pdf.

Health Professions Council of South Africa [HPCSA]. (2008a). *Guidelines for good practice in the health care professions: Booklet 14 – Guidelines on the keeping of patient records.* Retrieved from www.hpcsa.co.za/downloads/conduct_ethics/rules/generic_ethical_rules/booklet_14_keeping_of_patience_records.pdf.

Health Professions Council of South Africa [HPCSA]. (2008b). *Guidelines for good practice in the health care professions: Booklet 1 – General ethical guidelines for the health care professions.* Retrieved from www.hpcsa.co.za/downloads/conduct_ethics/rules/generic_ethical_rules/booklet_1_guidelines_good_prac.pdf.

Health Professions Council of South Africa [HPCSA]. (2008c). *Professional guidelines: Section 1 – Core ethical values and standards for good practice.* Retrieved from www0.sun.ac.za/rural-health/ukwandahome/rudasaresources2009/More/ProfessionalGuidelines.pdf.

Hebben, N., & Milberg, W. (2002). *Essentials of neuropsychological assessment.* New York: John Wiley & Sons Inc.

Kahn-Bourne, N., & Brown, R. G. (2003). Cognitive behaviour therapy for the treatment of depression in individuals with brain injury. *Neuropsychological Rehabilitation, 13*, 89–107.

Kapur, N. (2009). Advice to a newly appointed consultant neuropsychologist: Aspire for excellence. *The British Psychological Society Division of Neuropsychology Newsletter, 2*, 1–2.

Lezak, M. D., Howieson, D. B., Bigler, E. D., & Tranel, D. (2012). *Neuropsychological assessment* (5th ed.). New York: Oxford University Press.

Lishman, W. A. (1998). *Organic psychiatry: The psychological consequences of cerebral disorder* (3rd ed.). Abingdon, UK: Blackwell Science.

Louw, D. A., & Edwards, D. J. A. (1998). Psychological disorders. In D. A. Louw & D. J. A. Edwards (Eds.), *Psychology: An introduction for students in Southern Africa* (pp. 665–716). Johannesburg: Heinemann.

Luria, A. R. (1966). *Higher cortical functions in man.* London: Tavistock Publications.

Luria, A. R. (1973). *The working brain: An introduction to neuropsychology.* Aylesbury, UK: Penguin Books.

Luria, A. R., & Majovski, L. V. (1977). Basic approaches used in American and Soviet clinical neuropsychology. *American Psychologist, 32*, 959–968.

MacMillan, M. (2008). Phineas Gage: Unravelling the myth. *The Psychologist, 21*, 828–831.

Mateer, C. A. (2005). Fundamentals of cognitive rehabilitation. In P. W. Halligan & D. T.

Wade (Eds.), *Effectiveness of rehabilitation for cognitive deficits* (pp. 21–29). New York: Oxford University Press.

McDonald, A. (2009). A patient's journey: Living with a benign brain tumour. *British Medical Journal, 339*, 292–339.

Milne, D. (2009). *Evidence-based clinical supervision: Principles and practice.* Chichester, UK: BPS Blackwell.

Nasreddine, Z. S., Philips, N. A., Bedirian, V., Charbonneau, S., Whitehead, V., Collin, I., Cummings, J. L. & Chertkow, H. (2005). The Montreal Cognitive Assessment, MoCA: A brief screening tool for mild cognitive impairment. *Journal of the American Geriatric Society*, 53, 695–699.

Nell, V. (2000). *Cross-cultural neuropsychological assessment: Theory and practice.* Mahwah, NJ: Lawrence Erlbaum Associates.

Prigatano, G. P. (1999). *Principles of neuropsychological rehabilitation.* New York: Oxford University Press.

Robertson, I. H. (2005). The neural basis for a theory of cognitive rehabilitation. In P. W. Halligan & D. T. Wade (Eds.), *Effectiveness of rehabilitation for cognitive deficits* (pp. 281–291). New York: Oxford University Press.

Solms, M., & Turnbull, O. (2002). *The brain and the inner world: An introduction to the neuroscience of subjective experience.* New York: Other Press.

South African Mental Health Care Act. (No. 17 of 2002). Retrieved from www.info.gov.za/view/DownloadFileAction?id=68051.

Strub, R. L., & Black, F. W. (2000). *The mental status examination in neurology* (4th ed.). Philadelphia: F. A. Davis Company.

Swartz, L. (1998). *Culture and mental health: A southern African view.* Cape Town: Oxford University Press.

Van Horn, J. D., Irimia, A., Torgerson, C. M., Chambers, M. C., Kikinis, R., & Toga, A. W. (2012). Mapping connectivity damage in the case of Phineas Gage. *PLoS ONE, 7*, e37454.

Victor, M., & Ropper, A. H. (2001). *Adams' and Victor's principles of neurology* (7th ed.). New York: McGraw-Hill.

Walsh, K. W., & Darby, D. (1999). *Neuropsychology: A clinical approach* (4th ed.). Edinburgh: Churchill Livingston.

Wechsler, D. (1997a). *Wechsler Adult Intelligence Scale-III.* San Antonio, TX: The Psychological Corporation.

Wechsler, D. (1997b). *Wechsler Memory Scale-III.* San Antonio, TX: The Psychological Corporation.

Wilson, B. A. (1997). Cognitive rehabilitation: How it is and how it might be. *Journal of the International Neuropsychological Society, 3*, 487–496.

Wilson, B. A. (1999). *Case studies in neuropsychological rehabilitation.* New York: Oxford University Press.

INDEX

Page numbers in *italics* denote tables.